Radio Shack®

THE ART OF MASTERING CHESS
A Complete Course for Beginners

Adapted from

"A Crash Course in Chess"

by Robert Lin and Kaarlo Schepel

and

A Step-by-Step Program to Chess Mastery

Advanced Trainer Book by Saitek Ltd.

and

Russian Handbook of Chess Openings

by GM Eduard Gufeld & Nikolaj Kalinichenko

A Saitek Production

The Art of Mastering Chess

Cover by JoJo Design

Produced by The Alternative Press

for

Saitek Ltd.

Los Angeles, London, Paris, München, Zürich, Hong Kong

CONTENTS

FOREWORD

This book is aimed primarily at all those who have never played chess, but who would like to learn this mysterious and intriguing game. Purposely we have tried to keep the content as simple as possible; nothing is more discouraging to the uninitiated than reading a book you do not understand. But since we also discuss a lot of basic concepts that are not always included in books for beginners, we feel that it would be an ideal learning tool too for those readers who only know the moves and not much more.

We have tried to make it an enjoyable guide to chess for all you budding players who are aspiring to reach a level of Elo 1700 within a year or two. It explains what you have to do to get to that level of play, and what you can expect in setbacks and fun. We also explain what independent benefits you will get by playing chess. Research done in Eastern Europe, the Netherlands, England and other nations where chess has an enthusiastic following, proves that chess can be of great benefit for students and adolescents in general. In this book, we have attempted throughout to make our discussion of this game as clear and as interesting as possible.

THE GAME OF KINGS

Chess is often referred to as the royal game or the game of Kings. This is perhaps because it was played in court by Kings and their noblemen. It has also been referred to as a game of war because of its resemblance to a battlefield; and to become a good chess player, one has to possess fighting spirit when facing one's opponent over the chess board.

When and in which part of the world was chess invented ? That is a very difficult question. Chess historians cannot answer this question with certainty. It is generally assumed that chess was invented in Northern India around the end of the sixth century. Chronologically this fits in well with the mentioning of *"hsiang chi"* or Chinese chess in some Chinese literary works after the sixth century. *"Hsiang chi"* literally means "elephant chess" which does indicate its source of origin - The Land of the Elephants (in this case, India).

Following its invention in India, as a result of international trade and wars, the game of chess became popular throughout the world. Its popularity grew along two main channels of human communication at the time - one towards the east to China, where it was adapted to *"hsiang chi"*, the other towards the west to Arabia and later Europe, where it became international chess as we know it today.

WORLD CHAMPIONS

Readers naturally would like to know who the past and present World Champions are. It is hard to say who the first real world champion was. We have to draw the line somewhere. It is now generally accepted that Wilhelm Steinitz was the first World champion. Before his time chess matches were scattered individual encounters. Of course before Steinitz there were a number of great players of world champion calibre, such as the French composer François André Danican Philidor (1726-95), the Englishman Howard Staunton (1810-74), the Pole Adolf Anderssen (1818-79) and the tragic American hero Paul Morphy (1837-84).

Here is the list of world champions :

Wilhelm Steinitz	...	...	1886-1894
Emanuel Lasker	...	...	1894-1921
Jose R. Capablanca	...	...	1921-1927
Alexander Alekhine	...	...	1927-1935
		and	1937-1946
Max Euwe	...	...	1935-1937

(no World Champions after Alekhine's death until 1948)

Mikhail Botwinnik	...	...	1948-1957
		and	1958-1960
		and	1961-1963
Vassily Smyslov			1957-1958
Mikhail Tal			1960-1961
Tigran Petrosian			1963-1969
Boris Spassky			1969-1972
Robert (Bobby) Fischer			1972-1975
Anatoly Karpov			
(won by default from Fischer)			1975-1985
Garry Kasparov			1985 - present

There are at present two official World Champions, since Garry Kasparov and his challenger Nigel Short (who qualified through the International Chess Federation 'FIDE' cycle) broke away from FIDE in February 1993 to set up their own Professional Chess Association (PCA). Kasparov retained his title in their London match (Sept/Oct 1993), while Anatoly Karpov was just as decisive in winning the now vacant FIDE title in his match against Jan Timman of Holland, played in the Netherlands and Indonesia at the same time.

We sincerely hope that this book will serve you as a starting point for learning chess, and that it will help you to understand and and enjoy the game better.

PART ONE

The Basics of Chess

CHAPTER I

BASIC CONCEPTS

Contrary to what you may have thought, anyone can learn to play chess. Some people have a talent for it, and they often go on and start playing in tournaments or join a club. But it is easy enough to enjoy the game for its own sake, as long as you know a few basic concepts. And that is just what we are going to look at in the next three chapters.

It may come as a surprise to you that all serious chess players always analyse the game they just played with their opponents. The reason is - in the words of Grandmaster (= GM) Nigel Short, the past challenger for the World title - that chess is such a difficult game that none of us ever completely master it. Two chess players who play a game are creating a new game every time they sit down. There are so many different moves to choose from in the first ten moves, that unless you play according to accepted opening theory, you are really creating a new game. We shall discuss that in due course.

Chess is one of the cheapest recreations there is. It of course depends a bit on the quality of the set you buy, but your major expense will be a chess board and pieces. For as little as US$ 4-7 you are all set. And as soon as you know how the pieces go, all you need is someone who will function as your opponent or teacher or both.

As you can see in Diagram 1, a board is made up of black and white squares. If you put the board between yourself and your opponent, you must make sure that the square on the lower left side of your board is black. The empty board shown in Diagram 1, has ciphers written on the left side and letters under it. There is a good reason for it, because through it you can identify each square. We differentiate between files and ranks. Files and ranks are like streets in a city, except that this city has been perfectly built. Files run from the bottom to the top of the board (so these are drawn vertically in the diagram). Ranks run from left to right (horizontally in the diagram). All the squares on the left side of the board (vertically up from 'a') are on the a-file, in the next file (over 'b') on the b-file, and so on up to 'h'.

The squares closest to you (the ones horizontally to the right from "1") are on the 1st rank, the ones on the next rank are on the 2nd rank, and so on up to the 8th rank. By combining file and rank on the 1st rank, the squares are thus named from left to right a1-b1-c1-d1-e1-f1-g1-h1. In exactly the same manner you can name all the 64 squares (32 white and 32 black). This is important for writing down, reading and reproducing games.

Diagram 1

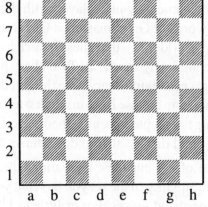

So, you see, learning and understanding all those rather confusing symbols you may have noticed in chess columns, is actually dead simple, like many of the other rules (or rather laws) of chess. Once you know how the pieces are named, what they do and how they are moved over the chess board, it is a question of learning. And that is a process that comes almost automatic, when you play and read chess books or chess columns, like in your daily newspaper. Experience shows that you retain very easily things that you understand **AND** are interested in. Like in any profession and any game, to do the job you must have the tools to work with. By understanding annotation, you will able to progress rapidly. We thus advise you to spend a bit of extra time on this. It will save you a lot of work later on.

As we already said, there are many additional benefits to be gained through playing chess. As ex-worldchampion Max Euwe of the Holland and former President of the International Chess Federation wrote before his death in 1981 : "Chess cultivates concentration and logical thinking, it promotes self-reliance and disciplined action. It demands the attention of many youngsters and gives them a game they can carry through life". He was himself a living example of that, and became after he won the world title (1935-37) also a professor of computer automation, in the first days of that science.

We shall first discuss the pieces used to play the game. Each player has 16 pieces that are each put on a fixed square at the start of the game. In the second diagram you will see all the pieces and where they have to be put.

Each player has 2 Rooks (= R), 2 Knights (= N), 2 Bishops (= B), 1 Queen (= Q), 8 pawns (no abbreviation, but identified only by the square on which it stands), and the most important piece of all, without which the game is lost: the King (= K).

Diagram 2

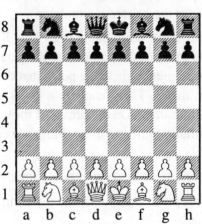

To help you to remember the name of the squares : White has Rooks on a1 and h1 (thus Ra1 and Rh1), Black : Ra8 and Rh8. White has Knights on b1 and g1 (thus Nb1 and Ng1), Black : Nb8 and Ng8. White has Bishops on c1 and f1 (thus Bc1 and Bf1), Black : Bc8 and Bf8. White has his Queen on d1 and his King on e1 (thus Qd1 and Ke1), Black Qd8 and Ke8. White has pawns on a2, b2, c2, d2, e2, f2, g2 and h2. Black has pawns on a7, b7, c7, d7, e7, f7, g7 and h7.

Please note that the White Queen stands on the white square and the Black Queen on the black square (isn't that easy to remember ?). Also make sure that, when you place the board between you and your opponent, squares a1 and h8 are black!

If you are uncertain about these rules later on when you are playing the games, don't hesitate to consult these two pages once more. Practice makes perfect! You will see that chess is as easy to learn as many other games.

Now that you are familiar with the rule that each piece has its appointed place at the beginning of the game, it is time to learn what will really set you apart from non-chess players. The knowledge of how to play a game, takes a bit more than just the initial position. We have to know exactly how the pieces go. That is the subject we are going to cover in the next six pages.

There are namely six pieces we play with. Once more, but now in order of importance: the King (= K), the Queen (=Q), the Rook (= R), the Bishop (= B), the Knight (= N) and the pawn (no abbreviation, but indicated by the square it stands on).

We shall start with the King. The King is the only really indispensable piece of the game. The King can never be taken. When you or your opponent gets to the point that the King can be taken, we call it 'check-mate'. This means that it has been put into a position where it cannot escape. On the previous move it will have been put in 'check'. Normally there are three things we could do, when a King is put in 'check':

1) the King tries to go to another square;

2) another piece is put between the King and the piece that gives 'check';

3) the piece that 'checks' is taken.

If you cannot do any of these, your King is check-mated and the game is over. The other way that a game normally ends is, when your position is so poor that you have no prospect of winning or drawing the game. A good chess-player will then resign his game and concede defeat.

As we mentioned before, one reason that the game of chess is called the game of Kings or the royal game of chess, is that it was played by Kings in the old days, and the struggle resembles what happens on the battle-field or in a war. The German word for chess is

'Schach' (in Dutch it is 'Schaak'; in Greek 'skaki', which is the same as the Persian word 'Shah' meaning 'King').

The King itself is thus essential for the game, and only rarely ventures anywhere until much later in the game. The first rule of strategy is that you protect your King first, before you start attacking the opponent. The King only can move one square at the time in any direction. But it has one special move called 'castling' which we shall cover under the rules for the Rook. The reason for this is that the King and the Rook 'castle' together. In the initial position the King stands on e1 (White) and e8 (Black). In the diagram below the moves are shown which the King can make all by itself. Thus it can move from the square e2 to : d1-e1-f1-d2-f2-d3-e3-f3, as long as it would not put itself in check, that is!

The next most important piece is the Queen. But as far as her potential goes, she is more versatile and more valuable than all other pieces. That is what Queens are anyway in a Kingdom. In chess she has even more power than the King, because she can do far more. It is wise as a chess-player to put a value on your pieces. The reason for that is that in chess you often have to exchange unequal pieces and you need to calculate how this will affect your chances. It does not happen often that you exchange your Queen for several minor pieces; however, quite frequently the Queen exchanged for two Rooks.

Diagram 3

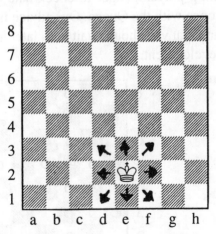

In every society there is a means of exchange. Normally this is money. The 'money' of chess is called 'pawns'. The King is too valuable to be expressed in pawns, because without him the game is lost. The Queen is worth 9 pawns. This may sound strange, because each player only has eight pawns. But it is only a figure of speech. We shall repeat this once more with every chess-man covered later on, but it is good to put it here together : the Rook is worth 5 pawns, the Bishop and the Knight each 3 pawns and a pawn is worth a pawn. That is, unless it reaches the 8th rank. That, however, is another story, and that we shall deal and entertain you later with!

The reason that the Queen is so valuable is that she can travel up and down the board in lightning speed, as long as no piece is put in her path. She can travel horizontally, vertically and along the diagonals. But because she is so valuable, it is important that you do not squander her.

Without her, you might as well stop playing (or 'resign' in chess), unless she is exchanged against the opponent's Queen. As a general rule, it is not easy to checkmate your opponent without some assistance of the Queen. The reason for it is that the Queen is so versatile and has so much power.

You need more chess skills to checkmate your opponent with a Rook and King, King and two Bishops or even King, a Knight and a Bishop. But even that is not too hard to learn once you know the rules. Many beginning players, eager to checkmate their opponent, start venturing at once with the Queen. Our advice is that this is not such a good idea and that you should wait until later in the game, until you have some development.

Diagram 4

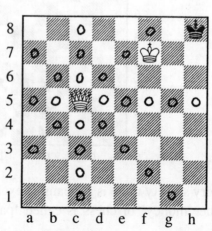

Diagram 4 illustrates the moves that the White Queen can make in the diagram. It can travel from square c5 to: c8-c7-c6-c4-c3-c2-c1 (vertically), a7-b6-d4-e3-f2-g1 or a3-b4-d6-e7-f8 (diagonally) and finally a5-b5-d5-e5-f5-g5-h5 (horizontally). The last move is without any doubt the best : Qc5-h5. In the diagram it delivers checkmate! The Black King cannot go anywhere, it cannot put anything in between, nor can the White Queen be taken.

After the King and the Queen the most important chess-man is the Rook. Its value is about 5 pawns. There are frequent occasions during a chess game that it is strategically sound to sacrifice the Rook for a Bishop or a Knight. This is in chess jargon called sacrificing the 'exchange'.

But if this happens involuntarily it is called 'losing the exchange'. Often it makes sense in a situation where you are in a bind and it is hard to find a good move, especially if you can win one or two pawns in the bargain.

This happens often at the end of the middle game or in the endgame. But we get to that in due course.

The Rook can travel from one to seven squares in just one move, both horizontally and vertically, as long as there is nothing in its path. Diagram 5 below shows the White Rook on square d2. It can go from there to: d1-d3-d4-d5-d6-d7-d8 (vertically) and a2-b2-c2-e2-f2-g2-h2 (horizontally). There is further a very important feature, which I already mentioned earlier under the King : the 'castling' or the 'rochade' of both the King and the Rook. It is meant to bring the King to a safe place, often to complete 'development'. Please remember this last word, because it is one of the most important words in chess.

In Diagram 5 White has already 'castled'. This is done by removing the King from e1 to g1, and at the same time bringing the Rook on h1 over to f1. This is called the 'short rochade' or 'castling short'.

There is also a long rochade or 'castling long', when you bring your King from e1 to c1 and at the same time your rook from a1 to d1. Better make sure that you are completely familiar with every aspect of this important rule, because it is a rare game where not at least one of the players castles.

Diagram 5

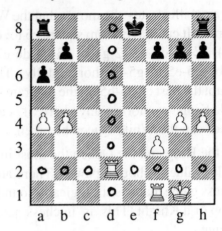

You only can do this 'castling' if you can comply with the following conditions :

1) your King has not moved yet and is not in check,

2) the Rook you wish to castle with has not moved yet,

3) there are no pieces in between your King and the Rook you wish to castle with,

4) your King does not cross (or put itself on) a square while castling that will put it in check.

Assuming that the Black King nor its Rooks have moved, before we arrived at diagram 5, Black can now castle short to g8, while his Rh8 moves simultaneously to f8. However, he cannot castle long, because the White Rook on d2 covers square d8. You can thus not comply with condition 4.

One last word of advice : When you castle, play the King first, then the Rook. A difficult opponent (yes, they exist) could demand that you only play the Rook, if you touch your Rook first. In competitive chess, if you touch a piece you must move it. If you move your King to g8 there is absolutely no misunderstanding that you wish to castle. Please don't forget. And most important of all, you will look so much more like a real chess player, if you do. The Bishop is a wonderful and very useful piece. As a matter of fact, Bishops go in pairs and stand in the initial position on c1 and f1 (for White), and c8 and f8 (for Black). Since they stand adjacent to the King and Queen, they are often called the King's Bishop or the

Queen's Bishop. You will see below that one starts on the the black squares (c1 resp. f8) and will remain on those squares throughout the game. The other one starts on the white squares (f1 resp. c8) and too will remain so throughout the game. It is important to remember this for a reason you will learn in due course, because of promotion of pawns, weak squares and strong squares and all sorts of most interesting concepts we shall discuss in the following sections of the book.

We promise that it will be an exciting voyage of discovery to see how many possibilities and hidden resources there are in chess. And you will understand everything, as long as you know the basic rules and especially know how the pieces go. The Bishop can only travel diagonally, thus in diagram 6 the white-squared Bishop on c4 can go to a6-b5-d3-e2-f1 or a2-b3-d5-e6-f7-g8. It can take any piece that is in its path, but must then stop.

Diagram 6

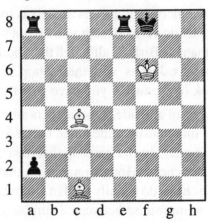

For instance it would make sense for White to take the pawn on a2. We have not covered this yet, but White is in a very dangerous position, because of the position of the Black pawn. White has, however, a big advantage: he can move. It is his turn. His second black-squared Bishop on c1 can travel to : b2-a3 and also to d2-e3-f4-g5-h6. This last move is by far the best, because it delivers checkmate : 1.Bc1-h6+!

As discussed before, if the King is in check, cannot go to another square, cannot put one of its own chess-men in between nor is able to take the piece that delivers check, it has been checkmated.

17

In diagram 6, Kf8 cannot move to e8 (as his own Rook occupies that square), nor to g8 or f7 (White's Bishop on c4 covers those squares, **see above**), nor to e7 or g7 (because of White's King on f6, which incidentally also covers f7). Nor can Black put anything in between, nor can Bh6 be taken. This sort of thing happens all the time in chess, and that makes it such an exciting game. From a totally lost game, you can snatch victory, as long as you have worked out a better plan than your opponent. To recapitulate : The Bishop only travels diagonally, it can go as many squares up or down the diagonal it is on, as long as its path is not impeded.

Of the minor chess-men the Knight is the most interesting, because it jumps in such a funny way: two squares forward and one square sideways, or two squares backward and one square sideways, or two squares sideways and one square forward or backward. It can jump over its own pieces and pawns as well as over those of the opponent. In closed positions (a concept you do not understand yet), it is more valuable than the Bishop, although they both are worth the equivalent of three pawns. Just as with the Bishop, if you lose the Knight, but win a Rook (= 5 pawns), you have won the "exchange".

By way of an aside, those readers who are familiar with Chinese chess will more easily understand the awkward jump of the Knight. There is a rather similar piece in that fascinating game. As a matter of fact, experience in Hong Kong shows that those players who excel in Chinese chess, do equally well in international chess. International chess is a compromise between a number of varieties that existed in Europe and the Middle East during the last 1,000 years. The present laws of chess are here to stay, though, because they have proved so enduring. Knowledge of the game on the other hand is still expanding with no end in sight.

You will see how useful the Knight is and how essential for a harmonious development of your pieces, if the Knight is well positioned, both for the defense and for the attack. In diagram 7 we show you the jumps a Knight can make: From square e4, it can travel to d6, f6, g5, c5, g3, c3, d2 and f2. That is a lot of possibilities. It often means that a Knight can control a whole position and becomes worth far more than three pawns. Also sometimes to get to the best square, you may have to move your Knight several times around.

Diagram 7

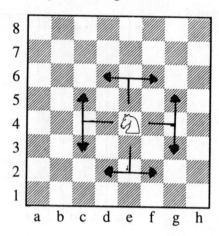

Some of these manoeuvres will win you games and we shall demonstrate that too later on.

The pawn is the toddler of the chess game, but don't be mistaken. He is small and not worth a lot, but he has seven brothers. He can make an awful lot of trouble if he gets half the chance, and can become very important. The strange thing about the pawn is that it does not capture in the same way as it moves over the board. We have already seen that all chess-men can capture other pieces, but they always do it in the same manner as they move. If it is their turn to move, and a chess-man of the opponent occupies a square they want to move to, they just capture that piece.

With the pawn it is a different story: it moves forward in a straight line, but captures diagonally forward. And the pawn is the only piece that is not allowed to take a step backward. It can only move forward. That makes a quite a difference! Something else that is funny about the pawn is that on the first move of the pawn you may choose if you want to push the pawn one or two squares forward! Isn't that surprising?

Thus White's pawn in diagram 8 can be played from square e2 to either e3 or e4. But during all further moves the pawn makes, its advance is restricted to one square forward at a time. Thus if you play it to e3 on the first move, it continues to e4, then e5, then e6 and so on during each subsequent move, unless it can take a piece on the d- or f-line.

Diagram 8

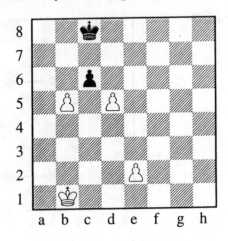

To make this point easier to grasp, we have left all other pieces off the board. If you have understood the above, you will know that Black can play his pawn on c6 to c5, but he can also take White's pawn on d5 or the pawn on b5. A pawn thus moves forward, but captures at an angle of 90 degrees.

Pawns can take any piece, even the Queen, but of course not the King. The pawn itself can be taken by any piece, including by the King and by a pawn of the opponent. And although the pawn is worth very little, it is good to be very careful with your little men. Grandmasters often win or lose games because they have one pawn more or less. And the more you learn, the more you will see that for you too it can be the difference between winning and losing in many games.

The reason you ought to be careful with your pawns, is that although there are eight of them and you would think that you would not miss one, they have a lot of potential.

True enough, they are the least valuable of the chessmen. But like a caterpillar transforms itself into a magnificent butterfly and the ugly duckling becomes a swan in the fairy-tale , the pawn when it reaches the eigth rank is promoted. As a matter of fact, you may choose to make it into any piece you like (except for the King, that is). Normally a promoted pawn is made into a Queen. To bring a pawn to the 8th rank in chess-language is called: to "queen" a pawn.

However, sometimes it is advisable to underpromote it to a Rook, Bishop or Knight. The reason for that would take us too far at this point, but will be explained in due course.

Diagram 9

In diagram 9 we see that White is in a very desperate situation and that checkmate is only one move away. Although we have not yet discussed in detail the co-ordination of the chessmen, to deliver checkmate often needs more than one piece. White's King on square h1 cannot move to g1, because this square is covered by the Knight on f3 (remember that the Knight controls all squares that it can move to with its funny jump). White cannot go to square g2, because of the fact that the Black Rook on c2 covers that square, and White most certainly cannot go to square h2, because this square is covered by both Rc2 and Nf3 (by the expression 'cover' we mean that a piece can go to that square in just one move).

And that is where the problem lies. Although White is not in check, he is as good as in check. He cannot avoid checkmate on the next move, because Black threatens to bring Rc2 to square h2. White cannot take the Rook, he cannot put anything in between, nor can he cover square h2 himself with one more piece. If he could do that, he could take the Black Rook if it moved to h2. There is, however, one big difference. White is not in check and can thus move any piece as long as the move is legal. And because he has his pawn on e7, he can 'queen' it and checkmate the opponent! Thus **1. e7-e8Q** checkmate.

That is the beauty of chess. You can suddenly win a lost game, if you see further than the opponent. And do not think it does not happen that way. It happens all the time. And not always through luck either. Ex-world champion Bobby Fischer once said : "The better player is always lucky". By this he meant that a more accomplished player normally reaches positions where his pieces co-ordinate better. This is then often the difference between a win and a loss when complications arise.

There are still a few points we have not covered yet with regard to pawns. And unless that is done, you would be faced with unexpected difficulties. We talked briefly about the fact that present International Chess is a compromise of several forms of chess that existed before. In order to play the game universally, to be able to have a World Champion and to organize tournaments where they would not quarrel over the laws/rules of chess, they had to agree on all details.

It is only about 200 years since the laws of chess have become uniform. Many other things have changed since then (the use of clocks, time-control, the organization of the Federations, how the World Champion is selected, etc.). These things will continue to change. The world of chess is dynamic and its popularity is growing rapidly, especially since chess computers were introduced. But the principles on which play is based are now uniform.

One of the last things to change were the rules that dealt with the pawns. In Indian Chess (still widely played on the Sub-Continent) the pawns still move only one square forward at a time. When they decided, on the first pawn move, to allow players to choose between either one or two squares forward in International Chess, many people felt this was not fair if you had a pawn on the fourth square yourself, as an opponent. It would prevent you from capturing the pawn that just had jumped past you. In diagram 10, White has a pawn on e2, Black one on d4. In diagram 11, White plays his pawn to e4. They decided 200 years ago that if such a thing happened, it would be fair if the opponent would be allowed - FOR ONE MOVE ONLY - to act as if the pawn was played to e3. If he did not take it, then he would forfeit the opportunity. In diagram 12 we see that Black indeed has taken the pawn "en passant". Now we have covered this last part, it is time to move to other things that will prepare you for your first game. Naturally it is really exciting for you to reach this point.

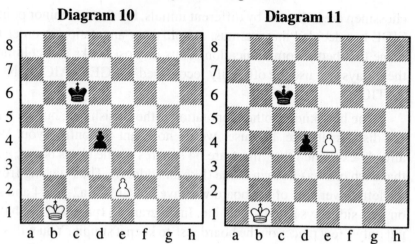

Diagram 10

Diagram 11

Diagram 12

So far we have discussed how the pieces go, what each chessman is worth and where the pieces stand at the start of the game. It is time to discuss the way we write down moves. In chess jargon this is called 'annotation'. More often than not, this part of chess is neglected. It is the language by which chess players converse with each other if they are not in the same room. If you do not know how to read annotation, you cannot follow the games in chess columns in newspapers or books. It is like being a musician who cannot read the music score. So please pay attention. In the past there were several different ways of writing moves down. In many countries the chessmen are indicated by different initials, but that is a minor point. FIDE has decided that we must simplify our annotation in order to come to a better communication. Thus in most books and columns these days, we use the officially recognised ALGEBRAIC ANNO-TATION.

The best-known other annotation is the British one, but we will not discuss it here, because we do not want to confuse you. We already explained that there are 64 squares on the chess board, and that each one has its own name (like an address). Thus starting from the left lower side of the board we have upward a1-a2-a3-a4 and so on, and sideways a1-b1-c1-d1 etc. In diagram 13 (page 25) we have put only a few pieces on the board just to keep it simple. You will see that we can learn and start playing chess at the same time. This is a very simple problem for which we shall give the solution on the same page. Our more experienced readers should be able to solve it.

In algebraic annotation the position reads : White - Kf7, Rf3, Bc5, Nc3; Black - Ke5, pawn f5. Do you recognize the squares on diagram 13, where the pieces are positioned ? If you do, well done ! It means you are on your way to become an accomplished player. The task in this diagram is : White to play and to checkmate in 2 moves against any defense.

Well, once you see the solution, do not be disappointed if you were unable to solve it yourself. The most important thing is that you understand the solution; it means that you are making progress, that you are learning the concepts we have discussed so far. And chess, as all sorts of research has borne out around the world, is a very powerful tool for learning. The way that your chess improves relates to the memories you retain from the games you play, the problems you study and understand and the insight you get into problem-solving. Just be content to understand for a start. You will learn very quickly as long as you do it systematically.

Black is lost in the position, because he is far behind in material, which his opponent captured during the game. He should have resigned. The position is, however, not from a game, but a problem composed by the Englishman G. Mott-Smith.

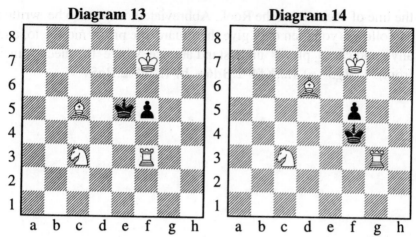

Diagram 13   **Diagram 14**

In problems we set ourselves a task, and in the process we discover the beauty of chess. In problems there is only one solution. In this one there are many ways to win, but only one that leads to checkmate in two moves. In diagram 14 we see the final position after the checkmate has been delivered. And by comparing diagram 13 with diagram 14, we can understand the annotation by which chess game records are kept.

The solution of No. 14: **1. Rf3-g3** and now a) **1...,Ke5-f4 2.Bc5-d6+** or b) **1..., f5-f4 2. Rg3-g5+.** Since the Black King is in check, it cannot take the piece that delivers check, cannot move to another square to get away from check and cannot put anything in between (remember those three rules ?), it is checkmate. And to give you an idea how beautiful this problem is, those who compose and those who solve and appreciate chess problems agree that a problem with "pure" mate is the best composition.

By this they mean that, when the King is mated, each square he moves to is covered by only one opposing piece. In this problem under a) squares g5, g4, f3 and e3 are only covered by the Rook, square e4 only by the Knight and square e5 is covered by the White Bishop. The Black pawn on f5 blocks the last route of escape. Under b) squares f6 and e6 are covered by the White King, squares d4 and d6 by the Bishop, square e4 by the Knight, square f4 is blocked by its own pawn, while squares d5 and f5 do not get the Black King out of the line of check from the Rook. Abbreviated, it can also be written as follows (you then only give the square the piece moves to, and any good chess player understand at once where the piece comes from): **1. Rg3 a) 1...,Kf4 2.Bd6+ b) 1...,f4 2.Rg5+**

* * * *

CHAPTER 2

OPENINGS

We have started out with some diagrams and simpler positions before playing actual games. It is good not to be impatient about that. The learning process actually will happen faster if the basics are fixed in your memory in simpler terms. It is easy to get confused when you have to think of too many things. That is why many people give up the more interestings things in life, just because it looks too difficult. What we are trying to do is to let you understand all concepts gradually. On the next page we shall start with an actual game. But before that we want to cover the last few things you absolutely need to know.

Chess is played by two players (White and Black) who sit on each side of the board. White plays first, then Black and the moves are played in turn, until one player resigns or is checkmated, or when players agree to a draw. In tournaments you can also lose on the clock, if you cannot finish the required number of moves within the set limit. This time limit may vary and depends on the organizers and on the level of players that are taking part.

As we already said, both players start off with 16 chessmen (8 pawns, 1 Queen and 1 King, 2 Rooks, 2 Bishops and 2 Knights). Diagrams you see in the paper are positions in a game where pieces have been captured or exchanged. Normally with players of even strength, pawns are exchanged for pawns, Rooks for Rooks, the Queens are swopped, and the Bishops are taken in exchange for Bishops and Knights. The positions we see are then rather even in material, but may be superior in positional strength. If you are ahead in material, you can normally win WITHOUT RISK by exchanging your pieces as described above. The advantage of one or two pawns or even a piece becomes proportionally bigger the less material there is on the chess board.

Another way to win is to use your positional or material advantage to win: a) even more material, b) to checkmate the opposing monarch (King).

Before we start on the subject of openings itself, we have to make some reservations. Although openings are the most essential part of the game (without an opening, there is no middle game or endgame), once you are able to get a good position on the board and at least EQUALIZE, the real game starts. There are many chess players who spend all their time trying to cram opening theory into their head, and neglect the middle and endgame entirely.

Bob Wade, one of the most accomplished authorities on how to teach chess to young people, stresses that a weekend spent working on simple endgames positions will produce more results (drawn positions being won and lost positions being drawn) than working on openings. As an international master and the coach who guided both Jonathan Speelman and Nigel Short to their first Candidate matches, he speaks from experience.

Please take now a board and pieces and set up the initial position from which both players start a game. To show that a game can end in just a few moves, we record the following game: **1.e2-e4,c7-c6 2.d2-d4,d7-d5 3.Nb1-d2,d5xe4 4.Nd2xe4, Nb8-d7 5. Qd1-e2** We have now reached the position shown in Diagram 15. White has set a trap, and you would be surprised how many good players overlook the idea behind an insidious move like that, when they play too quickly.

Diagram 15

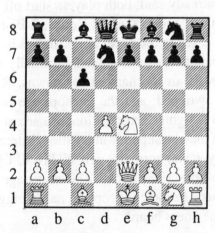

We are now going to introduce another new idea. In the course of these pages you will get acquainted with all the intricacies of chess in this manner. The idea behind this trap is called "the pin". It means that a piece cannot move because it protects the King itself. The tragedy in this case is that pawn e7 (the only chessman that would be able avoid checkmate) is 'pinned'. Black did not see the trap: 5....,Ng8-f6, to which White replied: 6.Ne4-d6 checkmate!

This sort of mate will not happen often in serious games but is not uncommon in lightning (also called 'blitz') chess, albeit seldom in the first few moves. 'Lightning chess' is a game in which a clock is set at 5 or 10 minutes for each player and all moves have to be played within that time frame. Since players only have a few minutes for the entire game, they may overlook such a trap. More often than not, the player plays a prepared variation in the opening he knows best, and that is where opening knowledge becomes valuable. The point we wish to make is that it is next to impossible to have more than a rudimentary knowledge of most openings, even for seasoned players. To progress you should choose an opening you want to be an expert in.

To return to the above example (a way every player wants to win occasionally), the so-called 'miniatures' or games that last less than 20 moves, can be encountered in every tournament. There are books that will give you many of these examples, and they are very helpful in making you aware of the dangers that exist in that opening. The authors have won (and lost) many of these miniatures. Chess players love these kind of games, but they are not the norm. It is good practice to analyse them, for the simple reason that it teaches you to find the best, shortest way to a win in similar positions. They also teach you the essentials and pitfalls of a certain opening, and here we come to an important part of our course.

Grandmasters (GM) and International Masters (IM) who teach chess stress that the serious student should concentrate on learning all there is to know about certain openings that interest them. That way they learn to become systematic in the way they think. The opening shown above is known as 'Caro-Kann'. It is an opening that was out of fashion until Mikhail Botwinnik used it in 1958 in his second match against Vassily Smyslov, and recaptured the world title which he had lost the previous year. The important element in this was surprise. Botwinnik had never played this opening before as Black. He almost always played **1...,e6** both against the K-pawn opening (1.e4) which is called the French Defense, as well as against the Q-pawn opening (1.d4). He would continue after **2.c4** with **2...,f5** (known as the Dutch Defense.)

Botwinnik was thus very efficient and economical in his openings. And here is an important lesson to learn. To become a good player, you have to be efficient in your learning habits. When you work through this book, chess magazines and chess columns, look for openings and defenses you would like to play. Try them out over the board, and study the theory.

Every opening has its great proponents. There are GMs who are particularly good in certain openings. Imitate their style. It is the quickest way to learn. Just follow the masters in chess. They got where they are in chess, because their system works.

When Botwinnik answered Smyslov's 1.e4 with 1...,c6, this created a lot of excitement in Moscow. He had prepared himself meticulously and introduced many novelties, which made him only the second man to recapture the World Championship in chess after Alekhine. It emphasized the importance of good preparation in chess and keeping up to date in opening theory.

Although this is not so essential in club play, at the GM level no one survives for long without a solid knowledge of openings. It is also important at their level to play one's own variation rather than the opponent's. Our advice is thus to follow the great chess teachers' advice and concentrate on just one opening for White: either 1.e4 or 1.d4 and find a main line to play against each answer; and one defense for Black against the main opening moves. The third section of this book, together with the (programmable) opening library of your computer will assist you in this endeavor.

Chess is not just attacking, sacrificing and winning in a few powerful moves. This is the impression one might get when reading most chess columns and diagrams published in the newspapers. No, on the contrary, the way most chess games are played at a level where opponents are of equal skill, is that one player obtains a slight advantage and slowly builds that into a positional or material equivalent.

But , for the purpose of keeping this volume interesting, there will be many 'tactical' manoeuvres and sacrificial attacks, and not only the 'strategic' ideas that we cannot do without. To continue with the Caro-Kann, let us just suppose the following game is played: **1.e2-e4,c7-c6 2.d2-d4,d7-d5 3.Nb1-c3** (or Nb1-d2 as in the previous game.) **3...,d5xe4 4.Nc3xe4,Nb8-d7** (White's move 5.Qd1-e2 is not the strongest as it blocks the Bishop on f1. The better move is a development move like Bf1-c4 or Ng1-f3. In this game White played the not so usual attacking move:) **5.Ne4-g5** (Black now should have continued with: 5...,Ng8-f6, but played instead:) **5...,h7-h6?** (What follows is a tactical move:) **6.Ng5-e6**. In this position, Black cannot take the Knight (6...,f7xe6??), because of the devastating **7.Qd1-h5+** checkmate!!

Every opening has many of these little traps, but some more than others. Both Botwinnnik and Mikhail Tal (World Champion 1961-62) particularly liked to play the Caro-Kann as Black. Others like GM John Nunn of England have a style that particular suits playing as White against the Caro-Kann. Nunn plays agressively.

Why would one play this defense or any other one where one gets under a good deal of pressure ? The answer is that White often tries to push his advantage, creates weaknesses in his own position and gets clobbered, when the game settles down. But others like Nunn or GM John van der Wiel of the Netherlands are like a fish in the water in such games. Let us just see how Nunn finished off his opponent GM Kiril Georgiev of Bulgaria in Linares, 1988. First moves (see above). **6.Ng5-e6,Qd8-a5+ 7.Bc1-d2,Qa5-b6 8.Bf1-d3,f7xe6??** (He had overlooked the following fatal combination.) **9.Qd1-h5+,Ke8-d8 10.Bd2-a5** (and here Black resigned, because the Queen is pinned, thus cannot move away and is lost).

To make clear what happens in games and use less space, chess columnists often use certain script-signs to indicate their comments. Thus '?' means a bad move, '!' a good move, '??' a losing (very bad) move and '!!' a winning (excellent) move. By '!?' they normally mean a move which deserves attention, while '?!' means a dubious move. These are the most common ones and we will stick to them during the course of this book.

Diagram 16

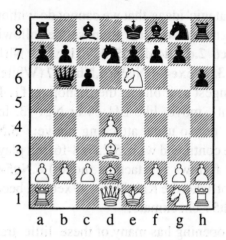

So far we have used long annotation, indicating at every move the square the moving piece is coming from, and the square it is going to. The short annotation mostly used in chess columns only will give the symbol of the chess-man and the square it is moving to. Once you get used to it, there is nothing to it. If there is some confusion (mostly with Rooks and Knights that both could go to the same square), you add either the rank or the line it is coming from as well.

Let us now give the game once more in short hand, just to show how easy it is, with script-signs as comment: **1.e4,c6 2.d4,d5 3.Nd2,exd4 4.Nxe4,Nd7 5.Ng5!?,h6? 6.Ne6!,Qa5+ 7.Bd2,Qb6 8.Bd3** (See Diagram 16) **8...,fxe6?? 9.Qh5+,Kd8 10.Ba5** (1-0).

In this way a whole story and a drama can be told in just a few lines. Some comments to go with it make it of course much more readable, but for the sake of brevity, very little is necessary.

Readers will be excused if, after reading the last few pages, they do not believe in the Caro-Kann as an option. What we have shown so far were games in which Black was beaten with very simple means in record time. This is the exception rather than the rule. Chess is a very dynamic game where new discoveries (novelties) are being made and introduced all the time. Creativity and analysis go hand in hand.

For the average club player it is impossible to keep up with all developments. Even for most professional chess players it is a real task to stay up to date. That is why sensible players specialize in certain openings and play their favourite variations with confidence. Only occasionally you get caught out, most of the time by experimenting in unknown territory.

To set the record straight, here a wonderful win for Black in the same Caro-Kann. Every tournament bulletin can provide a few games like the following miniature. They are like small gems. It is the spice that livens up all the prepared lines and the inevitable dull draws that occur with evenly matched opponents. Grandmaster Eduard Gufeld is in the habit of saying that each bad move (also called a 'lost tempo') is the equivalent of two years of your life. A chess game lasts on average 40 moves; humans live, if they look after their health, 80 years. Each move is important. In the following game White made one bad move and then overlooked the consequences.

White: Schuster Black: Carls (Oldenburg, Germany 1914)
1.e2-e4,c7-c6 2.d2-d4,d7-d5 3.Nb1-c3,d5xe4 4.Nc3xe4,Ng8-f6 5.Ne4-g3 (Here 5.Ne4xf6 is better.) **5...,h7-h5 6.Bc1-g5** (Not correct; with 6.h2-h4 White would get advantage.) **6...,h5-h4 7.Bg5xf6** (This will be refuted elegantly. Necessary was here 7.Ng3-e2) **7...,h4xg3 8.Bf6-e5** (The danger appears gone, but now follows a nasty surprise:) **8...,Rh8xh2** (start of a forced sequence that leads to a fascinating win).

Diagram 17

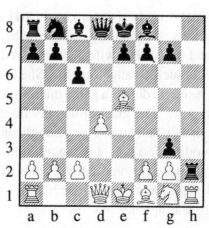

9.Rh1xh2,Qd8-a5+ 10.c2-c3,Qa5xe5+ (The point of the idea.)

11.d4xe5,g3xh2 and White resigned, as he is a piece down and Black will get his Queen back by promotion on h1 or g1 (0-1).

Although the advice in chess columns and in general chess books sometimes may seem contradictory, if not confusing,there is a logic behind it all. Chess is such a rich game that the possibilities in moves are almost infinite. There are many stories about the origins of chess and what happened over the many centuries that the game was played with those who became infatuated with it. Two of them are worth repeating in that they tell a lot about the game in just a few words.

The first one concerns the man who did a difficult task for the king, and was asked what he wanted to have for doing it. All he wanted was grains of corn using the squares of the chess board. He explained that he wanted 1 grain on the first square, 2 on the second, 4 on the third, 8 on the fourth and so on. He was granted his wish, until the king and his minister of finance realized to their consternation that by the twelfth square they were supposed to pay out 2048 grains.

Since there are 64 squares on the board, there would not be enough grain in the entire kingdom to pay the man. It taught a lesson to them not to agree too readily to things they did not understand. When we take into account that at every move each player can choose from many moves the multiplication of possibilities in chess is even more complex than this story.

The second story is about a king in Sri Lanka (Ceylon) who had to go to war every six months, because he had that sort of character, belligerent and proud. His wife got very tired of him being away so often and living such a dangerous life. She consulted a wise man and asked him if he could devise a game that would tame her husband and keep him at home. The guru came up with chess as the new game imported from a distant land. True enough, once the king learned the moves and understood that his aggression could be channeled in chess without need for physical violence, he played daily with all who wanted to play against him. He lived a long and fruitful life and never went to war again.

This story tells us that the impetuousness and frustrations that many of us have growing up or just living in a crowded city, can be used constructively by playing a game that captures the intellect and overcomes the basic animal instincts. What we are trying to say is that, despite the difficulties of learning to play chess well, there are many benefits that come as a result of playing this fascinating game. To improve your game is not that difficult and it becomes enjoyable, once you learn to see the art in the game.

Those who have studied the game in all its aspects call chess not only an art, a sport, but a science as well. Development of logic is a key element in chess. It helps you to understand why some games are won or rather lost quickly (inside 20 or 25 moves). Almost always the reason is that one of the players has not followed the accepted rules of chess. By that we mean that over the twenty centuries that the game has been played, and the thousand years that it has been played almost like we play it today, the masters have discovered and developed certain rules that need to be followed.

Of course you don't have to, but it is a good suggestion. If you do not, the chances are almost 100% that you will lose against an experienced player. As difficult as the game looks at times, it is not that impossible to make rapid progress. If you remember that a simple computer with as little as 16K can play with a rating of Elo 1850, then you with billions of brain cells should be able to do better.

The memory of a chess computer is very limited, but its program can discern the patterns in chess and produce play that will defeat the vast majority of chess players.

All you need is insight, caution and lots of solid experience.

One of the most important rules in the opening (mentioned in a previous chapter) is that you should develop your pieces quickly. As a rule do not play more than once in the opening with the same piece, unless it is accepted opening theory. Just follow the masters in openings. They have discounted the variations that do not work.

To go back to the Caro-Kann: let us show once more that White as well as Black can win quickly in the opening if the opponent takes risks. The following game was played in 1959 in Bled, Yugoslavia between Vassily Smyslov, just one year after he lost his World championship crown to Botwinnik, and Mikhail Tal, just two years before he won the crown from Botwinnik. Both of them were thus at the peak of their career. We have used the short annotation to save space. You will be excused if you do not understand the ideas at all behind several moves. If you play this game once more AFTER you finish the book, you will see how rapidly you learn!

White: Tal Black: Smyslov

1.e4,c6 2.d3,d5 3.Nd2,e5 (A bit better is 3..,dxe4 4.dxe4, e5 5.Nf3,Bc5 6.Bc4,Qe7 after which Black does well easily.) **4.Nf3,Nd7 5.d4!,dxe4 6.Nxe4,exd4 7.Qxd4,Ngf6 8.Bg5, Be7 9.0-0-0,0-0 10.Nd6,Qa5** (Both players are ready for battle. This is not going to be a draw.) **11.Bc4** (This adds fuel to the flames.) **11..,b5 12.Bd2,Qa6 13.Nf5!,Bd8** (Black has no time to take the Bishop on c4; he would lose Be7, a piece needed for his defense.) **14.Qh4,bxc4** (White has now sacrificed a piece, just to have one extra tempo in which he can threaten mate.) **15.Qg5,Nh5** (Black now has to give the sacrificed piece back in order not to lose and to get counterplay.) **16.Nh6+,Kh8** (Another case of a 'pin'; Black could not take the Knight, since pawn g7 was pinned.) **17.Qxh5,Qxa2** (This natural move loses quickly as White demonstrates. Also wrong would be to play 17...,gxh6 18.Bxh6 and Black is mated or loses material with interest, but that would take us too far. Correct was here 17..,Bf6! with fine chances for Black.) **18.Bc3,Nf6.**

Diagram 18

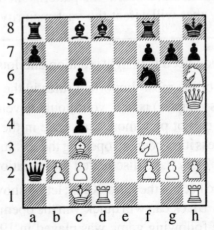

36

19.Qxf7!! (wonderful and the deciding stroke of genius.)
19..,Qa1+ (If here 19..,Rxf7 20.Rxd8+ etc. and if 19..,Rg8
20.Qxg8+!!,Nxg8 21.Nf7 checkmate) **20.Kd2,Rxf7 21.Nxf7+,Kg8
22.Rxa1,Kxf7 23.Ne5+,Ke6 24.Nxc6,Ne4+ 25.Ke3,Bb6+ 26.Bd4**
(1-0). Black is an exchange plus a pawn down, so there is no chance
of pulling any rabbits out of the hat.

In chess, the name of the game is winning. If you can force a
decision outright by checkmating the opponent, there is no need to
be careful with your pieces. Tal was willing to give his Queen. No
GM has won more high-quality 'sacrificial' games than him. If you
want to follow in his path, you must learn the ability to calculate
accurately. Make sure you do not blunder and lose instead; very easy
in a complicated game like we just saw. If you are not sure, it is far
better to play cautiously in a good position; you can then win without
taking risks, but it may take a bit longer. If you are wrong in a
decisive combination, there is no more chance to even draw the game.
That is the dilemma.

Experienced teachers say that in order to become good in
chess, you must be able to see tactical combinations of a few moves
deep. This normally involves a sacrifice of a pawn or more and you
only develop this ability by exercising it on a regular basis. Our
advice is to try to solve chess problems. Analyse them until you find
the correct combination. Don't waste more than half an hour, as it
sometimes involves a tactical theme you do not know yet. Study it
if it looks unfamiliar. Show them to your friends in school. There is
no better way to learn than by teaching others. And try to use the
tactical ideas in your games. You will see that the same kind of
combinations repeat themselves in chess, often when you least
expect them.

The above game may have been too complicated at this stage.
But pretty soon you will be able to understand all the ideas that
motivated the players to make those moves. After this relatively
difficult game that challenged your ability to understand ideas you
have only partially grasped, we shall make it easier. One of most
common defenses played today is the Sicilian. Over 80 % of all
serious games begin with either d4 (Q-pawn openings that often lead

to a closed, positional sort of game) or e4 (K-pawn which leads to an open, rather tactical kind of combat).

Black normally will answer in kind with d5 resp. e5. This is called symmetry. According to the American GM Reuben Fine who wrote several standard books about chess, there are two fundamental concepts in the opening: development and the center. If you neglect either of these, you will get into trouble rapidly.

Since White moves first, he has a slight advantage and often keeps the initiative for a little while. If Black does not play the strongest moves, White will be able to dictate the game. Black, however, can choose the defense and is seldom pressed into a system he does not like. The trick is thus to find and play openings that suit your style, and leave as little to chance as possible. Many players love to play 1...,c5 in answer to 1.e4 for the reason that it means that it breaks the symmetry. The Caro-Kann does the same, but the idea is to support the centre. In the Sicilian, Black starts an immediate counter-attack on the Queen's wing. In the following game one of the acknowledged masters who is almost impossible to beat in that defense is playing Black. He is the Swedish GM Ulf Andersson (at the time, rated 10th on the World Elo list). His opponent as White is the Estonian Jaan Ehlvest (then rated 11th in the world). He had analysed Black's games and really done his homework. Both players have been in the top 30 for many a year. It was a game played in Belfort, France five years ago in one of the World Cup tournaments. Mind you, the Sicilian is home ground for Andersson, but he is swept off the board in 19 moves! In the process we shall learn more about the basic opening concepts in general.

1.e4,c5 2.Nf3,e6 3.d4,cxd4 4.Nxd4,Nc6 5.Nc3,a6. (This is an idea of GM Miguel Najdorf, now established part of theory. It is to prevent Nb5. Of course the advantage of a pawn advance is that you capture space, but you also create a weakness on b6, because the pawn can never go back.) **6.Be2,Qc7 7.f4,Nxd4 8.Qxd4,b5 9.Be3,Bb7 10.0-0-0!?** (First surprise: White saves time, as Rd1 is already in place to strengthen his hold on the d-line. In the Sicilian, timing is everything. One tempo is often the difference between a win, a draw or even a loss) **10...,Rc8 11.Rd2!** (Defense and attack.)

11...,Nf6 (The immediate threat is: 12..,b4 and White loses a pawn.) **12.Bf3,Be7 13.Rhd1,0-0 14.e5!** (A real blow which catches Black unawares. Here only 14..,b4! would give satisfactory play. Instead Black played:) **14...,Bxf3? 15.gxf3,b4** (Too late. Now the g-line is open to a double attack by two White Rooks.)

Diagram 19

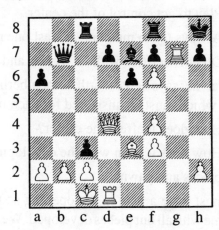

16.exf6!,bxc3 17.Rg2! (Not seen by Andersson. Again defense and attack. The saving tempo-winning threat 17...,cxd2+ is gone.) **17...,Qb7 18.Rxg7+,Kh8** (See diagram 19.) **19.Rg8+!!** Stunning, a full Rook sacrifice that decides the game. Black resigned (1-0) because he saw that 19..,Kxg8 20.Rg1+,Kh8 21.fxe7+,f6 22.exf8Q+,Rxf8 loses a piece and the game, while 19..,Rxg8 20.fxe7+,Rg7 21.Rg1,Qxb2+ 22.Kd1,Qb1+ 23.Bc1 mates.

One of the most enduring books about openings was written by the above-mentioned GM Fine. 'The ideas behind Chess Openings' first published in 1948. It has gone through many reprints. The serious student of chess will get a wealth of information about all relevant openings. Fine gives ten practical rules the beginning player should stick to:

1. Open with either e4 or d4.

2. Wherever possible, make a good developing move which threatens something.

3. Develop Knights before Bishops.

4. Pick the most suitable square for a piece and develop it

there once and for all.

5. Make one or two pawn moves in the opening, not more.

6. Do not bring your Queen out early.

7. Castle as soon as possible, preferably on the K-side.

8. Play to get control of the center.

9. Always try to maintain at least one pawn in the center.

10. Do not sacrifice without a clear and adequate reason.

Further he says it is worth remembering that there are two questions which must be answered for each move played:

1. How does it affect the center?

2. How does it fit in with the development of my other pieces and pawns.

We must have a plan in the opening so that we move into the middle game with all our pieces developed. We should be able to adapt it, depending on the play of our opponent. Those skills of strategy and skirmishing you develop by regular play. The plan is most easily acquired by analysing master games in the openings you favor.

We hope you understand by now that a loss in under 20 moves can happen to anyone, and that often this is not always due to a difference in strength. Fine combinations have been made in chess for hundreds of years, but it is only in the last 60 years that chess players have become systematic about tactics. We know now that there are many patterns to the combinations that decide a game. These are used to program computers and also to help young chess players to improve their game. We already mentioned developing your tactical skills by solving the daily chess problems in your paper.

Although this does not relate directly to openings, it may be useful to say something about Elo ratings. It is a term we have used several times already. A player with a certain rating has obtained it by virtue of the results, (i.e. performance) in the games he has played.

In general they are against other rated opponents as scored in tournaments. It corresponds roughly to the computer ratings in tennis. The terms has been derived from the name of its creator Prof. Arpad Elo of the USA. Internationally rated players have a rating of

2005 and higher for both men and women. FIDE originally stuck to 2205 for men, but lowered this last year for obvious reasons. Those players who have an Elo rating of 2300 for over a period of one year and who have been playing actively, become so called FIDE masters. Most international masters (IM) are rated over 2400, most grand-masters over 2500. The GMs over 2600 are generally referred to as Super GMs. Only Kasparov (the current champion until he dropped out of FIDE), Karpov, Anand, Ivanchuk, Kramnik, Shirov and Salov are rated over 2700 with resp. 2805, 2781, 2721, 2704, 2727 and 2711(April 1994).. Bobby Fischer, despite his return to chess is not rated. He was the first player to reach 2800!

But even on a much lower level than world champions or top GMs, fine games can be played and used to demonstrate the principle necessary to come to a winning position in the opening. Following are four short games played by one of the authors against slightly weaker opponents or adversaries who played without due care. What the following games demonstrate is exactly those principles we have discussed before: without a center you are in most cases quickly lost, and the player who has the better development will dictate the game. After you have played each game, compare notes with the ten rules on the previous page, and you will see that they work. There is thus a direct correlation between following these rules and results. All other things being equal, that will save you a lot of work and dis-appointment in the long run.

The first one is the Petroff (or Russian Defense) that leads to an almost even game: White - Kaarlo Schepel Black - Khalid Al-Attal (Kuwait), Asian Team Championship, Genting Highlands (1989). **1.e4,e5 2.Nf3,Nf6 3.Nxe5,d6 4.Nf3,Nxe4 5.d4,Be7** (Here 5...,d5 to defend the Knight is slightly better.) **6.Bd3,Nf6 7.c4,c6** (A bit too cautious.) **8.Nc3,0-0 9.Qc2,Nbd7 10.Bg5,Re8 11.0-0-0,Nf8 12.Rde1,Ng6 13.h4!,Bg4 14.Nh2!,Be6? 15.f4** (Black is already in trouble.) **15...,Nf8 16.f5,Bd7 17.g4,h6 18.Be3,N6h7 19.Nf3,Rb8** (Too late.) **20.g5!,hxg5 21.hxg5, Nxg5** (See Diagram 20. White has sacrificed just one pawn to open up the h-file. His Rooks are inter-connected, an important rule you should remember for an effective middle-game, and Rh1 can support the Queen, so she can travel into enemy territory) **22.Qh2** (Threatens 23.Qh8++.) **22...,f6**

23.Nf3xg5,f6xg5 24.Ne4,d5 (Here 24..,Bxf5 is better but would be answered by 25.Ref1 and mate is not far off.) **25.f6!** (Diagram 21.)

Diagram 20   **Diagram 21**

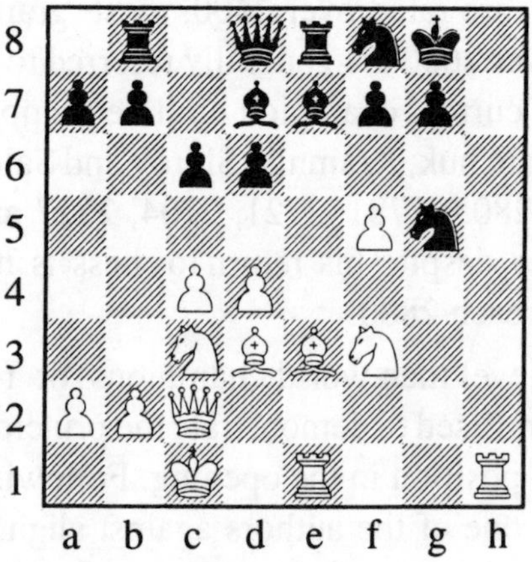

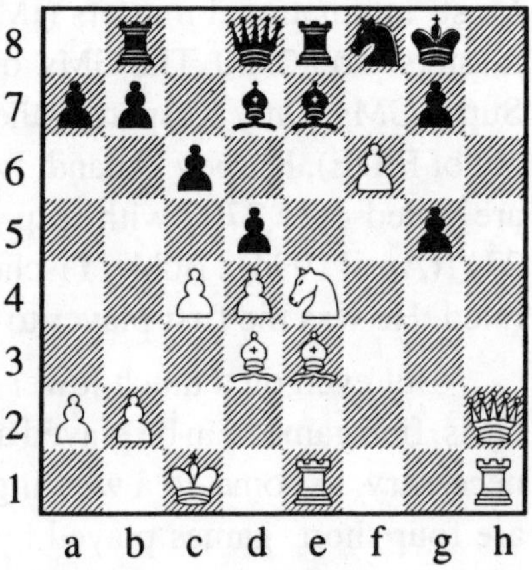

25...,gxf6 (If 25..,Bxf6 26.Nd6! and the Black King cannot escape; if 25...,dxe4 26.Qh8+,Kf7 27.Qxg7+,Ke6 28.Bxg5, Bxf6 29.Rxe4+,Kd6   30.Bf4+ etc.) **26.Qh8+,Kf7 27.Nxg5+,fxg5 28.Rh7+,Ke6 29.Bf4++** (1-0.) Here 29.Qe5+ would mate too. What is the reason that Black loses in all these different variations, you will ask. After all, he developed his pieces and defended reasonably well. Answer: the main reason is that he was weak in the center from the start, and that he lost several tempi. He would still have had a chance if he had tried to counter on the Q-side. That is also a vital rule in the middle game. Either you defend or you counter on the other wing. Black's 12th to 15th moves were a complete waste. After that he had never the chance to catch up. It was just a question of finding the right approach and then close the trap.

Another game that works on the same principle, (except that White tried to counter but ran out of time) was won by Black in the Exchange variation of the Ruy Lopez (or Spanish), the classic K-pawn symmetrical opening. White never had a chance after a few weak moves. He is quite a strong chess player and just did not have his day. White - Colin Madhavan (Malaysia) Black - Kaarlo Schepel (Genting Highlands, 1989)

1.e4,e5 2.Nf3,Nc6 3.Bb5,a6 4.Bxc6, dxc6 (the more usual line is 5.Ba4,Nf6 6.0-0,Be7 7.Re1,b5 8.Bb3,0-0 etc.) **5.0-0,Bg4 6.h3,h5!** (If 7.hxg4,hxg4 8.Ne1,Qh4!) **7.d3,Bd6** (If 8.hxg4,hxg4 9.Ng5,Nh6! and the White Knight is caught.) **8.Be3,Bxf3 9.Qxf3,Qe7 10.Nd2,0-0-0 11.Nc4,g6 12.c3,f5! 13.exf5,Rf8** (The point; Black has gained a tempo by using the already discussed pin.) **14.d4,e4 15.Nxd6+,cxd6 16.Qg3,gxf5 17.Bf4,h4! 18.Qg5,Qe6 19.c4,Ne7 20.Bh2,Rfg8 21.Qf4?,Qg6**. (See Diagram 22.)

Diagram 22

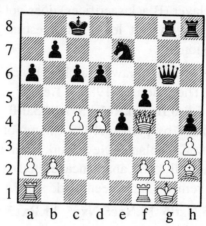

(If White had played 21.Qd2 then 22.f3 would have been possible. Now there threatens a mate in one by 22...,Qxg2; the reply is forced. Just like in the previous game, White did not do anything really wrong. He just wasted time, and thought still about attack when it was time to spend all energy on defending his King. That is now going to cost him the game.) **22.g3,hxg3 23.Bxg3,Rxh3 24.Kg2** (Or 24.Qxd6?? loses the Queen: 24..,Qxd6!, because Bg3 is pinned.) **24...,Qh5! 25.Rg1** (better, but still losing is 25.Rh1,Ng6 26.Qxd6,Qf3+ and mate; or 26.Qe3, Rxh1 27.Rxh1,Qg4! and there is no defense against 28...,f4! etc.) **25...,Ng6 26. Qxd6, Rxg3+!** and White resigned as it is mate in two moves (27.Qxg3,Nf4+ 28.Kf1,Qe2++ or 27.fxg3 or 27.Kxg3,Qf3+ and 28...,Rh8++).

Although this game was not decided by an early sacrifice, the two main principles are there again. Black took the initiative, had his pieces better developed and had the edge in the center after the pawn push e5-e4. Finally two more games in the same Spanish Opening, where the White players were not familiar with the variation. The value of a sacrifice at the right moment will prevent the adversary to develop his game normally. If you can delay the normal development moves of your opponent by 2-3 tempi, the sacrifice of a pawn is well justified. The established openings in which a pawn is sacrificed are called 'Gambits'. In the next two games we look at the best known and soundest gambit of the Spanish Opening. According to Kasparov, if accepted, it will give Black at least equal play. But often the White player (Black sacrifices) does not know all the complications that go with it. It leads to interesting games, thus well worth trying occasionally.

White - Mubiana Nawa (Zambia) Black - Kaarlo Schepel (Chess Olympics, Thessaloniki 1988). **1.e4,e5 2.Nf3,Nc6 3.Bb5,a6 4.Ba4,Nf6 5.0-0,Be7 6.Re1,b5 7.Bb3,0-0 8.c3,d5!?** (The famous gambit initiated by perpetual US Champion Frank Marshall in his game against Capablanca, New York 1918. He had waited 10 years to play it, but still lost. Capablanca refuted it over the board, but many solid improvements have been made since.)

9.exd5,Nxd5 10.Nxe5,Nxe5 11.Rxe5,c6 12.d4,Bd6 (12.g3 is considered the strongest move today to keep the Queen out.) **13.Re1,Qh4 14.g3,Qh3 15.Re4?,g5!** (Stops 16.Rh4 etc; this is theory, but hard to find over the board.) See Diagram 23.

Diagram 23

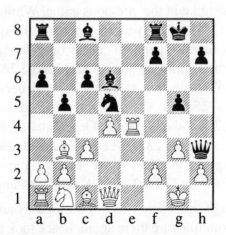

16.Bxg5? (Black's move was so quaint that taking the pawn is almost irresistible.) **16...,Qf5** (Suddenly material loss is unavoidable, both Re4 and Bg5 are threatened. White panics.) **17.Bh6,Qxe4**

18.Bxf8,Bh3 19.f3 (There is no defense left..) **19...,Qe3+ 20.Kh1,Qf2**
(1-0.)

The last game is based on the same principle. White has not
enough pieces developed and loses quickly when his most active
piece (the Rook) has to be given to avoid mate. The first nine moves
are the same: White - Lionel Wong Black - Kaarlo Schepel, Hongkong
Open 1989. **10.h3?** (White knows that the quick employment of the
Black Bishop-pair can be devastating. The move prevents 10....,Bg4,
but invites a host of problems. If White does not like 10.Nxe5 etc.
because of the tempo and development loss, then 10.d4 will solve
that.) **10....,e4! 11.Rxe4,Bf5 12.Re1,Bd3!** (Locks in Bc1, Nb1 and
Ra1, thus:) **13.Ne5,Nxe5 14.Rxe5,Nf4** (If now 15.Qf3,Bd6
16.Qxf4,Bxe5 17.Qxe5,Re8 etc.; if 15.Qg4,g5 16.g3,h5 17.Qf3,Nxh3+
18.Kg2,g4) **15.g3** (If the Knight moves, Rd5 gets rid of the
paralyzing Bishop.) **15...,Nxh3+ 16.Kg2,Bd6 17.Rd5,Be4+!**

Diagram 24

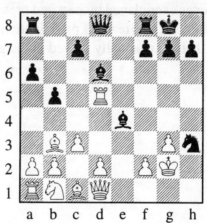

(See Diagram 24. Sacrifice of the Knight forces the White King
into a mating net.) **18.Kxh3,Qf6** (Immediate threats are 19...,Qxf2
etc. and 19...,Qe6+ 20.Kh2,Bxd5 wins the exchange. If 19.Kh2,Qh4+
20.Kg1,Qh1++.

Please note that the Queen cannot be taken,because g3 is
pinned by Bd6.) **19.Rxd6,cxd6** (Black has only one Bishop more on
the K-side, but it is enough for a win. Threat is 20...,Qh6+ etc.)
20.d4,Qxf2 21.Bf4,Bf3 and White lost soon. It is the loss of a Queen
or checkmate.

This short guide to openings is by no means complete. No book for beginners could possibly be. All the opening material you might possibly need in your first two years of play can be found in Part III of this book. We have tried to simplify this complex matter, so that a reader knows how to accumulate knowledge in a systematic manner. Basically chess players can be divided in naturally tactical and positional players. Try to find out what style you like, find one or two openings that suit your style, and gear your playing to one or more GMs who have a similar preference. By imitating their style and games you will learn quickly. Then try to improve your positional play (if you are tactically gifted), or your tactical play (if you possess common sense in positional games).

We turn now to the endgame. The middle game will need much more space to explain and is learnt best by analysing many annotated games. Part Two serves that purpose by introducing 11 of the most brilliant games ever played by past and present champions with very intensive analysis. The reader's participation is called for by guessing the moves that were actually played in the games.

*   *   *   *

CHAPTER 3

THE ENDGAME

Most dedicated chess players like the authors cannot help noticing over the years that most junior and even adult competitors have difficulties in converting a decisive advantage in an endgame into a win. We recently watched with amusement how a boy in the under-12 competition chased his opponent's lone King all over the board with a Queen. The game ended in stalemate.

Yes, endgame knowledge is essential for a chess player; you cannot expect to score well in competitions without it. That is why we include a special chapter on endgames. This is a vast subject and the space allotted is limited. We have thus taken the basic ideas that we think a beginner cannot do without. For further advancement, we strongly suggest that you consult authoritative works on the subject. In this respect we remind readers that all world champions, past and present, are great endgame masters. Capablanca is reputed to have studied thousands of endgames before he learned the theories of the chess openings, and before he became famous.

The study of endgames requires patience, but understanding the logic behind the moves makes the learning process a joy.

A) How to force checkmate with a Queen and King.

Diagram 25

Even a simple ending like this requires a plan to save time and energy. It has to be done in as few moves as possible. It is rather embarrassing and of no use to keep checking the Black King and chase him all over the board like a merry-go-round! The correct plan to force checkmate is to first restrict the movement of the opponent's King with both the Queen and the King. Please note that the White King (the winning side in this case) is an important attacking piece in endgames. The Black King has to be forced to the edge of the board or one of the corners, where he will be checkmated. The simplest way (starting in diagram 25) to carry out this plan is as follows: **1.Qe3,Kc4** (If 1...,Kd6 then simply 2.Qe4 further restricting the King's freedom.) **2.Kb2,Kd5** (if 2...,Kb4 3.Qc3+ and the Black King is confined to the a- and b-files) **3.Kc3,Kc6 4.Qe5!,Kd7** (If 4...,Kb6 5.Qd5) **5.Kc4,Kc6 6.Qd5+,Kc7 7.Kc5,Kc8** (First goal is achieved, the Black King is at the edge of the board.) **8.Kc6,Kb8 9.Qd7,Ka8 10.Qb7** mate.

Diagram 26

We talked about stalemate. By that we mean that it is a player's turn to move, but there is no "legal" move he can make (without putting himself in check). The rules of chess call that a stalemate, and one of the ways a game ends in a draw. It is not so uncommon as you would think, especially when there is time-trouble. Watch out for common stalemate positions, like when the lone King of your opponent is in a corner (see diagram 26). **1.Qb6??** or **1.Kc7??** Stalemate!

The correct approach is to restrict the Black King to the back rank with... **1.Qg7,Kb8 2.Kc6,Ka8 3.Qb7** mate (or 2...,Kc8 3.Qc7 or 2.Qg8 mate).

(B) How to force checkmate with a Rook and King.

Checkmating a lone King with a Rook is easy, but a plan is required to keep the number of moves to a minimum. The technique used is similar to that used with a Queen. The Black King is to be forced to retreat to the edge or corner of the board, where it is checkmated.

Diagram 27

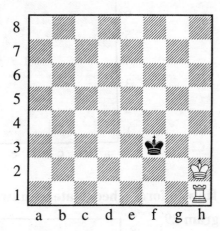

1.Re1! (An important move which saves tempi. The Black King is now confined to within a region of 3 files.) **1...,Kf2 2.Re8,Kf3 3.Kh3,Kf4** (If 3...,Kf2 4.Kg4,Kg2 5.Re2+,Kf1 6.Kf3,Kg1 7.Re1+,Kh2 8.Ra1!,Kh3 9.Rh1++.) **4.Kh4,Kf5 5.Kg3,Kg5** (Or 5...,Kf6 6.Kg4,Kf7 7.Re5,Kf6 8.Kf4 etc. with a similar end.) **6.Re5+,Kf6 7.Kf4,Kg6** (Or 7....,Kf7 8.Kf5!) **8.Re6+,Kf7** (If 8...,Kh5 9.Ra6!,Kh4 10.Rh6++.) **9.Kf5,Kg7** (If 9...,Kf8 10.Kf6 etc.) **10.Re7+,Kf8** (if 10...,Kg8 11.Kg6,Kf8 12.Kf6 etc.) **11.Kf6,Kg8 12.Re8+,Kh7 13.Ra8!** (A useful waiting move that settles the issue! The Black King is now in 'zugzwang': he has to move and finds himself in a mating net.) **13...,Kh6 14.Rh8++.**

(C) One Bishop with a King cannot win.

This should be quite obvious. Because the chess board consists of an equal number of white and black squares, the lone Bishop can only attack squares of its own color. The opponent King has a passage of escape along the squares not controlled by the Bishop.

(D) One Knight with a King cannot win.

One Knight cannot force a checkmate. The best the Knight can do, with the assistance of the King, is to corner the opponent King, resulting in a stalemate position as diagrammed.

Diagram 28

(E) How to force checkmate with two Bishops?

Diagram 29

Two Bishops together can attack and cover all squares on the chessboard. With the assistance of the King, the opponent King is forced to retreat to a corner where it is checkmated. From the position in diagram 29, the first practical step for White to take is to centralise his King and let the Black King choose into which corner he will be driven.

1.Kd2,Ke4 2.Kc3,Ke5 3.Bd3,Kd5 4.Be3,Ke5 (The Black King tries to stay in the center to prolong the struggle.) **5.Kc4,Kd6 6.Bd4,Ke6 7.Kc5,Kd7 8.Be4,Ke7 9.Bd5,Kd7 10.Be5,Ke7 11.Kc6,Kd8 12.Bf7,Kc8 13.Bf6,Kb8 14.Be6,Ka7 15.Be5,Ka6** (if 15...,Ka8 16.Bc8!,Ka7 17.Kc7!,Ka8 18.Bb7+,Ka7 19.Bd4++) **16.Bc3!** (Black's escape route via a5 has to be sealed off! The end is now not far away.) **16...,Ka7 17.Kc7,Ka6 18.Bc4+,Ka7 19.Bd4+,Ka8 20.Bd5++.** A tedious process, someone might say. But in a real chess struggle, there are no easily earned points. The true beauty of the art is normally hidden under the meticulous execution of scientific principles.

(F) Two Knights (and a King) cannot force checkmate.

In diagram 30, the Black King is already confined to the corner. But the White King cannot force checkmate, because stalemate will result if you try to confine the opponent further. This is a peculiar situation: you cannot win despite having such a vast material advantage!

Let us see ....

1.Nf6+,Kh8 2.Ng5 (intending 3.Nf7 mate?) Black has no legal moves left and is thus stalemated, thus the game has ended in an automatic draw.

Diagram 30

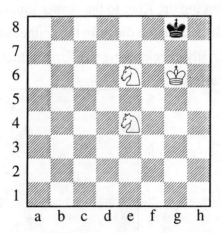

In order to avoid stalemate or a repetition of moves (also an draw, as long as one of the players claims it, according to the 'laws' of chess, when three times in succession the same position is on the board with the same player to play), White simply has to free the Black King from the corner.

The interesting thing is that if Black has a pawn on, say, e2 in the above diagram, then there is no stalemate and White wins as follows: **1.Nf6+,Kh8 2.Ng5,e1=Q 3.Nf7++.**

(G) How to force checkmate with Bishop and Knight.

The laws of chess allow a maximum of 50 moves for mating an opponent without the capture of any piece; when the 50-move limit is exceeded, the game is counted as a draw (as long as one of the players claims it).

You can force checkmate with Bishop and Knight against a lone King, but the process of checkmating generally takes well over 30 moves with precise execution! Needless to say, you should know exactly how to go about it to claim victory with such a material advantage.

Let us start with a position that is 'most favourable' for the defense (as is customary the defending side is Black). The winning process involves three stages:

(1) forcing the opponent's King to the edge of the board.

(2) forcing the King to the corner square controlled by the Bishop (in the diagram thus either a8 or h1) and,

(3) finally checkmating the King in that corner.

Diagram 31

52

1.Be2,Kd4 2.Kd2,Ke4 (Naturally the Black King resists being driven back.) **3.Nc3+,Ke5 4.Ke3,Kf5 5.Kd4,Kf4 6.Nd5+,Kf5 7.Bd3+,Ke6 8.Nf4+,Kf6 9.Kd5,Kg7 10.Ke5,Kf7 11.Bc4+,Kg7 12.Kf5,Kh6 13.Bd5,Kg7 14.Kg5,Kh7 15.Ne6,Kh8.**

The harmonious co-operation of the King, Bishop and Knight has driven the Black King back to the edge of the board. But now he deliberately retreats to the corner not controlled by the White Bishop (an important strategy to remember if you are yourself on the losing side!). White's next task is to drive the opponent now to the opposite corner (a8), where he can be checkmated:

16.Kg6,Kg8 17.Ng5+,Kh8 18.Be4!,Kg8 19.Nf7!,Kf8 20.Kf6,Kg8 21.Bf5,Kf8 22.Bh7!,Ke8 23.Ne5,Kf8 24.Nd7+,Ke8 25.Ke6,Kd8 26.Kd6,Ke8 27.Bg6+,Kd8 28.Nc5,Kc8 29.Bh5,Kd8 30.Nb7+,Kc8 31.Kc6,Kb8 32.Kb6,Kc8 33.Bg4+,Kb8 34.Bf5,Ka8 35.Nc5,Kb8 36.Na6+,Ka8 37.Be4++.

A long process, isn't it? Chess is a hard game, but very satisfying when you succeed in winning such a game. And that is why it is so fascinating.

The (B+N) checkmating technique demands the harmonious co-ordination of the Bishop, Knight and King. It is a good practice to set up (B+N) positions and to try to force the opponent's King to the checkmating corner. Have a try with a friend and have fun!

(H) The value of a single, meager pawn advantage.

In chess the value of the pawn is the least of all pieces at the beginning of the game. However, in the endgame the relative value of a pawn is completely different. With the assistance of his King or any of the pieces, a (so called) 'passed pawn' may be pushed to the eighth rank and be promoted into a Queen, a Rook, a Bishop or a Knight as preferred. An extra pawn in the endgame often means victory.

In the following sections we present you with the most basic and common types of endgame that illustrate the extraordinary hidden benefit of a meagre pawn advantage.

(I) King + Pawn versus King

In studying this type of endgame we have to understand the concepts of 'opposition' and 'zugzwang'.

(a) Opposition

When the two Kings are facing each other with one square separating them, the side whose turn it is not to play, is said to have the opposition. In King + Pawn vs. King endings, White can only win if he has the opposition in the diagram (and similar positions) shown; otherwise the game should end in a draw because of stalemate. Let us have a look.

Diagram 32

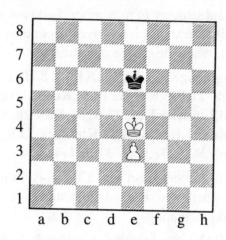

(1) White has the opposition:

It is Black's turn to move, which means that he has to concede vital squares to White. The game should continue as follows:

1...,Kd6 2.Kf5,Ke7 3.Ke5,Kd7 4.Kf6,Ke8 5.e4,Kd7 6.e5,Ke8 7.Ke6 (White maintains the opposition! Note that White should never play 7.e6??,Kf8! and now it is Black who has the opposition, and the game ends in a draw because of 8.e7+,Ke8 9.Ke6 and it is stalemate.) **7...,Kf8 8.Kd7,Kf7 9.e6+,Kf8 10.e7+,Kg7 11.e8=Q** White wins.

2) Black has the opposition:

It is White's turn to move and the game should end in a draw.

1.Kd4,Kd6 2.e4,Ke6 3.e5,Ke7 4.Kd5,Kd7! (Black maintains the opposition. He should never play 4...,Ke8?? 5.Ke6!, when White gains the opposition and wins.) **5.e6+,Ke7 6.Ke5,Ke8!** (Again, Black has to be extremely careful! For if 6...,Kf8?? 7.Kf6! and White wins. And if 6...,Kd8?? 7.Kd6,Ke8 8.e7 and White wins because of opposition.) 7.**Kd6,Kd8** (or 8.Kf6,Kf8 draws in the same way.) **8.e7+,Ke8 9.Ke6** stalemate!

3) Rook pawn - the exception:

You should note that with a Rook pawn White cannot win even if he has the opposition, because of stalemate in the corner. The Black King cannot be forced out by the extra tempo.

Let us proceed from diagram 33:

Diagram 33

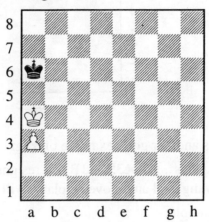

1...,Kb6   2.Kb4,Ka6   3.a4,Kb6   4.a5+,Ka6   5.Ka4,Ka7 6.Kb5,Kb7   7.a6+,Ka7   8.Ka5,Ka8   9.Kb6,Kb8   10.a7+,Ka8 11.Ka6 stalemate!

(b) Zugzwang:

This word in German means 'obligation to move'. In chess it denotes a situation where you have to move because it is your turn; but any move you make is a bad one!

Zugzwang is a common motif in the middle game, especially in positional games. But in the endgame the correct use of zugzwang often helps the superior side in claiming a swift victory. The situation we discussed under (a) "the opposition", is thus just a special case of zugzwang. The following (diagram 34) is a composed problem by Richter, based on the theme of zugzwang: **1.Kb7+!,Kh7** (Black has to protect his Queen.) **2.Qh2+,Kg8 3.Qa2+,Kh7** (If 3...,Kf8 4.Qa8+ wins the Queen) **4.Qf7!** (Now Black is in zugzwang; and he has no choice but to move his Queen to a bad square!) **4...,Qg8**

(Please note that every other square is covered by the White pieces; g8 is the only square left.) **5.Qh5++** mate.

Diagram 34

Here is another good example of 'zugzwang' (diagram 35):

White plays .... **1.Qe3!!** and Black resigns. Why? Because Black is in 'zugzwang' and any move he plays will simply lose the game!

For example:

a) **1...,g5 2.Qe1+,Qg3+ 3.Qxg3++**

b) **1...,Qg5 2.Qh3++**

c) **1...,Qf5** (or other Q-moves)

   2.Qg3++

Diagram 35

(J) Some illustrative examples of pawn endings:

a) Two connected passed pawns should win. The way to win in diagram 36 is quite simple:

1.c6!,Kd6 (Black cannot take the pawn by 1...,Kxd5 because of 2.c7 and the pawn will queen on the next move.) **2.Kf6** (Putting Black in 'zugzwang'.) **2...,Kc7 3.Ke7,Kc8 4.d6,Kb8 5.Kd7**, and White will promote his c-pawn into a Queen in two moves by 6.c7 and 7.c8Q.

Diagram 36

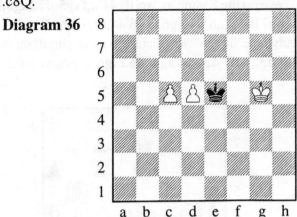

b) Two passed pawns with distance between them usually win (diagram 37):

1.f6! (Not 1.c6??,Kxc6 2.f6, Kd7 3.f7, Ke7 draw.) **1...,Kxc5 2.f7** (White wins.); or **1.f6,Ke6 2.c6,Kd6 3.f7,Ke7 4.c7** (White wins, as the the Black King is helpless. He cannot guard against two passed pawns at the same time.)

Diagram 37

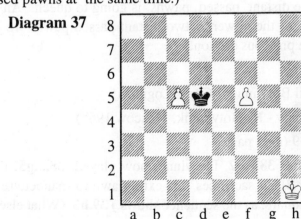

(c) Capablanca shows his artistry in a pawn ending (diagram 38).

(Capablanca - Conde, Hastings 1919)

Position after **38...,Kd7**. Now Capablanca played a stunning move:

39.b4!!,axb4 (if 39...,cxb4 40.Kxd4 also wins) **40.a5**. (The distant passed pawn diverts Black's King to the Q-side. This needed very careful calculation.) **40...,Kc7 41.g5!** (Now, White is creating another passed pawn on the K-side as well!) **41...,fxg5 42.fxg5,hxg5** (What can Black do? If 42...,h5 43.g6,fxg6 44.fxg6 and Black cannot cope with the advance of the two distant pawns simultaneously.) **43.hxg5,b3 44.Kd3!,Kd7 45.g6,fxg6 46.fxg6** (resigns 1-0.)

Diagram 38

(One of the distant passed pawns is going to queen. An excellent example of the power of two distant passed pawns we just discussed in the previous section.)

(d) Mikhail Botwinnik - Chess Logician!

(M. Taimanov - M. Botwinnik, Moscow 1967)

Diagram 39 (next page)

Position after **38.Kg2**. Botwinnik now played: **38...,g5!** (The winning move! Black sacrifices his extra pawn to manoeuvre his King to a vital square, as the sequence shows.) **39.h5** (What else? If

39.hxg5,Kg6 and Black wins simply.) **39...,Kg7 40.Kg3,Kh7!!**
(Accurate tempo calculations are absolutely necessary in endgames.
If 40...,Kh6, as most beginners would normally do, then 41.Kxg4 and
it is Black who is in 'zugzwang'! But after the ingenuous text move
Black's victory is near.)

Diagram 39

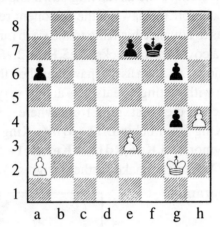

41.Kxg4,Kh6 42.e4; and here White resigned later after
making this sealed move at the adjournment at the end of the first
time-control. The reason is obvious to experienced chess players:
after 42...,a5 43.a3,e6 44.a4,e5 45.Kf5,Kxh5 46.Kxe5,g4
47.Kf4,Kh4 48.e5,g3 49.Kf3,Kh3 50.e6,g2 51.e7,g1=Q
52.e8=Q,Qf1+ 53.Ke4,Qe1+ winning the Queen.

This endgame is another excellent example of the 'zugzwang'
motif in an actual tournament game.

(K) Rook and pawn vs. Rook endgames

After the middlegame struggle and simplifications, Rook +
pawn vs. Rook are possibly the most common of endgames. Because
of space limitation we can only present you with the most basic,
essential knowledge of this type of endings. Any chess player should
know at least how to play the famous 'Philidor' and 'Lucena' positions.

(a) The Philidor Position:

This is a drawn position (see diagram 40) established by the great
French 18th century chess master and musician. It is this type of po-

sition the defending side has to strive for. He can then can secure a draw with careful play, though he is a pawn behind and his King is confined to the eighth rank.

The characteristic features of the position is that the Black King is in front of the advancing pawn and the Black Rook is on the sixth rank before the pawn of the opponent reaches it. In order to win, White has to advance his King to the sixth rank. So he tries to use his pawn as a cover from checks: **1.e5,Rh6 2.e6,Rh1!** (This is the most critical move. As soon as the pawn reaches the sixth rank, White will play Kd6 with mating threats. It is at this very moment that Black has to advance to the first rank from where he can start to check the White King from behind. The White King cannot hide behind the pawn anymore.) **3.Kd6,Rd1+ 4.Ke5,Re1+ 5.Kf6,Rf1+** (There is no way that White can make further progress.)

Diagram 40

The following position (see diagram 41) is another drawn position worth discussing. White's Rook on b6 is misplaced, giving Black the opportunity to play for a draw following the Philidor technique.

It is a draw even if it is White's turn to move:

(i)   If **1.Rb7,Ra6+ 2.Kf5,Ra1** (Draw as Black can check White's King from behind.);

(ii)   If **1.Kf5** (Black simply plays:) **1...,Ra1** (as above);

(iii) If **1.f7,Rc8** (And it is a draw.)

Diagram 41

(b) The Lucena Position:

This winning position was established by the then famous Spanish chess master and writer Lucena, as early as 1497! It is this type of position the winning side should strive for. From the diagrammed position (diagram 42) White wins by playing ....

1.Rf4 (The key and winning method of 'building a bridge in the Lucena position.) **1...,Rc1 2.Ke7,Re1+ 3.Kd6,Rd1+ 4.Ke6,Re1+ 5.Kd5,Rd1+ 6.Rd4** (And White proceeds to queen his pawn)

Diagram 42

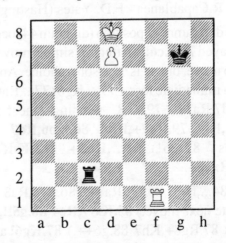

(c) Cutting off the defending King from the queening square.

From the position in diagram 43, the simplest way to win is to cut off the Black King from the queening square of the advancing pawn, in order to achieve the Lucena position, Thus ....

1.Rg2!,Rc1+ 2.Kd6,Rd1 (There is not much Black can do to stop the pawn advance.) **3.Ke6,Re1+ 4.Kd7,Rd1 5.d6,Kh7 6.Ke7,Re1+ 7.Kd8,Rd1 8.d7** (White has succeded in getting into the Lucena position.) **8....,Re1 9.Rg4** (The Rook is 'building a bridge', the characteristic winning technique of the Lucena position. And White now proceed to win as in b.)

Diagram 43

L) Some Illustrative examples of R + P endings:

a) J.R.Capablanca - F.D. Yates (Hastings, 1930)

The diagrammed position (diagram 44) occurred after: **76....,Ra7.** 'Capa' played **77.Kc6!!** (After this simple move Black is in zugzwang! He has to move, but it is Hobson's choice. Any move he makes will lead to an immediate loss.) **77...,Kg6** (77...,Ra6+ is no better, because of 78.Kd7,Ra7+ 79.Ke8 winning the f-pawn and the game.) **78.Rg8+,Kh7 79.Rg7+,Kh8 80.Kb6,Rd7 81.Kc5!** (Now White threatens 82.e6!) **81...,Rc7+ 82.Kd6,Ra7 83.e6!,Ra6+ 84.Ke7,Rxe6+**.

(If 84...,fxe6 85.f7!,Ra7+ 86.Kf6,Ra8 87.Kg6 followed by checkmate next move.) **85.Kxf7,Re4 86.g5!!,hxg5** (Forced as White threatens 87.Rg8+,Kh7 88.g6++.) **87.Kg6!** and Black resigns. The fatal threat is 88.Rh7+,Kg8 89.f7+,Kf8 90.Rh8+ followed by queening of the pawn. Black cannot parry this threat with 87...,Re6 because of 88.Re7! When analyzing this endgame, one cannot help admiring Capablanca's perfect endgame technique.

Diagram 44

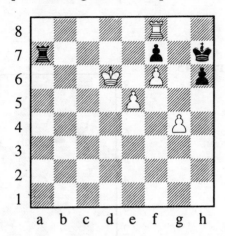

b) Max Euwe - Alekhine, world championship match 1937

The diagrammed position (diagram 45) occurred after **35.Ke2**. Let us have a look at the position. White is a pawn ahead, with an active Rook. And with three pawns against one pawn on the K-side, White can convert the K-side majority into two connected passed pawns, which is sufficient for a win. This winning strategy is easy to understand; but how to carry it through is quite a different story! Let us learn something from the Dutch world champion 1935-37 Max Euwe.

35...,Kf7 36.Rh4,Kg6 37.Rf4,Rb3 38.Rc4,Rb6 39.Ke3 (White activates his King towards the centre.) **39...,Kf5 40.g4+,Ke6** (If 40...,Kg5 41.f3 followed by 42.Rc5+ forcing the Black Monarch to retreat.) **41.f4,Kd5 42.Rd4+,Ke6** (If 42...,Kc5 43.f5 etc. winning easily.) **43.f5+,Ke7 44.Re4+,Kf7 45.h4,Rb1 46.Kf4,Rc1** (Black's only hope is to protect his c-pawn and march it forward.) **47.Ra4,h6 48.Ra7+,Kg8**.

Please note that the White Rook takes complete control of the dominating 7th rank, one of the most important features in Rook + Pawn endings. This control has definite positional advantages for the following reasons: (1) The Rook on the 7th rank confines the opponent to the back rank. (2) The Rook can attack advancing pawns from behind when necessary. For example, when White plays **Rc7**, Black's Rook is tied up for the defense of his c-pawn while the White

Rook enjoys freedom of space.

Diagram 45

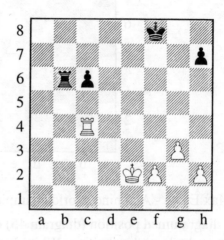

(Also note that in the game Black cannot play 48...,Kf6 because 49.Rh7 wins at once the h-pawn and the game.) **49.g5,Rc4+ 50.Ke5!** and here Black resigned (1-0). If 50...,hxg5 51.hxg5 and White has realized his plan of creating the connected passed pawns. And if 50...,Rxh4 51.g6! and checkmate is unavoidable after 52.Kf6.

c) K.Langeweg - M.Botwinnik, Beverwijk, 1969.

Position in diagram 46 after 36.**Rxg7**. In his last tournament before 'really' retiring, the ex-world champion Botwinnik found the best move: **36...,d4!** (The 'obvious' 36...,a4 is risky because of 37.Rxh7,a3 38.Ra7,b4 39.g5 and White's g-pawn will become extremely dangerous.) **37.Rxh7** (An error committed in time-trouble. Necessary was 37.exd4 to stay in the fight. After 37...,Rxh3 Black has at least a chance. Now Black's d-pawn will queen.) **37...,d3 38.Rh8** (So that if 38...,d2 39.Rd8+ winning the pawn.) **38...,Kc7!** (Nice and simple.

Diagram 46

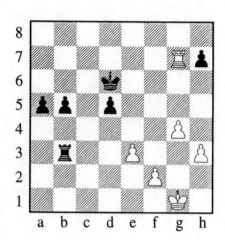

Now White's Rook cannot go to d8. White resigned.) The likely sequence would be: 39.Rh7+,Kc6 40.Rh6+,Kc5 41.Rh5+,Kc4 and White has no more checks left and the d-pawn will queen. And if 39.Kf1,Rc1+ and the White King is forced to go to g2.

* * * *

PART TWO

Developing Your Skills Through 11 Illustrated Games

CHAPTER 1

DEVELOPING YOUR SKILLS

This section illustrates some of the most famous games ever played in chess history. So what can you learn from these games? Obviously some of the conclusions to be drawn are pretty advanced. Remember that you are watching the efforts of the finest players the game has known. But there are many lessons for the casual player as well.

Once you are able to read a chess game and visualise it like many experienced chess players, the number of diagrams in the text will even allow you to play the games without a board or computer; a bit like blindfold chess. If you know brilliant games like these by heart, you will see their ideas will be most helpful during similar positions you may encounter over the board in your own games.

The Meaning of Elo Ratings

Elo rating	Description
1000 - 1200	Amateurs/Beginners
1200 - 1400	Weak club players
1400 - 1600	Average club players
1600 - 1800	Strong club players
1800 - 2100	Tournament players
2100 - 2400	Masters to strong International Masters

DEVELOPMENT

One of the most important factors in successful play is the proper development of your pieces, something we already discussed extensively in part One. After looking at games 1, 2, 3 and 7 you are bound to realize that the side that develops its forces quickly and effectively is the one that usually comes up with the winning combinations. Just count how many pieces each player has developed in the opening, i.e. how many pieces he has moved from their initial position to a more promising square, and you can usually guess pretty accurately which side is leading. Remember that castling is counted as an important developing move:

In game 2, Black neglects his development to the extent that he is unable to castle, and thus falls victim to a devastating attack.

So remember: More games are lost through lack of development than through any other single factor. Do not concentrate on shallow attacking moves that can easily be countered by the opponent. They usually help him to develop his pieces. Try not to move a piece twice in the opening (unless there is a very clear reason to do so) and put off your attacking plans till after your pieces are on good squares: Center pawns advanced and well-protected, Knights on c3 and f3, Bishops on long diagonals, King castled in safety, Rooks on open files (or files which might be opened shortly) and connected with each other. Developing the Queen comes last, since this valuable piece is usually driven back if prematurely thrown into the fray. In short, all the most important rules we discussed in Chapter 2. These are so important that we cannot emphasize them often enough. Here another refresher course:

KING SAFETY

"Great players never castle," wrote a Swedish chess teacher in 1784. This was probably the worst piece of advice in the history of chess. The study games prove that amply. Castling early is not a sign of timidity, it is the cornerstone of healthy play. Only when your King is in safety, can you undertake raids on the enemy position. If the Monarch is unprotected in the middle of the board, you will find you are wasting all your efforts warding off the opponent's threats - or even succumbing to them, as demonstrated in games 2 and 7.

CENTER CONTROL

In the initial phase of most games, the battle is for control of the center. "Without the center you have nothing," is an old chess adage! The best example is in game 5 whereas in game 7 Black fails to show that neglecting center control for a while (as advocated by the 'hypermodern school' at the beginning of this century) is a viable alternative. Remember that the Knight is most effective when it can operate from the center of the board. Note how Capablanca's Knight hops around the center in game 4, causing no end of problems for his opponent; or how powerful Fischer's Knight becomes in game 6 when it can move to a central square and from there infiltrate the enemy position.

LONG-RANGE PIECES

Knights are best moved to the center of the board, but Rooks and Bishops - and of course the Queen - are also effective at long range. Two Bishops working together can paralyse the opponent's position, and they are especially dangerous when posted on long diagonals that end around the enemy King! Games 3, 6 and 8 illustrate the power of Bishops. Rooks are most effective when they double up on an open file, as in game 5. A favourite place for the Rook is the 7th rank, where it attacks the enemy's pawns. Rooks and Queens will often threaten 'back-rank mate' - see games 2 and 5, in which this is the central them. The Queen is always good for double attacks - in game 1, Morphy reduces his opponent's position to shambles with such threats.

PAWN POWER

Many beginners tend to neglect their pawns, giving them away freely. But remember that at master level most games are decided by a single pawn! Take a look at Spassky's pawn in game 7, or Garry Kasparov's in game 8.

You will realize that pawns can be very powerful attacking pieces. And even in the spectacular game 5 a 'lowly' pawn is the cornerstone of White's development advantage.

OPENINGS

The first few moves of a chess game are of great importance since this is where a little study will bring the quickest results. Most beginners know just one or two openings and are easily outwitted by opponents with a more diversified repertoire. But this situation can be easily remedied - the computer will help you! It knows a large number of sound openings, ones that lead to good positions and exciting games. They are openings that the great masters of the game have devised over the centuries.

Playing through the study games will already give you a good cross-section of the best-known openings. In the first game, you will encounter the 'Philidor Defence', one of the oldest openings known, which begins with the moves **1.e4,e5 2.Nf3,d6**. White can play energetically with **3.Bc4** or **3.d4** (as Morphy did in game 1 and Adams in game 5), a continuation that usually leads to an exciting battle.

Another 'old' opening - the Italian Game (or 'Giuoco Piano') is to be seen in game 2: **1.e4,e5 2.Nf3,Nc6 3.Bc4**, usually leading to solid positions in which neither side must fear surprise attack. If you play 3.Bb5 (instead of 3.Bc4) things become more dangerous. This opening is known as the 'Ruy Lopez' (or Spanish Game) after the Spanish priest who first played it in the 16th century; it is very popular in modern chess. An excellent example is to be found in game 4.

Or perhaps you would like to try one of the more dashing openings, the 'Queen's Gambit': **1.d4,d5 2.c4**. White offers the opponent a pawn - not a very sincere offer, since after **2...,dxc4** he can win it back immediately with **3.Qa4+** and **4.Qxc4**. So the offer is usually rejected ('Queen's Gambit Declined'), as by Kasparov's opponent in game 8. You should study this opening very carefully, as it is one of the most common in present-day chess.

Of course there are more 'off-beat' openings, some of which could come as a nasty surprise to your friends. Take a look at the 'Grünfeld Defence' which Fischer used to trounce his opponent in game 6. It goes **1.d4,Nf6 2.c4,g6** preparing to put the Bishop on g7 and attack White's center pawns from the sidelines. Less recommended is the 'Larsen Opening' **1.b3,e5 2.Bb2**. Look at what happened to its inventor in game 7!

> **HINT**:When you reach a study position, do not look at the diagram that shows the actual move played until you have carefully thought about it.

THE CHESS COMPUTER: A TIRELESS AND PERFECT PARTNER
How to improve your game with a chess computer

The fusion of chess as an art and the advances of technology have produced a range of chess computers — such as RADIO SHACK, FIDELITY, KASPAROV, MEPHISTO, ... — that have been programmed with features and capabilities, advantageous to both beginners and proficient players.

For the beginner, owning a chess computer means that you can go through all the basics as often as you want: testing your chess abilities, sharpening your skills in the game and even getting a reliable evaluation of your performance from the computer! If you have just learned the moves, you can play simple games against the computer at its lowest level, knowing that your opponent will correct any illegal moves you may make, warn you when a piece is attacked or when you are in danger of losing material. Even if you are in a spot and do not know what to play, the computer will happily suggest a move for you.

As your level of skill increases, you can switch to higher levels and play serious games against the computer. You will learn to look after all your pieces as computers never miss the opportunity to capture undefended chessmen! You will also learn to watch for sneak attacks. In fact, the computer will be able to warn you when you have overlooked a trap. You will soon discover all the little tricks and combinations that lead to success in chess. Unlike a human opponent, though, this perfect partner will take defeat graciously and be always ready for another game!

Even if you are already a fairly proficient player, the computer will help you to sharpen your wits and learn sophisticated chess strategies. You can test your openings and work on difficult end-games. The computer will always allow you to take back unsound moves and try alternatives that promise greater success. Today's sophisticated chess computers have been programmed to show you on demand some of the most famous games ever played. These games and study positions are a further incentive to increase your skill and enjoyment of the game.

Whether you are an eager beginner or proficient player, the chess computer can both improve your skills and bring you additional hours of joy in the art of mastering chess!

ILLUSTRATED GAMES

CHAPTER 2

PAUL MORPHY (1837-1884)

In the middle of the last century, European chess was dominated by the Englishman Howard Staunton, self-proclaimed 'world champion', and by the German contender Adolf Anderssen, one of the most formidable attacking players of all time. The New World never produced a great chess master.

Then suddenly a star appeared the likes of which the chess world had never seen. Paul Morphy, born on June 22, 1837, in New Orleans was a child prodigy. He learnt the game by watching his father, and by the age of 12 he had beaten the strongest players in the city - and even demolished the visting Hungarian master Jacob Lowenstern. He was an extremely bright lad who went on to study law and graduated when he was 19 with the highest honours ever awarded to a law student. He was admitted to the bar of the state of Louisiana on the condition that he would not practise until he was 21.

In those two years, from 1857 to 1859, he completely transformed the chess world. "In the most charming and modest manner imaginable, he spent that brief period spreading goodwill and destruction wherever he went, giving the game of chess a glory which none had ever dreamed," says William Hartston. With the exception of Staunton, who studiously avoided a confrontation, Morphy beat all the leading masters in Europe in such a convincing fashion that it became clear that he was by far the strongest chess player alive. Then, after this short career, he suddenly retired from chess, never to play again.

Game 1 - Paul Morphy - Duke of Brunswick & Count Isouard de Vauvenargues, Paris 1858

(Philidor Defence - initial position, Diagram 1.)

This game is a true classic. It was played in an opera box in Paris, during the staging of the 'Barber of Seville', with Morphy's aristocratic opponents consulting with each other over their moves. The game combines the elegance and romanticism of a previous century with a precision and correctness so modern that you can still learn a profound lesson from it today. **1.e4,e5 2.Nf3,d6 3.d4,Bg4** (Diagram 2. In one of the oldest openings known, the Duke and the Count in consultation play an inaccuracy, refuted with style by Morphy. Correct is 3...,Nd7 - a solid move; 3...,Nf6 - counterattack; or 3...,exd4 - clearing the tension in the center. Now in the game, White can get ahead in development. What did Morphy do?)

(**Diagram 3**. This forced Black to give White two plusses: an advantage in development, as well as the advantage of two Bishops in an open position. Of course, Black could just give up the pawn, but he would lose the right to castle too after: 4...,dxe5 5.Qxd8+,Kxd8 6.Nxe5,Be6. Black could also resort to odd Queen moves like 4...,Qe7 which are an invitation to trouble.) **4...,Bxf3 5.Qxf3,dxe5 6.Bc4,Nf6** (**Diagram 4**.) Black plays too mechanically, overlooking a powerful double attack. Can you spot Morphy's move?) (**Diagram 5**. Attacking f7, an elementary weak square as we already learned; and b7 - surely Black now misses his light-squared Bishop he just exchanged! Note that normal development like 7.Nc3; or 7.0-0; or 7.Bg5 would give Black chances based on 7...,c6 and 8...,Qc7; or 7...,Bb4 with or without check.) **7...,Qe7 8.Nc3,c6** (**Diagram 6**. It looks as if Black has saved the day. White did not want to win just one pawn and have the Queens exchanged after 8.Qxb7,Qb4+ etc. Of course, Black could not play 7...,Qd7?? 8.Qxb7,Qc6 9.Bb5 and the Queen is lost. But Morphy concentrates on development. By the way, 8.Bxf7+,Qxf7 9.Qxb7 is also strong and wins a lot of material. Morphy never really seems interested in quantity! What did he play next?) (**Diagram 7**. Again some players and computers would simply castle 0-0, and after 9...,b5 would move the Bishop to d3. This might weaken Black's pawns, but White could lose the initiative, the momentum. Morphy has other ideas!) **9...,b5** (See **Diagram 8**. A provocative situation! It looks as if White must retreat his Bishop, when Black continues with 10...,Nbd7 and 11...,Nc5, with genuine counterthreats. For example, where should White put his Queen? But Morphy never gave his opponents time to catch their breath! What happened next?)

(A truly regal move! See **Diagram 9**. Giving up a piece for two pawns, White effectively prevents the opponents from catching up in development and getting the King safely castled. One could almost play this move on principle. Morphy probably played it on instinct.)**10...,cxb5 11.Bxb5+,Nbd7 12.0-0-0,Rd8**(See **Diagram 10**. In retrospect, 11...,Kd8 looks to be 'objectively' to be Black's best

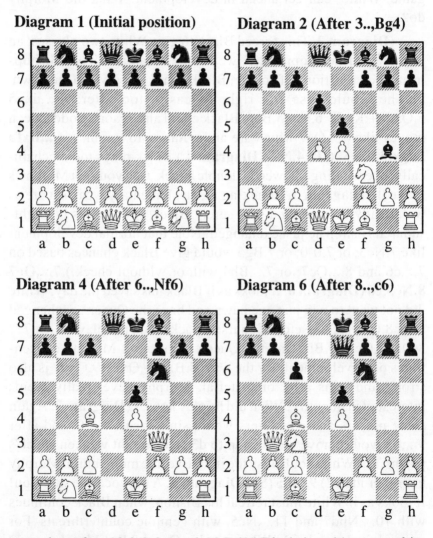

Diagram 1 (Initial position)

Diagram 2 (After 3..,Bg4)

Diagram 4 (After 6..,Nf6)

Diagram 6 (After 8..,c6)

move, but after 12.0-0-0+ and 13.Rd3! Black is subject to a big attack.Now White can win 'slowly', but Morphy, true to style, finds a brilliant move that shatters Black's dream of consolidating the

Diagram 8 (After 9..,b5)

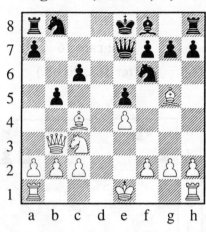

position. Can you guess what he played?) (**Diagram 11**. The real point of White's play.

Once again, he leaps ahead of his opponents' step-by-step plan, bringing his last not yet developed piece Rh1 into the game without loss of time. Actually 13.Rd3 is also good enough, as 13...,Qb4   14.Qxb4,Bxb4 15.Bxf6,gxf6 16.Rhd1 will win back the piece with 2 extra pawns in the ending.

Perhaps the romantic atmosphere of the Opera - as well as the constraints of time - propelled Morphy to a Grand Finale.)

Diagram 10 (After 12..,Rd8)   **Diagram 12 (After 14..,Qe6)**

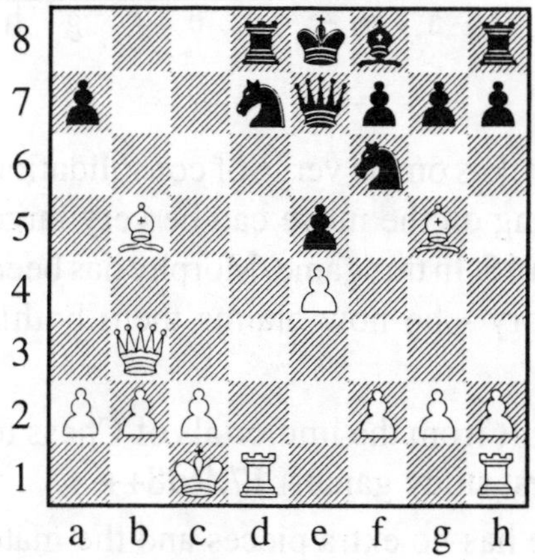

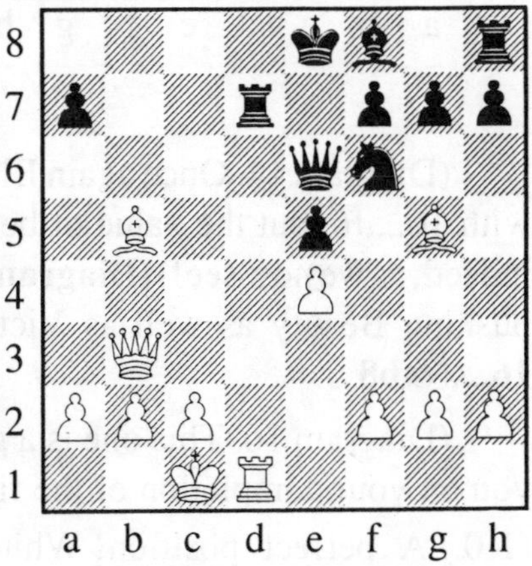

13…,Rxd7 14.Rd1,Qe6 (**Diagram 12**. By now it is just a question of how to lose for Black; 14...,Qb4 15.Bxf6,Qxb3 16.Bxd7++ mate would be nice, while 15...,gxf6 16.Bxd7+ would hardly be a graceful end, but the end nonetheless. Morphy can win material in various ways, but once again he has his eye on the final objective: Checkmate. What next?) (**Diagram 13**. White chooses the most pleasing win, leading to a quick mate; 15.Bxf6 and 15.Qxe6+ followed by 16.Bxf6 are good enough, but these continuations 'just' win material.) **15...,Nxd7**

Diagram 14

(After 15.., Nxd7.)

Diagram 16

(After 16.., Nxb8.)

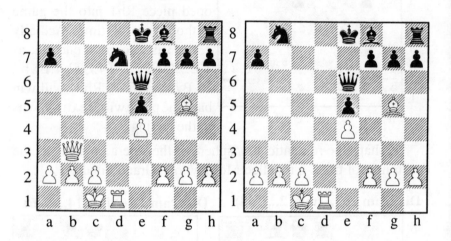

(Diagram 14. Once again Black is on the verge of consolidation with 16...,f6, but the value of being on the move can be very large indeed, as we now see!) (**Diagram 15**. In this game, Morphy has been pushing Beauty as well as Victory - he now claims them both!) **16...,Nxb8**

(Diagram 16. This one is a gift from the immortals of Chess to you on your completion of the first study game!) **17.Rd8++**

(1-0.) A perfect position! White has no extra pieces and the mate looks like the end of a composed problem. There are many great players for whom beauty and elegance are unimportant; only the result interests them. But for most of us, chess involves enjoyment as well as competition. These classic games can be as entertaining as they are instructive.

Diagram 3
(After 4. dxe5)

Diagram 5
(After 7. Qb3)

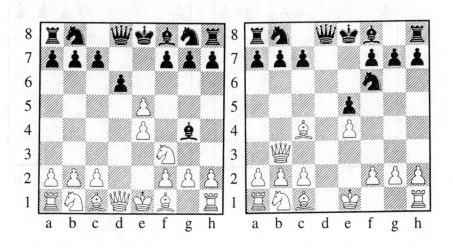

Diagram 7
(After 9. Bg5)

Diagram 9
(After 10. Nxb5)

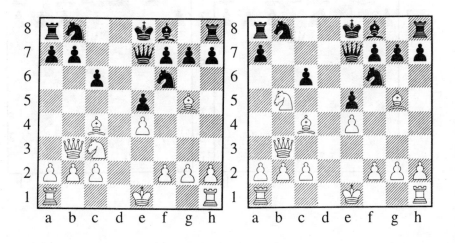

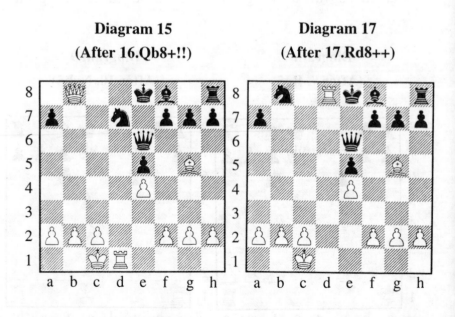

Diagram 11
(After 13.Rxd7!!)

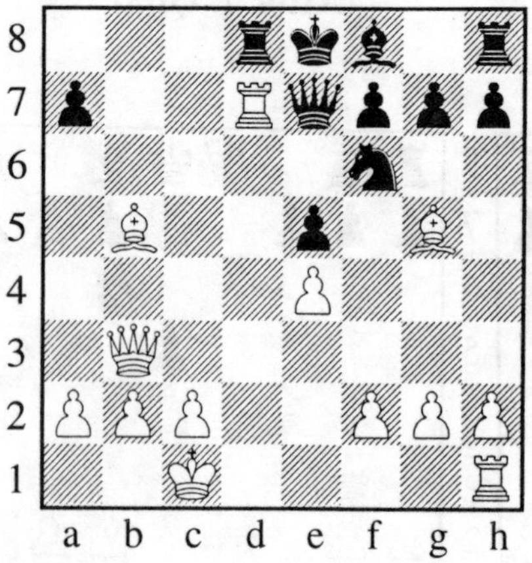

Diagram 13
(After 15.Bxd7+!)

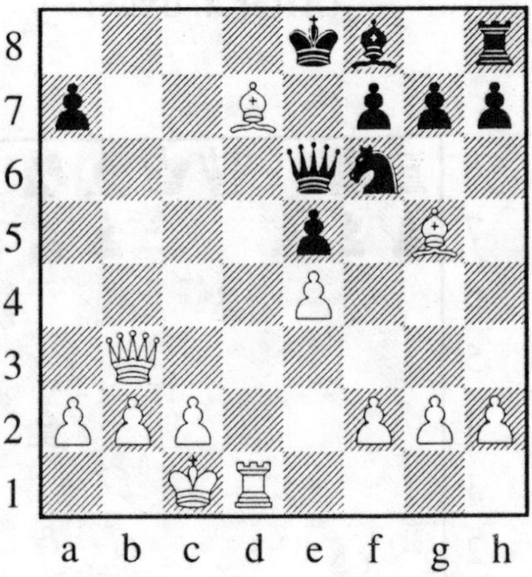

Diagram 15
(After 16.Qb8+!!)

Diagram 17
(After 17.Rd8++)

*   *   *   *

WILHELM STEINITZ (1836 - 1900)

In the "romantic" era of chess, dominated by Adolf Anderssen and Paul Morphy (the American genius), the prime goal was attack, the sudden lethal raid on the enemy position. But in the latter half of the 19th century, a player rose to the top of the chess world who considered strategy more important than tactical brilliance.

Wilhelm Steinitz began his chess career as a reckless player - in fact he was nicknamed "the Austrian Morphy". But he soon developed a totally different style, based on cold logic, more subtle and profound than the vicious attacking play of his predecessors that depended on the mistakes of the opponent. He articulated the principles of a scientific and logical brand of chess which strives for accurate moves that are immediately beneficial for full-scale development, a sound pawn structure, a foothole in the centre and "an accumulation of small advantages". If we take his match with Anderssen as the start of his supremacy, (and not the match with Zukertort in 1886) then he had an an unparalleled reign of 28 years (his successor Lasker got very close with 27 years). He not only became the first official "World Champion" but also proved that his methodical brand of chess was ultimately more beautiful than anything which had gone before. In the period of his reign, he won every tournament of chess or match he played in. Steinitz is rightly considered to be "the father of modern chess."

Game 2 Steinitz - von Bardeleben

One of the most spectacular games he played (as White) was in Hastings 1895 against von Bardeleben (Italian Game): (**Diagram 18** - initial position.) **1.e4,e5 2.Nf3,Nc6 3.Bc4,Bc5 4.c3,Nf6 5.d4,exd4 6.cxd4,Bb4+ 7.Nc3,d5** (Taking by Nxe4 is dangerous. Black chooses the most effective way to counter White's attacking chances, but ends up in a pin.) **8.exd5,Nxd5 9.0-0,Be6 10.Bg5,Be7 11.Bxd5,Bxd5 12.Nxd5,Qxd5 13.Bxe7,Nxe7** (Black has defended solidly and just needs to castle to complete his development and to connect his Rooks.) **14.Re1,f6 15.Qe2,Qd7 16.Rac1,c6?** (**Diagram 19**. Too slow but it is not clear what is the better move. 16..,Kf7? fails after 17.Qc4+. Now follows a hailstorm of beautiful moves. Can you find White's best move?) (**Diagram 20**. The key; note the advantages gained: White has an open c-line, square d4 is available for his Knight ready to jump at e6; at the same time Black's Ne7 is stuck.) **17...,cxd5 18.Nd4,Kf7 19.Ne6,Rhc8** (Here 19..,Nc6 is refuted by: 20.Nc5 with the threats 21.Qe6+ as soon as Qd7 moves as well as Nxb7.) **20.Qg4!,g6** (**Diagram 21**. No choice. Now it is all down-hill; all moves are forced for Black. But first you must find the key-move that Steinitz played.) (**Diagram 22**.) **21...,Ke8** (If Black had played 19..,Rac8 then he would have lost here immediately by 22.Rxc8+. Study the position carefully. Steinitz is a pawn down and his Q and N are 'en prise'. With his next move he increases the odds even further, but he already knows the outcome: 13 moves deep!! **Diagram 23**. What did he play?) (**Diagram 24**. The moves thus far were all logical up to a certain extent, but for this move you need a deep insight in tactical finesse. Some people have a natural talent for it. Most of us can learn a satisfactory degree by studying games like this.) **22...,Kf8!** (22..,Qxe7 loses after 23.Rxc8+ etc; while 22..,Kxe7 23.Re1+,Kd8 24.Ne6+ and 25.Nc5+ is also disastrous. Please note that Qd7 is safe as Black threatens 23..,Rxc1+ and mate! **Diagram 25**. What is the next move following the same pattern of thinking?) (**Diagram 26**.) **23...,Kg8** (Only move for both players. **Diagram 27**. What next?)

(**Diagram 28**. By now you should have the idea! White is trying to take the Black Queen with check, so that Black will not have a chance to deliver mate. In that case everything else on Black's side will fall. The game hangs on each move!) **24..,Kh8** (**Diagram 29**. No choice. If 24...Kf8 then 25.Nxh7+,Kxg7 26.Qxd7+ decides. What did Steinitz now play, or did he offer a draw, since both do not have enough time to

Diagram 18 (Initial position)

capture?) (**Diagram 30**. Here Black resigned but legend has it that Steinitz, not to be cheated of his achievement, played out the

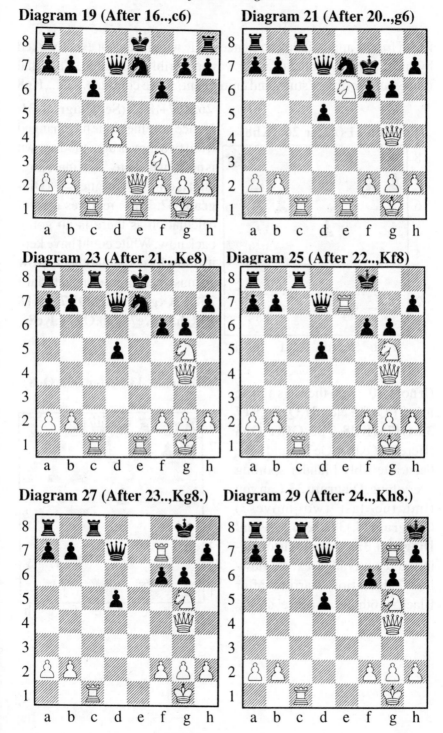

Diagram 19 (After 16..,c6)

Diagram 21 (After 20..,g6)

Diagram 23 (After 21..,Ke8)

Diagram 25 (After 22..,Kf8)

Diagram 27 (After 23..,Kg8.)

Diagram 29 (After 24..,Kh8.)

finish for the appreciating audience. He was a man not exactly liked by most of his opponents as he was so terribly conceited. The final moves are worthy of study and enjoyment, so we continue.) **25...,Kg8**

Diagram 31 (After 26..,Kh8)

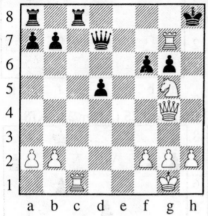

26.Rg7+,Kh8 (See Diagram 31. Notice how the game has changed from two moves ago: the h-pawn is not longer there. The final King-hunt is on. Can you guess?) (**Diagram 32**. This requires careful calculation as there is no going back now. White could have kept it a draw by perpetual check. Now he must mate or lose on material.) **27...,Kxg7   28.Qh7+,Kf8   29.Qh8+,Ke7   30.Qg7+,Ke8**

(If now 30..,Kd6 then it is a mate in 2: 31.Qxf6+etc.) **31.Qg8+,Ke7 32.Qf7+,Kd8   33.Qf8+,Qe8** (Here 33.Qxf6+, Qe7 would have been a terribly blunder spoiling everything. **Diagram 33**. Can you find the last two moves?) (**Diagram34**.)**34..,Kd7** (**Final Diagram 35**). A truly astonishing and unrivalled exact, flawless calculation starting after Black's 16th 'weak move' c6.)

Diagram 33 (After 33..,Qe8)

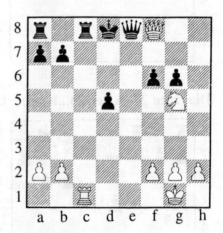

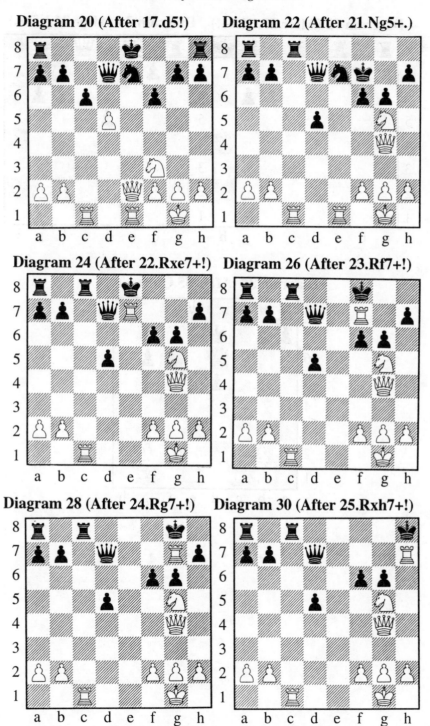

Diagram 20 (After 17.d5!)

Diagram 22 (After 21.Ng5+.)

Diagram 24 (After 22.Rxe7+!)

Diagram 26 (After 23.Rf7+!)

Diagram 28 (After 24.Rg7+!)

Diagram 30 (After 25.Rxh7+!)

Diagram 32 (After 27.Qh4+!) **Diagram 34 (After 34.Nf7+.)**

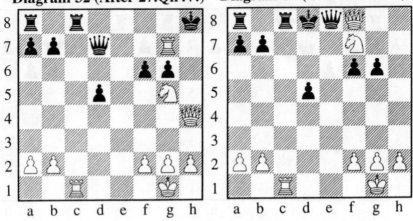

Diagram 35 (After 35.Qd6++.)

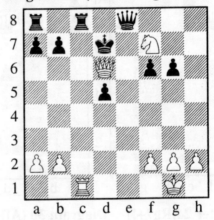

* * * *

GAME 3 ROTLEVI - A. RUBINSTEIN, LODZ (POLAND) 1907

(QUEEN'S GAMBIT, TARRASCH DEFENSE VARIATION)

While known as one of the best endgame virtuosi of all time, Rubinstein shone brilliantly in all phases of the game. Here his opponent tries to play quietly, only to go down in history to one of the most amazing and brilliant cascading sacrificial attacks ever seen. Even strong players will have a difficult time finding all the moves in this one.

1.d4,d5 2.Nf3,e6 3.e3,c5 4.c4,Nc6 5.Nc3,Nf6 6.dxc5,Bxc5 7.a3,a6 8.b4,Bd6 9.Bb2,0-0 10.Qd2,Qe7 11.Bd3 (White's sixth and tenth moves were weak. On both occasions he could have played the better cxd5. Now again 11.cxd5,exd5 12.Be2 would keep White's Queen relatively safe on d2. Now Black removes this possibility and gains the advantage. **Diagram 37. What did Rubinstein play?**)

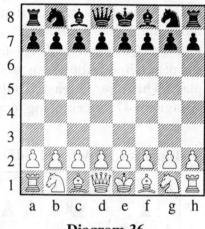

Diagram 36

(Initial position)

(Rubinstein is content with a symmetrical pawn structure, since he is ahead in development. **Diagram 38.**)

(By now you should be noticing that in virtually all these study games, it is the side who develops quickly and effectively that comes up with the winning combinations.) **12.Bxc4,b5 13.Bd3,Rd8 14.Qe2,Bb7 15.0-0** (Thanks to those earlier inaccuracies White has effectively lost two moves! Rubinstein still has to bring his Queen-Rook into play, but there are other more important things to do as well. **Diagram 39. What is next?**) (First he plays this excellent move, with two immediate goals: He trades off the one piece defending White's King, and secondly he opens up the diagonal b7-f3-g2 for the Bishop. An attack is looming! **Diagram 40.**) **16.Nxe5,Bxe5 17.f4** (**Diagram 41.** White has to avoid the threat of 17...,Bxh2+

18.Kxh2,Qd6+ and 19...,Qxd3. However, there was a healthier defense: 17.Rfd1,Qc7 18.f4,Bxc3 19.Rac1. Rotlevi gains time by f4 by attacking the Bishop, but weakens his King's position in the process. **What did Rubinstein reply?**) (**Diagram 42.** An important piece to save! White now compounds his unjustified optimism and his consequent problems by completely opening up the diagonals to his King.) **18.e4,Rac8 19.e5,Bb6+ 20.Kh1** (**Diagram 43.** Black has all his pieces perfectly poised for the assasult. He now goes all out and hurtles towards White's King. **Can you guess?**) (**Diagram 44.** Again a double purpose: The Knight has to move or is lost but goes on the offence aiming at both f2 and h2. Next move in the plan would be 21...,Qh4 and White is mated or must give the Queen. If 21.Qxg4 then 21...,Rxd3. White played instead:) **21.Be4** (Allows his next defensive move. What did Black play? **This one is easy. Diagram 45.**) (**Diagram 46. 22.g3**) (**Diagram 47.** Succumbing to a blind mating attack.)

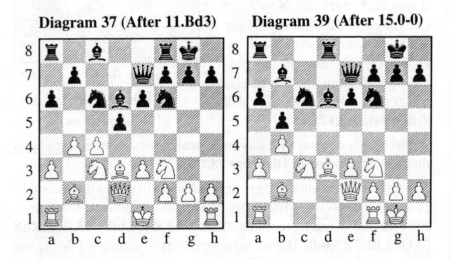

Diagram 37 (After 11.Bd3)   **Diagram 39 (After 15.0-0)**

(The only glimmer of hope lay indeed in 22.h3, but after 22...,Rxc3 to eliminate the defense of e4, White would lose after 23.Bxc3,Bxe4 24.Qxe4,Qg3 with mate next move. The alternative is not taking back after 22...,Rxc3 and White is mate by 23...,Rxh3+ etc; or 23.Bxc3,Bxe4 24.Qxg4,Qxg4 25.hxg4,Rd3 and Black mates on h3 next move or retains after 26.Kh2 two Bishops for the Rook and

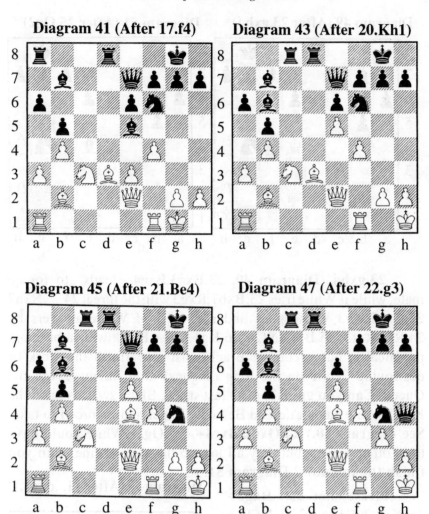

Diagram 41 (After 17.f4)

Diagram 43 (After 20.Kh1)

Diagram 45 (After 21.Be4)

Diagram 47 (After 22.g3)

will win. After the text move 22.g3, however, the situation is even more critical - Black's Queen as well as his Bb7 is under attack, but Black has a way to take advantage of the new weakness on the long diagonal. After all, even if you have a single piece left to deliver mate and your opponent almost all his original soldiers, you win the game! **What happened next?**) (**Diagram 48** No turning back! Again this move destroys White's security on the long diagonal, but what about the Queen, you will ask?)

Diagram 49 (After 23.gxh4)   **Diagram 51 (After 25.Qg2)**

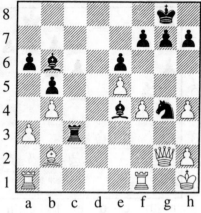

23.gxh4 (Diagram 49. 23.Bxc3,Bxe4+ leads to forced mate, while if White tries 23.Bxb7,Rxg3 with the threat 24....,Nxh2 25.Qxh2,Rh3 White goes under as well; if White answers by 24.Rf3,Rxf3 25.Bxf3,Nf2+ 26.Kg1,Ne4+ Black wins a bit more prosaically, but it counts! Black must now finish the work of destroying White on the long diagonal after having given the Queen. **Can you guess?**) (The last straw; Black swarms in on the King. White cannot defend Be4 any longer and is forced to take. **See diagram 50.) 24.Qxd2,Bxe4+ 25.Qg2** (White could have tried other moves, but they all lose to the same theme. **Can you finish the job now? Diagram 51.**)

(Please, not 25...,Bxg2+? 26.Kxg2,Ne3+ 27.Kf3 or 26...,Rc2+ 27.Kg3 with the better game for White! Now mate on h2 is unavoidable. **See final diagram 52.**)

Diagram 38 (After 11..,dxc4.)

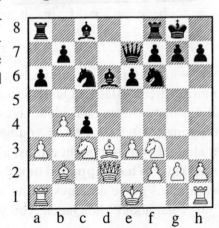

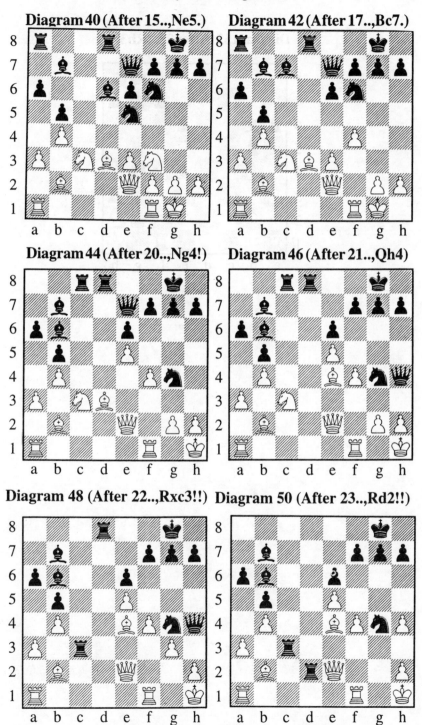

Diagram 40 (After 15..,Ne5.)

Diagram 42 (After 17..,Bc7.)

Diagram 44 (After 20..,Ng4!)

Diagram 46 (After 21..,Qh4)

Diagram 48 (After 22..,Rxc3!!)

Diagram 50 (After 23..,Rd2!!)

Diagram 52 (After 25..,Rh3!)

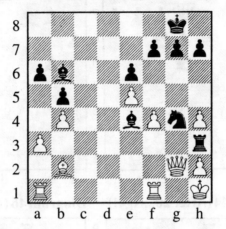

* * * *

CHAPTER 5

JOSE RAUL CAPABLANCA (1888 - 1942)

José Capablanca was probably the greatest natural talent in the history of the game. The Cuban began his career as a true chess prodigy: he learnt the moves at the age of four, just by watching his father play, and by the age of 12, he was already the strongest player in his country. He won his first international tournament at 22, ahead of the best player in the world. Soon he was regarded as a challenger to world champion Emanuel Lasker's throne. The latter demurred and it was only ten years later that Capablanca got his chance. He won the match convincingly to become the third 'official' world champion.

Capablanca "worked" as a diplomat in the Cuban Foreign Office - actually, his only duty was to travel around the world playing chess and acting as an ambassador of goodwill for his country. He invested less study into the game than any of his contemporaries, and still outplayed them with bewildering ease. He had a fantastic natural 'feel' for positions, rarely risked spectacular attacks but relied on the crystal clarity of his chess understanding to turn the game in his favor. Very often he seemed to win 'automatically', almost by chance. He gained a reputation of being completely invincible. "The chess machine", they called him; indeed he lost only 36 games in his entire career. During a ten year period (1914-24) he only dropped one game, and that merited headlines throughout the world: "Capablanca loses game!"

Game 4 - Capablanca - Tanerov, New York, 1910

Here the Cuban genius is seen at work at his most nonchalant. Every time Black comes up with another idea, 'Capa' has the answer. The moves have a compelling continuity, giving you the sense that you have to solve the problems as they arise. At the same time it leaves you suspect-

Diagram 53 (Initial position)

ing that he had everything under control from the start.

(Spanish Game also called the Ruy Lopez. Initial position - Diagram 53.)

Diagram 54 (After 3..,Nf6)

1.e4,e5   2.Nf3,Nc6 3.Bb5,Nf6 (White's e-pawn is attacked. What is the best defense? **Diagram 54.**) (**Diagram 55.** This move keeps open White's options of d4 and Nc3, while after 4...,Nxe4 White can easily regain his pawn with 5.Re1 or 5.d4,exd4? 6.Re1 fatally pinning the Knight.)

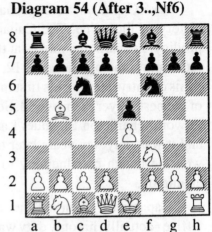

Diagram 56 (After 10..,0-0.)   **Diagram 58 (After 12..,Nd7.)**

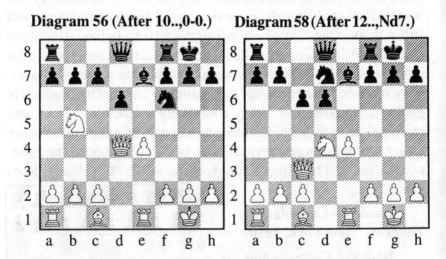

4...,d6 5.d4,Bd7 6.Nc3,Be7 7.Re1,exd4 8.Nxd4,Nxd4 9.Qxd4,Bxb5 10.Nxb5,0-0 (**Diagram 56.** Perhaps Black should not have ignored Nb5. Capa takes deft advantage of this by encouraging a weakness. **Can you guess the next move?**) (**Diagram 57.** Here Black should probably have tried 11...,Ne8 but he plays right into Capa's plan:) **11...,c6 12.Nd4,Nd7** (Black intends 13...,Ne5 and also ...Bf6, making his remaining two light pieces more active. **Diagram 58. What is the strongest reply?**)

(**Diagram 59.** Certainly the best square for the Knight; coincidentally, it threatens mate!) **13...,Bf6** (The logical reply: defense and attack. **Diagram 60. What is the best, most effective square for the Queen?**) (Of course! Keeping up the pressure on g7 while attacking pawn d6 at the same time. **Diagram 61.**) **14...,Ne5   15.Bf4,Qc7 16.Rad1,Rad8 (Diagram 62.** All natural moves. Still, Black should have played 16...,Rfd8.

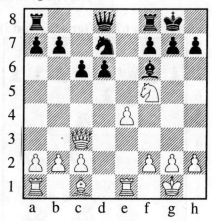

Diagram 60 (After 13..,Bf6)

But how was he to know what White was going to play? **Can you do better and find the move Capa played?**) (A pretty little combination exploiting the fact that the second defense of Ne5 is removed by this capture. It looks as if White wins at least a pawn. Black may have seen it, and thought that he could catch Capablanca in return. **Diagram 63.** Instead he finds himself the victim in the end.) **17...,Rxd6 18.Bxe5,Rd1 19.Rxd1,Bxe5 (Diagram 64.** Of course 18...,Bxe5 would have been fatal. Black, however, should have played 18..,Qa5! after which 19.Bc3 is forced: 19..,Bxc3 20.bxc3,Rg6 21.Ne7+,Kh8 22.Nxg6+ would give White a definite advantage, but he must work hard to win. Now Capablanca finishes off the game with a series of sharp blows. **What is next?**) (**Diagram 65.** This move only makes sense if you can see what follows.) **20...,Kh8** (White can force Black in a position where a combination exposing the back rank is decisive. **Can you see it yet? Diagram 66.**) (If Black does not take back, he will be a full Knight down. **Diagram 67.**) **21...,Qxe5 (Diagram 68.** The board is set for the finale. **Do the job for us!) 22.Nxf7+! (Final position - diagram 69.** Black can choose between mated after 22..,Rxf7 23.Rd8+ or remaining a Knight and two pawns down. Tanerov wisely resigned.

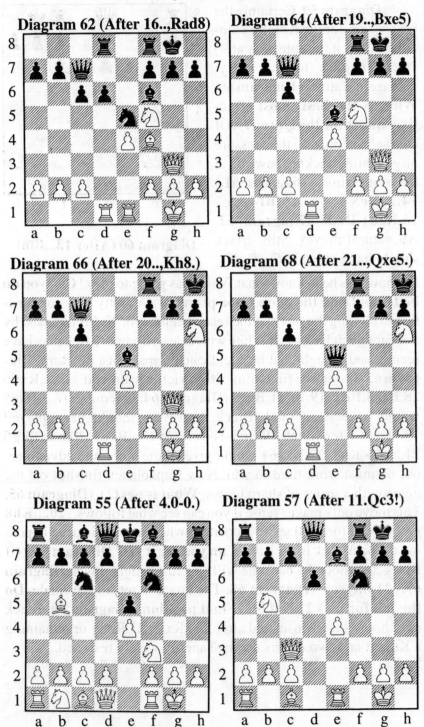

Diagram 62 (After 16..,Rad8)

Diagram 64 (After 19..,Bxe5)

Diagram 66 (After 20..,Kh8.)

Diagram 68 (After 21..,Qxe5.)

Diagram 55 (After 4.0-0.)

Diagram 57 (After 11.Qc3!)

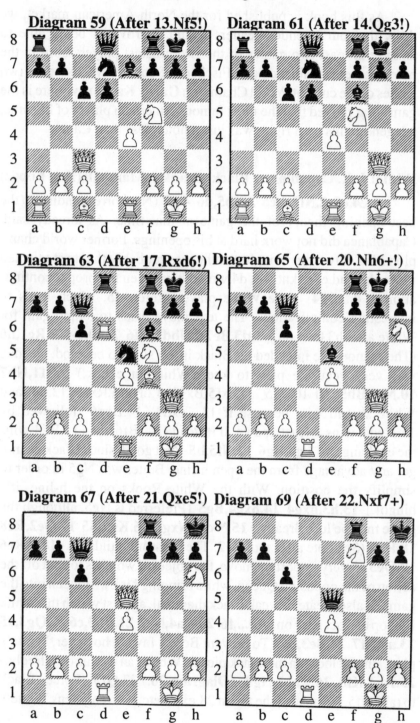

Diagram 59 (After 13.Nf5!)

Diagram 61 (After 14.Qg3!)

Diagram 63 (After 17.Rxd6!)

Diagram 65 (After 20.Nh6+!)

Diagram 67 (After 21.Qxe5!)

Diagram 69 (After 22.Nxf7+)

As this book is published for the North American market, we think that our intended readers would approve of being able to analyse at least two games of the two greatest players born in the hemisphere: Capablanca and Fischer. Of course, we also give two games of the current World Champion **Garry Kasparov.** Here is the game that proved that the most famous American player of his time, a legend in his own right, was just a notch less than Capa.

White: J. R. Capablanca Black: Frank J. Marshall (Ruy Lopez)

1.e4,e5 2.Nf3,Nc6 3.Bb5,d6 4.c3 (Not corresponding to the best opening theory of the game at that time. As already said, Capablanca did not work hard at his openings. Former world champion Max Euwe too thought that he was probably the most talented player he had ever known; d4 would have been the proper continuation.) **4...,Bg4** (The White player prefers f5, which leads to interesting complications. The text move leads to tempo gain for White after h3 later on.) **5.d3,Be7 6.Nbd2,Nf6 7.0-0,0-0 8.Re1,h6** (The manoeuvre intended by Black is too slow to be good. Needed was very accurate play to keep White in check.) **9.Nf1,Nh7 10.Ne3,Bh5** (If 10...,f5 11.exf5,Bxf5 12.Nxf5,Rxf5 13.d4 and White should win, because if 13...,exd4 14.Bxc6 followed by 15.Nxd4, wins at least a pawn. If instead 13...,Bf6, then 14.Bd3 wins the exchange.) **11.g4,Bg6 12.Nf5,h5** (Not good, since Black cannot get any advantage from the open h-line. Better was Ng5 in order to simplify the position. With the White Rooks on the h-line, it's bingo!.) **13.h3,hxg4 14.hxg4,Bg5** (Preferred is Ng5, although the game may be lost already.) **15.Nxg5,Nxg5 16.Kg2,d5 17.Qe2,Re8 18.Rh1** (See note after move 12. The pressure builds up.) **18...,Re6 19.Qe3** (A very important move, the object of which is to shut off the action of the opposing Queen, while bringing his own Queen into the game. It also creates a weak Black diagonal, against which the White Bishop can act later on.) **19...,f6 20.Ba4,Ne7 21.Bb3,c6 22.Qg3,a5 23.a4,Nf7 24.Be3,b6** (To prevent Bc5. It favors, however, White's plan, since it locks in the Black pieces. White can use his own freely.) **25.Rh4,Kf8 26.Rah1,Ng8** (**Diagram 70.**) **27.Qf3** (Forces Black to take Nf5, because of the threat 28.exd5 etc. It strengthens White's position even further.) **27...,Bxf5 28.gxf5,Rd6 29.Qh5,Ra7 30.Qg6** (No defense available. If 30...,Ne7 31.Rh8+,Nxh8 32.Rh8+,Ng8 33.Qh7,Kf7 34.Bxb6 wins. Thus:) **30...,Nfh6 (Diagram 71.) 31.Rxh6,gxh6 32.Bxh6+,Ke7 33.Qh7+,Ke8 34.Qxg8+,Kd7 35.Qh7+,Qe7 36.Bf8,Qxh7 37.Rxh7+,Ke8 38.Rxa7,** resigns (1-0). Capablanca then writes: "Except for the opening, it would be difficult to see where White could have improved his play. This is one of my best games. Capablanca was only 21 years old (12 years before he became world champion).

Diagram 70 (After 28..,Ng8.)   Diagram 71 (After 30..,Nfh6.)

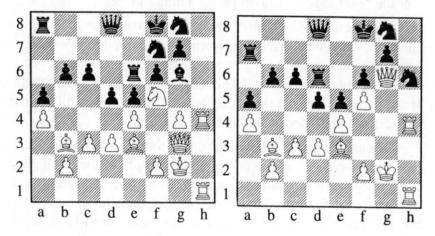

*   *   *   *

CHAPTER 6

QUEEN SACRIFICES

Quite often in a game of chess, a player will 'sacrifice' material, i.e. he intentionally gives away a piece in return for a better position or a strong attack. The commonest sacrifice is a pawn, of course, and there are many 'gambit' openings (see Section 3 of this book) in which one side will invest a pawn for positional reasons. The best known are the 'Queen's Gambit' (1.d4,d5 2.c4) and the 'King's Gambit' (1.e4,e5 2.f4). In the middle game, you can sometimes sacrifice a piece - a Knight or a Bishop, usually for one or two pawns - or the "exchange", i.e. a Rook for a minor piece.

But the ultimate dream of every chess player is the most regal of them all: the Queen Sacrifice. Normally the opportunity comes at most just once a year (if you are a regular club player), but for occasional players it is more like once in a life-time and, if successful, it always is a cause for celebration. Really, the fine and well-justified Q-sacrifice is as spectacular as a 'hole-in-one'.

In our next game, you will see one of the most astonishing series of Queen sacrifices ever recorded in the history of the royal game. Look at each study position carefully and try to appreciate why the opponent each time refrained from accepting the offer. It is one of our all-time favorite 'classic' games and one of the most famous brilliancies on record.

The first Queen sacrifice is astonishing, but once you got over the initial amazement, what about the next five! Because the study positions in this game are linked by a common idea, even a beginner can have the thrill of playing beautiful moves. (**Initial position - Diagram 72**)

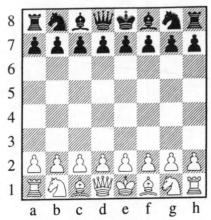

Diagram 72
(Initial position)

Game 5: Adams - C.Torre (Philidor Defense, played New Orleans 1920)

1.e4,e5 2.Nf3,d6 3.d4,exd4 4.Qxd4,Nc6 5.Bb5,Bd7 6.Bxc6, Bxc6 7.Nc3,Nf6 8.0-0,Be7 9.Nd5,Bxd5 10.exd5,0-0 11.Bg5,c6 (**Diagram 73**. Trying to swap off the powerful d5-pawn. **How does White keep his presence here?**) (**Diagram 74.** Recognizing the cornerstone of his advantage, the pawn, he supports it.) **12...,cxd5 13.cxd5,a5 14.Rfe1,Rfe8 15.Re2,Rc8** (Black tries to develop the Q-side to counteract the doubled Rooks on the e-line. Best was 15...,h6 to secure his back rank.) **16.Rae1,Qd7** (White now senses a once-in-a-lifetime opportunity and reaches for it. **Diagram 75. It is necessary to act immediately, or Black will secure his back rank. Can you find the move?**) (See **Diagram 76**. Of course 17...,gxf6 would be horrendous: Black's Bishop would be locked in, so Black played the 'natural' move and replied without a second thought.) **17...,Bxf6** (**Diagram 77.** Now it looks as though the Rooks will be exchanged after White's Queen moves, leading to some advantage for Black. He has carefully guarded e8 in preparation for this plan, but incredibly it is not as solidly guarded as one might think. There is a nasty surprise: **Can you find the killer move?**) (**Diagram 78.**)

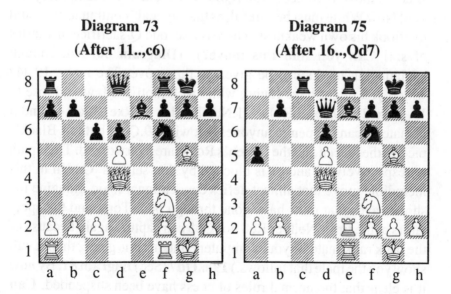

Diagram 73

(After 11..,c6)

Diagram 75

(After 16..,Qd7)

Diagram 77

(After 17..,Bxf6.)

Diagram 79

(After 18..,Qb5.)

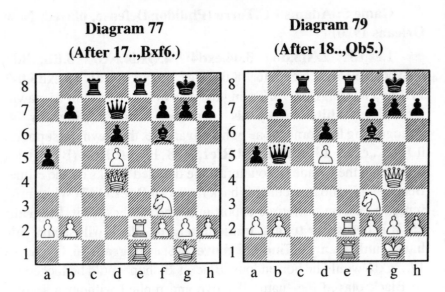

(The 18.Qg4!! Queen sacrifice challenges the opponent's defense. Black cannot capture the 'unprotected' offered Queen because of: 18...,Qxg4?? 19.Rxe8+ and mate next move; while 18...,Rxe2 is simply answered by 19.Qxd7,Rxe1+ 20.Nxe1 with a huge material advantage, more than enough to ensure an immediate win. Thus Black's move is forced.) **18...,Qb5 (Diagram 79.** A temporary haven! Now White must be careful, as the "logical" continuation would overlook his own weakness. There is a second Q-sacrifice in a series of six! **Can you find this move?)** **(Diagram 80.** Not enough exclamation marks can be given to this move. The move 19.a4? which you might have found, while well motivated, would lose to 19...,Qxe2! 20.Rxe2,Rc1+ 21.Ne1,Rxe1+ 22.Rxe1,Rxe1++ and it is mate; it can happen to anyone! But with 19.Qc4! both of Black's pieces, the Queen and the Queen's Rook, are overworked. Their path to respectively e2 and c1 is blocked by the 'selfless' Queen in this incredible move that almost defies conventional logic. Imagine the shockwaves that must have gone through poor Torre and the spectators at the time. Neither Rc8 nor Qb5 can capture again because of the back rank mate. If your computer contains this game, then it will show you the mate that follows.) **19...,Qd7** (See **Diagram 81.** By now it is clear that the normal rules of chess have been suspended. **Can**

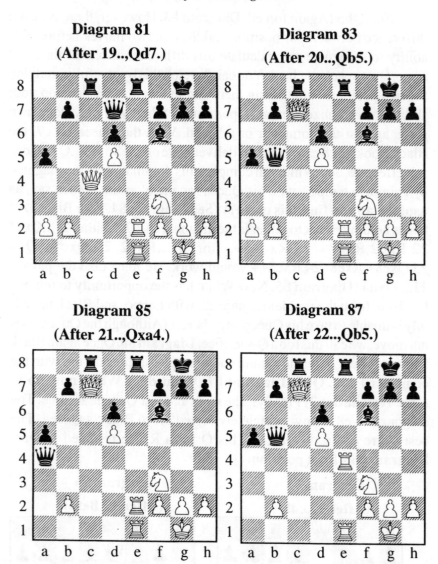

Diagram 81
(After 19..,Qd7.)

Diagram 83
(After 20..,Qb5.)

Diagram 85
(After 21..,Qxa4.)

Diagram 87
(After 22..,Qb5.)

you find White's next shocker? It is one of the most dazzling moves in the history of the game.) (**Diagram 82.** This move is a simple application of the same principles as before: White is trying to push Black's Queen off that diagonal, no matter what. This bombshell makes Newton's law irrelevant for chess defying accepted logic. Please pause and study the position carefully. Is it not amazing that the Queen can go there? Again neither piece dare take her Majesty: try this against the computer. So the Black Queen runs away once more.)

20...,Qb5 (Again forced. **Diagram 83.** However, there is now a difference between our position and the one two moves before. The ability to recognize and calculate this difference is one of the most important aspects of chess. You can develop this by carefully studying the two positions, comparing them and in this manner develop your ability to recognize similar opportunities when you play your own game against the computer or a friend. With the Queen on c7, the Black Rook on c8 can no longer deliver mate on c1. So the ...Qxe2 idea is ineffective, and White can complete his domination of the diagonal by gaining a tempo - with his Queen 'en prise' as the French say, **as usual! Can you find this move?**) (See **Diagram 84.** Poor Black! All that is holding Black together is the diagonal a4-d7. Neither 21..,Qxe2 22.Rxe2,Rxc7 23.Rxe8++, nor 21..,Rxe2 22.Qxc8+,Qe8 23.Qxe8+,Rxe8 24.Rxe8++ would work. He must take the pawn:) **21...,Qxa4** (**Diagram 85.** Now White has the opportunity to remove his Rook from the problem square e2, with tempo, and Black incredibly is unable to take his Queen anywhere.) (Although the Queen does not move, we call this too a Q-sacrifice. **Diagram 86.** Once again Black has one retreat only and cannot capture - please check it out with the computer.) **22...,Qb5** (**Diagram 87. What does White now do to force resignation?**) Finally! The sixth and last Queen sacrifice. The diagonal a4-e8 is now completely sealed off to Black's Queen. The best Torre could do was lose his Q for a R. He resigned instead. **Diagram 88 - final position.**

Diagram 74
(After 12.c4!)

Diagram 76
(After 17.Bxf6)

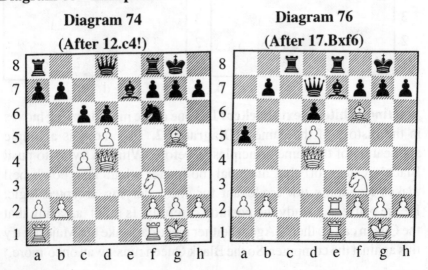

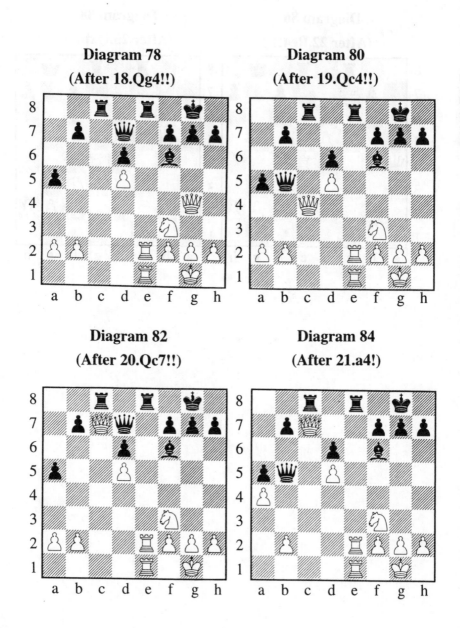

Diagram 78
(After 18.Qg4!!)

Diagram 80
(After 19.Qc4!!)

Diagram 82
(After 20.Qc7!!)

Diagram 84
(After 21.a4!)

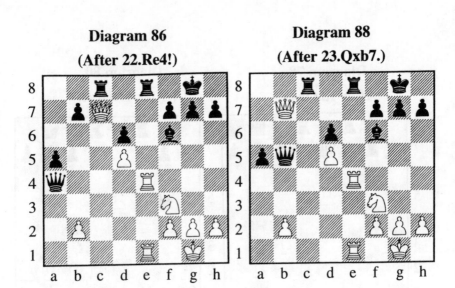

Diagram 86
(After 22.Re4!)

Diagram 88
(After 23.Qxb7.)

* * * *

ROBERT JAMES FISCHER (BORN 1943)

Is there any chess player, professional, amateur, weak or strong, who has not heard of Bobby Fischer?

The American is doubtlessly the most extraordinary phenomen in the history of the game. He began as a prodigy who outperformed all chess prodigies before him. At 12 he was playing at master strength, at 14 he won the U.S. Championship, at 15 he became the youngest Grandmaster in the history of the game, and the youngest Candidate for the World Championship.

The latter record still stands, the former only now (35 years later) has been broken by Judit Polgar of Hungary and just a few month ago by Peter Leko from the same country. But these players were discovered at a very early age and were completely nurtured to succeed. Bobby was basically self-taught! Indeed if he had not been so rigorous in his demands for better and fairer conditions in top-level chess, he would surely have become the youngest World Champion of all time.

His tournament and match results were phenomenal. In his storm to take the crown from the reigning Champion Boris Spassky (of the former USSR), he won twenty games in a row, wreaking havoc among the best players in the world. He beat his fellow world championship candidates Mark Taimanov and Bent Larsen 6-0 each and swept past ex-champion Tigran Petrosian to challenge Spassky in the 'Match of the Century' as it was called at the time, in Reykjavik (Iceland) in 1972. There Fischer became the first non-Russian World Champion since Max Euwe (1935-37).

The final game against Spassky was also his last public game of chess for exactly 20 years. He went into sullen retirement and in 1975 forfeited his title to challenger Anatoly Karpov of Russia. His return two years ago in Serbia and Montenegro (former Yugoslavia) to give extra publicity to the raging war, was even more controversial than what happened in the early seventies. He played Boris Spassky for an absolute record (in chess) of US$5 million in a 'return-match of the century' and convincingly beat him.

Now unable to return to the USA (where he had been living in self-imposed isolation in the Los Angeles area) he lives somewhere in Hungary. His much reported love-affair with a local chess beauty, one of the reasons he reputedly returned to chess, has also come to an end. However 'impossible' he has been both in his demands for better conditions and in his personal life, no one disputes his unrivalled genius. Here one of his most superlative games, also one of the most beautiful ever played. With unequalled logic and grace, Black pursues and achieves the highest goal. The final position is a coup-de-grâce study in its own - GM spectators, on hearing that the game was over, thought that Fischer had resigned! But Byrne was merely the second person to appreciate the truth of the position. If you can do as well, you will have truly graduated into the world of chess.

Game 6 Robert Byrne - R.J. Fischer
U.S. Championship (1963-64)
(Grünfeld Defense)

1.d4,Nf6 2.c4,g6 3.g3,c6
4.Bg2,d5   5.cxd5,cxd5
6.Nc3,Bg7 7.e3,0-0 8.Nge2,Nc6
9.0-0,b6 10.b3 (The game has started out quietly, but now Fischer starts to roll. First he completes his development, putting his last pieces on promising squares. **Question: Which piece goes where? See diagram 90.**) (The Bishop has much more scope here than after the mechanical move 10...,Bb7. **Diagram 91.**) 11.Ba3

Diagram 89
(Initial position)

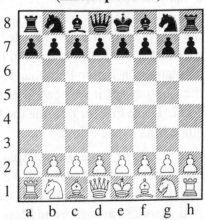

(What you can do, I can! White also plays his Bishop according to the position. Now how does Black take advantage of the difference in the squares where the two King's Knights are located? **Diagram 92.**) (**Diagram 93.** Because White's Knight is on e2 instead of f3, Black can more readily pursue the pawn advance to e5. This push is double-edged, as it gives a weak d-pawn. One of the things to remember at all times in chess when you advance a pawn, is that - unlike the other pieces on the board - you can never retreat pawns. Look at the weaknesses it leaves and see if the advantage of pushing a pawn outweighs the negatives.) **12.Qd2** (White intends to capture the d5-pawn after d4 has been exchanged on e5. **Diagram 94. Must Fischer abandon his original plan?**) (**Diagram 95.** No, he plays straight into White's intentions because he has looked a bit further! Of course Byrne need not take, but he thought he had accounted for his young opponent's activity.) **13.dxe5,Nxe5 14.Rfd1?** (**Diagram 96.** This is actually the losing move, but it may be too harsh to add a question mark to it. It seems perfectly plausible to want to place the Rooks on d1 and c1, but moving this Rook away from the Kingside proves fatal. Fischer takes advantage of this in such an unbelievable and direct way that it could only have come as a complete shock to his opponent. **What happened next?**) (This seems premature after White's logical next move. **Diagram 97.**) **15.Qc2** (**Diagram 98.** Now the Knight must retreat as Black otherwise will lose two light pieces for a Rook, more than enough material advantage for White to win the game. And if Nd3 retreats, then pawn d5 falls. **Or does it?**)

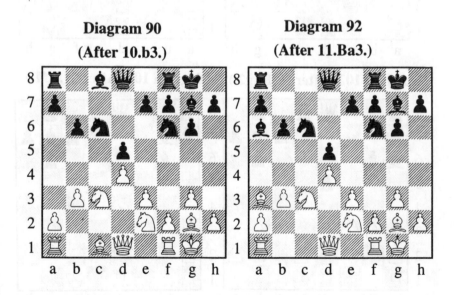

Diagram 90

(After 10.b3.)

Diagram 92

(After 11.Ba3.)

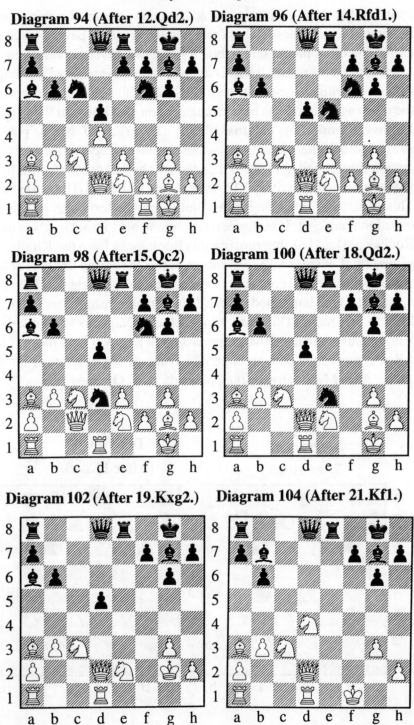

Diagram 94 (After 12.Qd2.)

Diagram 96 (After 14.Rfd1.)

Diagram 98 (After 15.Qc2)

Diagram 100 (After 18.Qd2.)

Diagram 102 (After 19.Kxg2.)

Diagram 104 (After 21.Kf1.)

(**See diagram 99**. The game takes on a whole new color. Where a moment ago, White had Black scrambling for cover, now he himself is coming apart at the seams. But isn't this costing Black a Knight?) **16.Kxf2,Ng4+ 17.Kg1,Nxe3** (Remember what we said about sacrifices: "In the middle game, you can sometimes sacrifice a piece - a Knight or a Bishop, usually for one or two pawns." It seems that Bobby is following our advice to the letter!) **18.Qd2 (Diagram 100.** Byrne still has reason to be satisfied. After Black regains the exchange on d1, he will recapture with Ra1 and the d-pawn will finally fall as planned. The material count of Bishop and a Knight versus Rook and pawn would then be a little better for White, who would be fully developed. So Black's combination was just an exchange to equalize, thought Byrne. **Are you of the same opinion, or have you got a better move than 18...,Nxd1?**) (Again two exclamation marks are in order. In fact, Fischer sees a more epic goal; the petty recovery of a small material loss is irrelevant to his plan. **Diagram 101.**) **19.Kxg2** (Now note that the White King is a little bit lonely. Given time, Byrne will surely move his pieces towards his Kingside. But Fischer has absolutely no intention of giving him time. He is relentless like a hawk diving on its prey! He presses on steadily, further opening the lines to White's King for a showdown. **Diagram 102. What was Fischer's next move?**) (**Diagram 103.** Preparing to return the Bishop to the first ignored, but now-vulnerable diagonal b7-g2.) **20.Nxd4,Bb7+ 21.Kf1 (Diagram 104.)**

Diagram 91 (After 10..,Ba6!)   **Diagram 93 (After 11..,Re8!)**

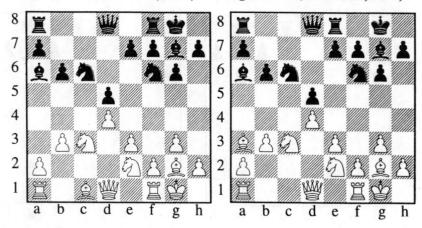

Diagram 95 (After 12..,e5!) **Diagram 97 (After 14..,Nd3!)**

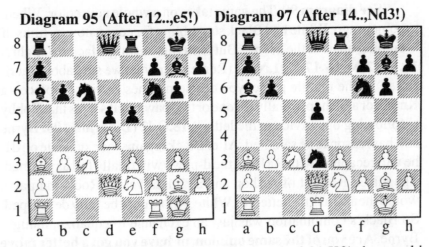

If White had played 21.Kf2 instead of 21.Kf1, he would have met with the same punishing reply, while 21.Kg1 allows 21...,Bxd4+ 22.Qxd4,Re1+ 23.Kf2,Qxd4 24.Rxd4,Rxa1 with a won endgame in a well-known combination exposing one of the weaknesses on the back rank and punishing the heavy workload of Rd1. Please study the position carefully. It was here that the commentator in the analysis room told the spectators that Fischer was completely lost!! But with an amazing 'quiet' move Fischer completely turns the tables. **Can you do the same?)** (**Final position - Diagram 105.** Here White resigned. He is completely lost despite his overpowering material advantage. The main

Diagram 99 **Diagram 101**

(After 15..,Nxf2!!) **(After 18..,Nxg2!!)**

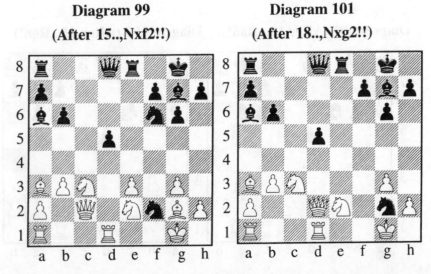

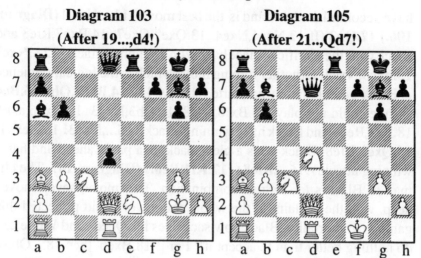

Diagram 103
(After 19...,d4!)

Diagram 105
(After 21..,Qd7!)

point is that Black will move his Queen to h3 with check and win material by threatening mate on g2.

Here another game of Bobby.

D. Byrne - Bobby Fischer (New York, 1956). Bobby was only 14 years old when he won the U.S. Championship, ahead of Samuel Reshevsky (in his time also a prodigy) and other American masters. When he won the following brilliant game against D. Byrne (the brother of the above GM Robert Byrne) Bobby was only 13 years old.

(Grünfeld Defense) **1.Nf3,Nf6 2.c4,g6 3.Nc3,Bg7 4.d4,0-0 5.Bf4,d5** (This again transposes into the Grünfeld, a favourite opening of Fischer against White's Q-pawn opening; since then also Kasparov and Karpov have started playing it regularly as both White and Black.) **6.Qb3,dxc4 7.Qxc4,c6 8.e4,Nbd7** (Books on openings these days recommend the more active 8...,b5 9.Qb3,Qa5 as better for Black.) **9.Rd1,Nb6 10.Qc5** (The White Queen is here misplaced and exposed to attack. Either 10.Qb3 or 10.Qd3 should be played.) **10...,Bg4 11.Bg5?** (Already the losing move which allows the 13-year old to conceive a most brilliant and far-sighted combination. It is worth remembering that in the opening pieces have to be developed and co-ordinated as soon as possible in order to fully fulfill their potential of attack and defense. In this case the simple 11.Be2 would have accomplished that and is the best move.) **11...,Na4!! (Diagram 106.) 12.Qa3** (If 12.Nxa4,Nxe4 13.Qxe7,Qxe7 14.Bxe7,Rfe8 and Black wins the sacrificed piece back with a winning attack.) **12...,Nxc3 13.bxc3,Nxe4!** (Another forcing move which is the logical sequence of Black's combination that started at move 11.) **14.Bxe7,Qb6 15.Bc4** (White could not play 15.Bxf8,Bxf8 16.Qb3,Nxc3 17.Qxb6,axb6 18.Ra1,Re8+ and Black has a winning attack.) **15...,Nxc3! 16.Bc5** (If 16.Qxc3,Rfe8 Black wins a piece back, is a pawn ahead and has a winning attack.) **16...,Rfe8+ 17.Kf1,Be6!! (Diagram 107.** The climax of Black's far-sighted combination. This move, seven moves deep, won the acclaim of the whole chess world and projected this game to immortality. Black now sacrifices his Queen and White can do nothing better than to accept it!! For if 18.Bxe6 then 18...,Qb5+ 19.Kg1,Ne2+ 20.Kf1,Ng3+ 21.Kg1,Qf1+ 22.Rxf1,Ne2++. Therefore White played:) **18.Bxb6,Bxc4+ 19.Kg1,Ne2+ 20.Kf1,Nxd4+ 21.Kg1,Ne2+ 22.Kf1,Nc3+ 23.Kg1,axb6 24.Qb4,Ra4 25.Qxb6** (If 25.Qd6,Nxd1 26.Qxd1,Rxa2 and Black also wins easily.) **25...,Nxd1** (White might just as well resign here, as Black now possesses an overwhelming material advantage with a crushing attack to follow. Still for the inexperienced player it is very instructive how the future world champion, at this tender age already a master at his craft, finishes off his opponent.) **26.h3,Rxa2 27.Kh2,Nxf2 28.Re1,Rxe1 29.Qd8+,Bf8 30.Nxe1,Bd5 31.Nf3,Ne4 32.Qb8,b5 33.h4,h5 34.Ne5,Kg7 35.Kg1,Bc5+ 36.Kf1** (It is interesting to note that, with Black's Rook on the seventh rank, White's King movement is restricted to his back rank. Black now proceeds with a series of checks to drive the White Monarch into a mating net.) **36...,Ng3+ 37.Ke1,Bb4+ 38.Kd1,Bb3+ 39.Kc1,Ne2+ 40.Kb1,Nc3+ 41.Kc1,Rc2++** Checkmate!

A masterpiece from a 13-year old genius! This game was voted by many chess writers the game of the 20th century.

Diagram 106
(After 11...,Na4!!)

Diagram 107
(After 17...,Be6!!)

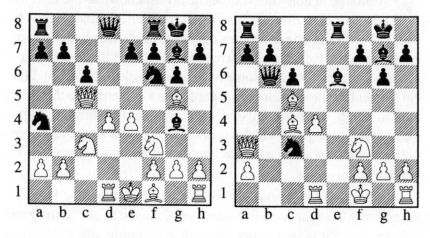

* * * *

BORIS SPASSKY (BORN 1937)

Although in non-chess circles he is best known as the man who lost (now twice) to Fischer, Boris Spassky is an all-time great of the chess board - and one of the most amiable ex-world champions one could imagine. He began his career as a 'Wunderkind', becoming at 18 the youngest Grandmaster ever (before Fischer appeared). In his early twenties, he was already regarded as a contender to the crown and in 1966 narrowly missed ousting world champion Tigran Petrosian. Three years later he was successful and would have been able to look forward to a long reign - if Fischer had not become the challenger.

After losing in Reykajavic in 1972, Boris changed his life-style completely. He married a Frenchwoman, moved to her country and decided that chess should not be an all-consuming affair. Always a slightly lazy player, he relied on his natural talent for the game and his all-round abilities to maintain his position at the top of the chess world. Instead of concentrating his efforts on regaining his title, he preferred to build a beautiful house in the French Alps and spend as much time as possible with his family. Today it is easier to talk him into a nice game of tennis than a foray at the chess board.

Still he remains a top Grandmaster, always able to rise to the occasion and teach any young upstart a lesson or two. His universal style and his charming personality have made him one of the most popular players on the international chess circuit. His match against Fischer in Yugoslavia will be forgiven in due course.

Game 7: Bent Larsen - Boris Spassky (Belgrade 1970 in the match 'World versus the USSR')

(Larsen Opening) This minature shows in graphic form the danger of ignoring the

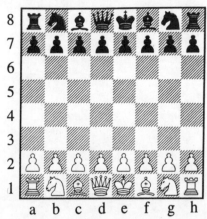

Diagram 108 (Initial position)

basics of opening play, i.e. development, occupation of the center and securing the safety of the King. While Larsen, admittedly one of the great modern players and experimenters, pursues his esoteric goals, Spassky calmly brings all his pieces to correct, effective squares. When the position is ripe, he strikes brilliantly to expose Larsen's plan as a failure. Played on board one in the celebrated 'World vs. USSR' match, this game shows us that even the world's greatest players are not immune to disaster.

1.b3,e5 2.Bb2,Nc6 3.c4,Nf6 4.Nf3 (Larsen plays the opening named after him, delaying occupation of the center in true 'Hypermodern' style.

Meanwhile Spassky develops classically, following the recommendation "Knights before Bishops." But now Larsen tries too soon to establish a Knight in the center. Spassky sees that this plan can be blocked. **Diagram 109**. What did Spassky answer?) (**Diagram 110**. Any passive defence of the e-pawn would give the initiative to White. So Black decides to attack the attacker. In a game against Spassky one month later, Larsen played the more careful 4.e3 leading eventually to a draw.)

5.Nd4,Bc5 6.Nxc6 (**Diagram 111**. Black must choose with which pawn he will recapture. Guess!) (**Diagram 112**. Spassky prepares to bring his Bishop on c8 to a good square in a hurry. He already has the advantage in development - two pieces versus Larsen's one - so he wants to press in that direction.) **7.e3,Bf5 8.Qc2,Qe7 9.Be2** (**Diagram 113**. This was Larsen's chance for the natural move 9.d4 but now Spassky takes even that away. Notice how he played his Queen to e7 to prevent White from ruining Black's pawn structure with Bxf6? What happened next?) (**Diagram 114**. Black has built a beautiful game! Nevertheless, White could have completed his development by playing 10.Nc3 or even 10.Bxf6,Qxf6 11.Nc3. However, Larsen decides on a faulty plan, thinking it could proceed smoothly.) **10.f4** (**Diagram 115**. The idea is to eventually play g4, supported by Rg1 and h3. If successful, he would push back Spassky's pieces. This plan is Larsen's downfall! Still, it is not easy to demonstrate the way. Spassky's answer was probably considered by Larsen. What did Spassky reply? It showed he had seen the plan.)

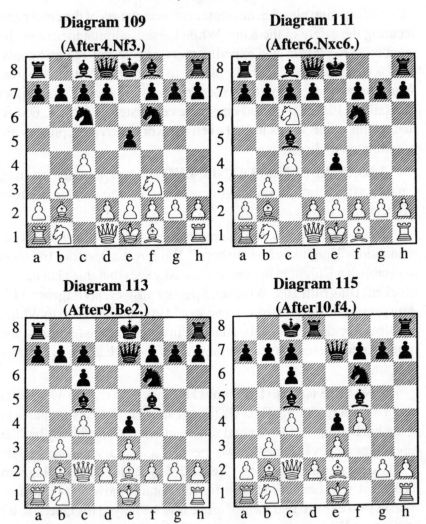

Diagram 109

(After 4.Nf3.)

Diagram 111

(After 6.Nxc6.)

Diagram 113

(After 9.Be2.)

Diagram 115

(After 10.f4.)

(**Diagram 116**. Preparing to attack with ....Qh4. Larsen thought it would just help his plan, or at least that he would avoid the worst with 11.0-0, Qh4 12.Bxg4. The Knight has to be taken; if 12.h3 to avoid mate, then 12...,h5 would step up the attack.) **11.g3 (Diagram 117**. Now you must consider how you are going to answer 12.h3 and 13.g4. Like Spassky did when he played 16...,Ng4, there must be a plan or else the Knight move was senseless.) (**Diagram 118**. Of course! This will prevent g4 after h3. But actually, Spassky had much grander intentions. He is thinking about taking advantage of the weakness produced by the push g3. Can you see how that will come

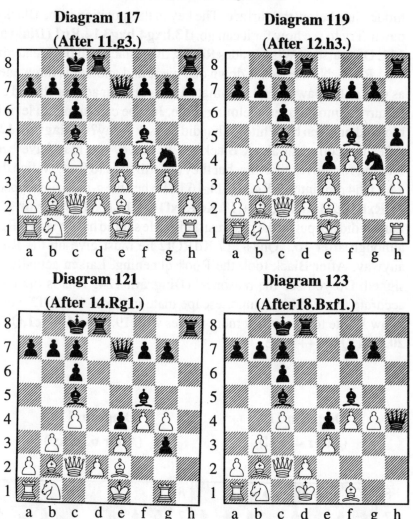

Diagram 117
(After 11.g3.)

Diagram 119
(After 12.h3.)

Diagram 121
(After 14.Rg1.)

Diagram 123
(After18.Bxf1.)

about? Larsen continued:) **12.h3** (**Diagram 119**. If White had not played this, then Black would certainly play 12...,h4, opening the h-file. With the Q-side so undeveloped, White's King would be unable to get away. But now after the Knight moves, 13...,h4 can be met by g4, keeping the K-side closed and forcing more of Black's pieces back. Spassky has considered this and is ready! What did he play?) (**Diagram 120**. Sacrificing a piece or two is fine with Spassky who occasionally plays the King's Gambit! More important is the caving in of White's K-side. The lesson here is to recognize promising ideas, even when they at first seem to lose quickly, and see if there is not something hidden just below the surface. The key in this position is the Black h-pawn. Try to see how far it can go.)**13.hxg4,hxg3 14.Rg1 (Diagram 121.** Of course, if White trades Rooks, then Black will be threatening 15...,Rh1+. Now Black is down one piece and another is threatened, as well as the pawn on g3. But that pawn is also far advanced, and can be turned into an overwhelming force. Just be careful not to let it be blocked or taken by White! What did Spassky play?) **(Diagram 122.** After the comment about Black's 12th move, you may have been looking for moves like this, but they are still hard to find! Notice that 14...,Qh4 runs into 15.Rg2,Qh1+ 16.Bf1 when the g-pawn is stopped.) **15.Rxh1,g2 16.Rf1,Qh4+ 17.Kd1,gxf1Q+ 18.Bxf1 (Diagram 123.** Larsen did not put up the best resistance. He should have tried 16.Rg1, although after 16...,Qh4+ 17.Kd1,Qf2 he must give up the Rook anyway. After Black took the Rook queening, Larsen actually resigned. Do you see the reason?) **(Diagram 124.** This is the most accurate. Now White cannot escape mate in three! 18...,Qf2 would allow White to steal a few more moves with 19.Qc3.) **19.Kc1,Qe1+ 20.Qd1,Qxd1++** mate.

Diagram 110
(After 4..,e4!)

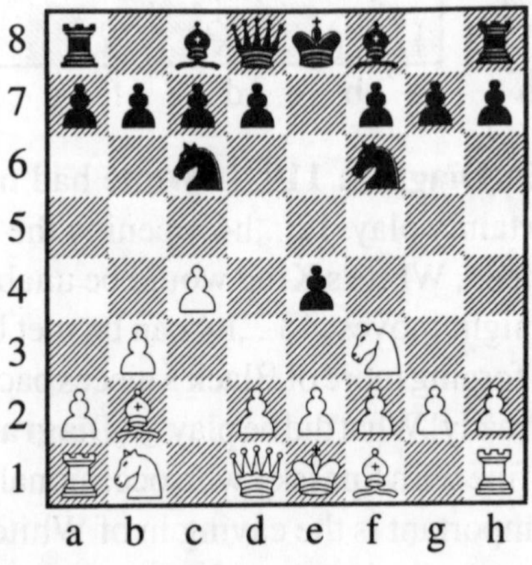

Diagram 112
(After 6..,dxc6)

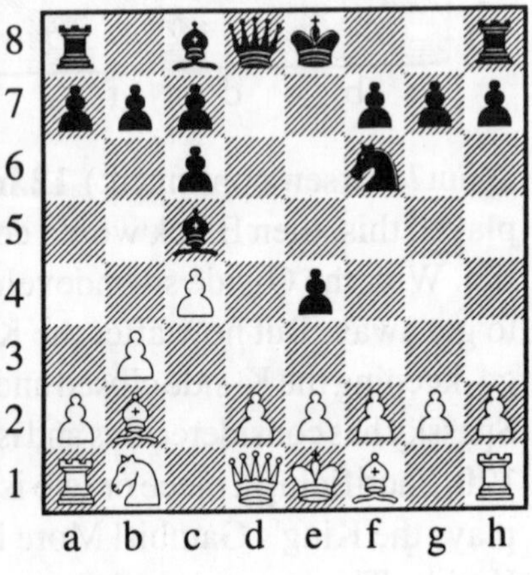

Diagram 114
(After 9.., 0-0-0)

Diagram 116
(After 10.., Ng4!)

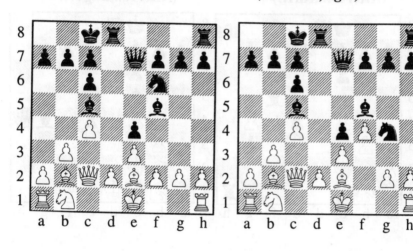

Diagram 118
(After 11.., h5!)

Diagram 120
(After 12..., h4!)

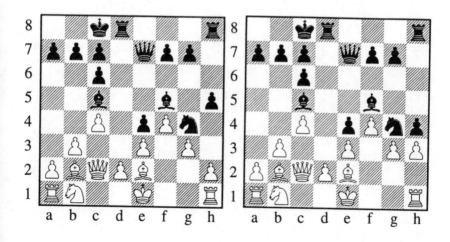

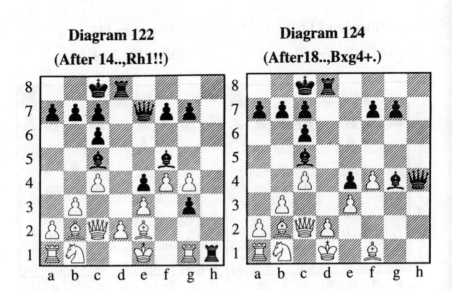

Diagram 122
(After 14..,Rh1!!)

Diagram 124
(After18..,Bxg4+.)

* * * *

GARRY KASPAROV (BORN 1963)

When Bobby Fischer retired from chess in 1975, there was a universal moan of disappointment. Would the world ever see a player of that calibre again - or one with Fischer's charismatic personality? The reign of Anatoly Karpov, though he was very successful and very active as a tournament player, did little to fire the imagination of a new chess generation.

While Fischer was scaling the highest pinnacles of chess, a little boy of Jewish-Armenian descent was following every game with great interest. His talent had been discovered at the age of five, and before he had reached his teens his teacher, ex-world champion Mikhail Botwinnik predicted: "In him lies the future of chess." Within a few years it became clear to everyone who knew him that a World Champion was in the making.

In a series of matches (first two as challenger, the next two as defending champion) starting from 1984 and ending after 144 games (!) in 1990, Garry Kasparov defeated his rival Anatoly Karpov to claim the title of World Champion in 1985, the youngest in history. Garry's forceful personality and his incredible genius at the chess board - he has taken on entire national teams in simultaneous displays - have made him today's superstar of chess. Already he rivals Fischer as the greatest player the game has ever seen.

Game 8 - G. Kasparov - S. Begun, Minsk 1978.

(Queen's Gambit, Semi-Tarrasch)

Diagram 125 (Initial position)

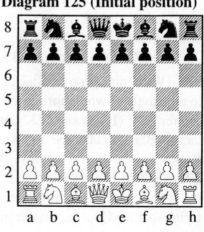

It is very difficult to find an appropriate game by the current World Champion. He sees so deeply that it is hard to guess his moves! And, frankly, that is what his opponents feel. World class chess of today is an extremely refined battle. But here is a game from one of Kasparov's first successes, when he was all of 14 years old. In it we can see him form an energetic plan, and we can follow this plan straight to mate!

1.d4,d5 2.c4,e6 3.Nc3,Nf6 4.Nf3,c5 5.cxd5,Nxd5 6.e3,Nc6 7.Bd3,Be7 8.0-0,0-0   39.Nxd5,Qxd5 10.e4,Qd8 11.dxc5,Bxc5 12.e5,Be7 13.Qe2,Nb4 (**Diagram 126**. White clearly stands at least a little better, thanks to the problems Black has in developing Bc8. With his last move, Garry takes aim at his opponent's King - of course he intends 14.Qe4, provoking the weakening pawn move g6. Black tries to prevent this by attacking the Bishop at d3. How does White continue?) (**Diagram 127**. Garry is willing to block Ra1 in order to be able to play Qe4 with the most force. When one can set up a battery towards the opponent King, it is usually better to have the Queen in front: then the threat will be checkmate!) **14...,Bd7** (**Diagram 128**. Black finishes his development with a little trap, which hardly enters Garry's mind. Now White chooses just the right move order to prevent Black from getting his pieces to good squares. What is next?) (**Diagram 129**. Did you consider 15.Qe4,g6 16.Qxb7? This does not win a pawn but loses the Queen after 17...,Bc6; where does the Queen go? Of course Garry did not fall for the trap.) **15...,Nd5 16.Qe4,g6 17.Bh6,Re8** (**Diagram 130**. White has made progress by forcing Black to open up the dark squares around his King, but it will take more pressure to make real inroads. Garry decides to bring yet another reserve into the battle. Can you figure out which one that will be? The move played is a key idea in this kind of position.) (**Diagram 131**. One would think that White would try to win on the dark squares, but Black's pieces still cover them well. Therefore, White throws his little pawn into the attack, with the idea of trading off on g6, thus loosening up the structure around the King. After that, there will be sacrifices in the air!) **18...,Qb6** (**Diagram 132**.)

(With this Q-move, Black tries to distract White by threatening to take the b-pawn, ignoring ancient warnings to avoid it. What was the reply?) (**Diagram 133**. Garry goes straight for the throat. He tempts Black to take the b-pawn and thus win time to bring his own Rooks into position against the Black King. So if 19...,Qxb2 20.Ra2,Qb5 21.Qg4 with the idea of sacrificing his Bishop on g6 - the whole idea of pushing the h-pawn; Black would try 21...,Qa4 trying to trade Queens, answered by 22.Qg3 after which taking on g6

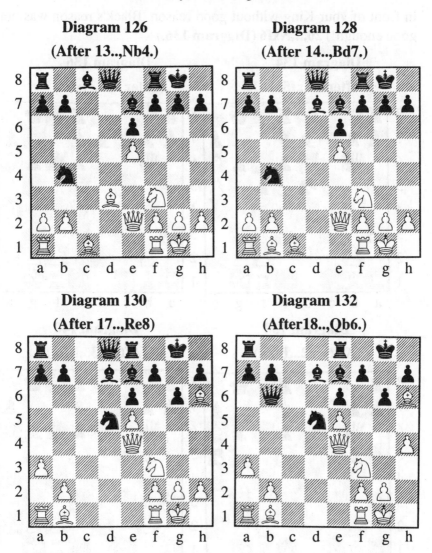

Diagram 126
(After 13..,Nb4.)

Diagram 128
(After 14..,Bd7.)

Diagram 130
(After 17..,Re8)

Diagram 132
(After18..,Qb6.)

and bringing a Rook to g4 via d4 remain threats.) **19...,f5 (Diagram 134**. If the last note was too complicated for you, so was it for Begun. He sees that after 19...,f5, if the Queen moves, the pressure will lessen, while if White takes 'en passant' by 20.exf6,Nxf6 the 'battering ram' h5 can be taken next. Can you see as far as Garry?) (**Diagram 135**. Granted, the pawn on h5 will disappear, but a new piece can now aim for g6: the Knight! And meanwhile the position of Black's King looks unhealthy. Steinitz warned a century ago not to push the pawns in front of your King without good reason. Black's reason was not good enough!) **20...,Nxf6** (**Diagram 136**.)

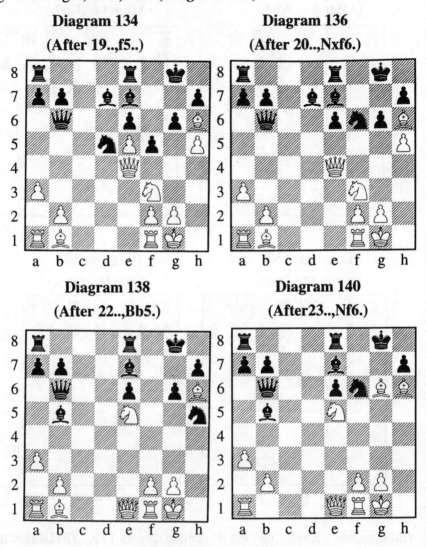

Diagram 134

(After 19..,f5..)

Diagram 136

(After 20..,Nxf6.)

Diagram 138

(After 22..,Bb5.)

Diagram 140

(After 23..,Nf6.)

(Now Kasparov finds a truly wonderful move. He has to move his Queen, but he still want to use her against Black's King shortly. However, he does not want Black using the threat to take it or exchange it to slow the attack. So he finds the perfect waiting move - a mirror of the first study on move 14. Can you see it after comparing the two positions?) (**Diagram 137**. Avoiding all problems! After Qe2, there was 21..,Bb5 possible; while after Qe5, Black could play

21....,Nxh5 followed by 22...,Bf6. All other squares were unsafe. So this move is just a question of calm thinking.) **21...,Nxh5 22.Ne5,Bb5** (**Diagram 138**. Considering what is going to happen next, Black looks somewhat silly for trying to win a Rook for a Bishop; but there was no defense against the coming storm. Garry gets the chance to finally prove that his plan was right all along! Can you see the demise of Black?) (**Diagram 139**. Black's defenses crumble. Apparently, 23.Nxg6 looks just as good, but did you see that after 23..,hxg6 24.Qe4,e5! Black's Queen defends g6? As played, the Knight prevents that and peeks at f7!) **23...,Nf6** (**Diagram 140**. After 23..,hxg6 White mates after both 24.Qe4 or 24.Qb1; yes, 21.Qe1 was that good! Garry plays the most forceful move, causing his opponent to resign immediately. What was that move?) (**Final position - Diagram 141**. Now 24..,Kxh7 25.Qb1+ leads to mate, as does 24..,Nxh7 25.Qe4,Nf8 26.Qg4+ - try both against the computer!) A most instructive game. The ideas that Garry used: setting up the Queen and Bishop; the h-pawn push, the sacrifice on g6; retreating with the idea of attacking; are all useful building blocks for advanced chess strategy!

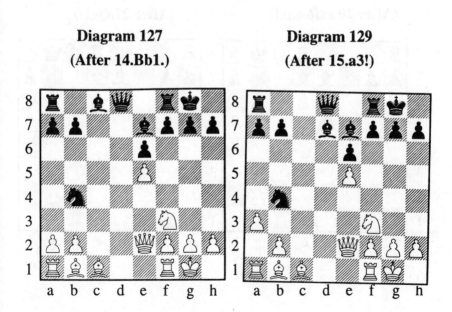

Diagram 127

(After 14.Bb1.)

Diagram 129

(After 15.a3!)

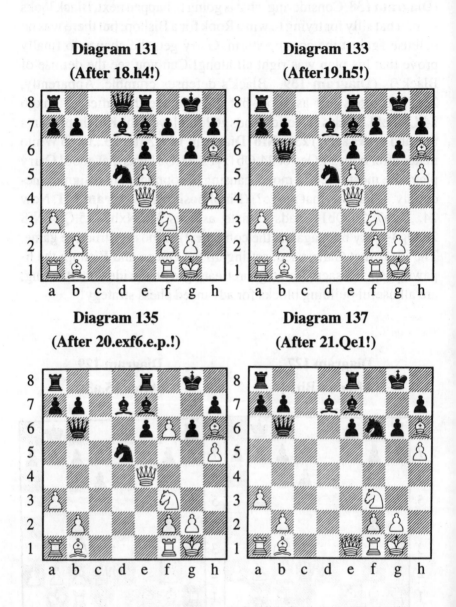

Diagram 131
(After 18.h4!)

Diagram 133
(After19.h5!)

Diagram 135
(After 20.exf6.e.p.!)

Diagram 137
(After 21.Qe1!)

Diagram 139	Diagram 141
(After 23.Bxg6!)	(After24.Bxh7+)

Another game of Garry Kasparov

Since he assumed the title in 1985, Kasparov has asserted his authority over the board against all leading GMs. Vassily Ivanchuk is one of the super GMs, but has lost the majority of his games against the World Champion.

White: G. Kasparov Black: V. Ivanchuk (English Opening)

1.c4,Nf6 2.Nc3,e5 3.Nf3,Nc6 4.g3,Bb4 5.Bg2,0-0 6.0-0,e4 (Both players have completed the most essential development. Black gets a bit more space by this pawn push, but has to give the King's Bishop in return.) **7.Ng5,Bxc3 8.bxc3,Re8 9.f3,exf3** (9..,e3?! 10.d3 and White is better.)**10.Nxf3,d5** (The liberating move, better than 10...,Qe7?! 11.e3,Ne5 12.Nd4!,Nd3 13.Qe2,Nxc1 and 14.Rxc1 which proved better for White, as played in Kasparov-Karpov, 1987.) **11.d4!**

(Novelty. To an equal game would lead 11.cxd5,Qxd5 12.Nd4,Qh5!) **11...,Ne4 12.Qc2!,dxc4 13.Rb1!!** (**Diagram 142**. Exclamation marks are from Kasparov. White is better. The open b-file prevents Black's response Bf5.) **13...,f5 14.g4!,Qe7**

(If here 14...,fxg4 15.Ne5,Nxe5 16.Bxe4,Ng6 17.Bxg6,hxg6 18.Qxg6 with a strong White attack.) **15.gxf5,Nd6** (Or 15...,Bxf5

16.Ne5,Nxe5 17.Rxf5,Ng4 18.h3,g6 19.Rf3,Ngf6 20.Re3 and White has the upper hand.) **16.Ng5,Qxe2 17.Bd5+,Kh8 18.Qxe2,Rxe2 19.Bf4** (Diagram 143. Despite or because of the exchange of Queens, Black is now in dire straights. White has achieved a decisive advantage, because he has managed to exchange

Diagram 142

(After 13.Rb1!!)

Diagram 143

(After 19.Bf4.)

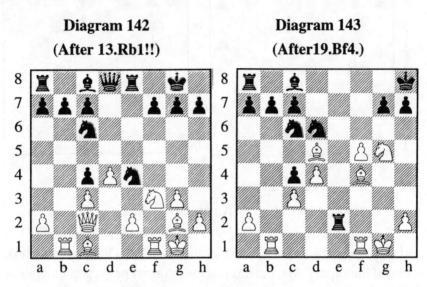

Black's most active piece. Black's Queen wing has no part in the game.) **19...,Nd8** (The alternative was 19...,Bxf5 20.Bxd6,Bxb1 21.Nf7+,Kg8 22.Nd8+,Kh8 23.Rf8++.) **20.Bxd6,cxd6 21.Rbe1!,Rxe1 22.Rxe1,Bd7 23.Re7,Bc6 24.f6** after which Black resigned (1-0), because the end is inevitable :

24...,Bxd5 25.Re8+,Bg8 26.f7,Nxf7 27.Nxf7++.

*   *   *   *

PART THREE

A Small Encyclopaedia of Openings

PART THREE

INTRODUCTION

The previous two parts of this book have given the begining chess player as well as those who have some experience adequate advice how to go about studying openings. It is better to concentrate on just a few than to drown in the sea of information that is available from many sources. Only the top 2% of all chess players spend an enormous amount of time expanding their knowledge on a wider basis.

A chess computer has on average at least 100,000 opening data stored in its memory, and will be able to guide you through whatever opening takes your fancy. There are a number of encyclopaedias that provide an even broader view. We have incorporated into Part Three a sizable part of up-to-date opening theory originating from Russia collected and edited by one of the great chess teachers from that country GM Eduard Gufeld who is known as the man who made Maya Chiburdanidze the youngest female world champion at age 17.

The data are not only useful as a practical guide to prepare for a serious game or to consult afterwards, but come in very handy if your computer has a 'programmable function'. You can then 'feed' it a lot of the opening lines, and use it for sparring sessions with your computer. You will find that your practical knowledge will expand rapidly.

In this section, we had to limit ourselves to the openings that will be most beneficial to the average club player. We have given a short description of the peculiarities of each opening/defense. Included are alphabetically the main lines of:

The Caro-Kann, Catalan & Dutch Defenses, the English Opening, the French Defense, the Italian Game (and related openings), the King's Gambit, the King's Indian and Pirc-Ufimtsev Defenses, the Queen's Gambit, the Ruy Lopez (Spanish) and Scotch Openings, the Sicilian and Slav Defenses and the Vienna Game.

PLEASE NOTE:

In Part Three, we have used the commonly accepted chess symbols (the first six of the following list) that were introduced in Part One. A number of other ones that are used in most chess publications are given below seven to 17).

To keep the material fresh and alive, we have only used them in the main tables. In the annotations that further explain the tables with examples from GM games and analysis from noted authorities on these openings, we chose text instead of symbols although the meaning is almost the same.

THE SYMBOLS

!	—	strong move
!!	—	splendid (often winning) move
!?	—	deserves consideration
?!	—	doubtful move
?	—	erroneous move
??	—	bad move or blunder
±	—	White has a slight advantage
∓	—	Black has a slight advantage
±	—	White has the advantage
∓	—	Black has the advantage
+−	—	White has a decisive advantage
−+	—	Black has a decisive advantage
∞	—	unclear position
∞̄	—	with compensation for the sacrificed material
Δ	—	with the idea
↑	—	with initiative
→	—	with attack

How to read Part Three to best advantage.

Choose one of the openings or defenses that you already encountered in the previous pages and that has taken your fancy. Start with the main table and play systematically through all the variations. Please note that the move for White is placed above the same move for Black. A '**4**' means the fourth move, a '**5**' means White's or Black's fifth move.

Select after that once more the first two lines and play through these moves.

By using two boards at the same time, you can save a lot of effort and time by continuing on the second board with the annotation below the table. The superscripted numbers in the table correspond to the notes below. If in these notes the first move is underlined, it means this (and similarly underlined moves) are valid alternatives.

If additional notes are given under the same number after the first analysis and start with a later move (i.e. the next section has move 17, while the previous one had move 14), then this means that this additional note refers to the analysis that immediately precedes it. It all comes down to common sense, and if in doubt, please do not hesitate to ask a more experienced chess player you know to help you become familiar with this system.

*   *   *   *

CARO-KANN DEFENSE 1.e4,c6

It would be appropriate to call this popular defense (already discussed in Part One) the Defense of World Champions. It was the favorite weapon of Capablanca; Botwinnik used in in his title bouts, Petrosian, Tal and Smyslov had it as part of their repertoire and most other champions (including Karpov and Kasparov) have used it at least occasionally as Black or made contributions to theory when faced with it as White.

Although it has a reputation of being dull, the theory has developed to such a degree that some variations (especially the Advance) can get you in really chaotic positions. The Classical System occurs after **2.d4,d5 3.Nc3,dxe4 4.Nxe4,Bf5.**

Diagram 1

2.Nc3,d5 3.Nf3,Bg4

Diagram 2

Main line: after 9...,Re8.

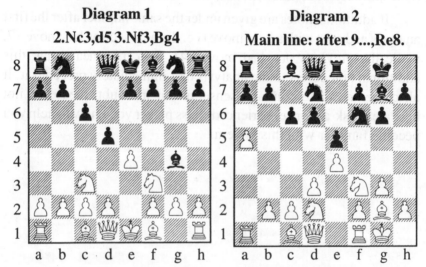

The Two Knights Variation (see **Diagram 1**) leads to interesting positions, while the Exchange Variation (after **2.d4,d5 3.exd5,cxd5**) is yet another alternative (both used with success by Fischer) to sharpen White's weapons. Combined with **4.c4** (the Panov-Botwinnik Attack), it demands that Black is keenly aware of the transpositional options (i.e. that he suddenly lands in another opening) to equalize.

1.e4,c6

2	3	4	5	6	7	8	9
d3	Nd2 [2]	Ngf3	g3	Bg2	0-0	a4	a5
e5 [1]	Nf6	d6	g6	Bg7	0-0	Nbd7	Re8 [3] ∞
c4	exd5	cxd5	Qa4 [6]+	Nc3	Nf3 [7]	Qb3	Bc4
d5 [4]	cxd5	Nf6 [5]	Nbd7	g6	Bg7	0-0	Nc5 [8] ±
Nc3	Nf3	h3	Qxf3	d3 [11]	Qg3 [12]	Be2	e5
d5	Bg4	Bxf3 [9]	Nf6 [10]	e6	Nbd7	Bb4	Nxe5 [13] =
--	--	Ne4	Ng3	Bc4	h3	Qxf3	Qe2
--	dxe4 [14]	Bf5 [15]	Bg4	e6	Bxf3	Nd7	Ngf6 [16] ±

1. 2..,d5 3.Nd2,g6 4.Ngf3,Bg7 5.g3,e5 6.Bg2,Ne7 7.0-0,0-0 8.Re1,Nd7 9.b4,a5!? 10.bxa5,dxe4 (10..,Qxa5 11.Bb2,Qc7 12.a4 and White is a bit better.) 11.Nxe4,Qxa5 12.Bb2,Qc7 was unclear. Bischoff-Grünfeld, Graz 1981.

2. 3.g3,Nf6 4.Bg2,d5 5.Nd2,Bd6 6.Ngf3,Nbd7 7.0-0,0-0 equalises. Stein-Barcza, Tallinn 1967; 3.Nf3,d6 4.g3,Nf6 5.Bg2,Be7 6.0-0,0-0 7.Re1,Nbd7 8.d4,Re8 9.c4,exd4 10.Nxd4,Ne5 11.Na3!?,Qb6 12.Re3! (12.h3?,Bxh3!) 12..,Bg4 13.f3 and White was slightly better in Ljuboevic - Speelman, Barcelona, World Cup, 1989.

3. 10.b4,Rb8 11.Bb2,b5 12.axb6,axb6 13.Ra7,Bb7 14.c4,Qc7 15.Qb3,Ra8 16.Rxa8,Bxa8 (16..,Rxa8 17.d4 is also good for White says Ljuboevic) 17.Ra1,d5 18.cxd5,cxd5 19.Ng5! and White has an edge in Ljuboevic - Karpov, Amsterdam 1988.

4. 2..,e5!? 3.d4,Bb4+ 4.Bd2,Bxd2+ 5.Qxd2,d6 6.Nc3,Qf6!? (6..,Nf6 is good for White) 7.Nge2,Ne7 8.0-0-0,0-0 9.f4,Bg4 10.f5,Nc8!? = Sax - Miles, Lugano 1989.

5. 4..,Qd5 5.Nc3,Qd6 (5..,Qa5!? 6.d4,Nf6 7.Nf3,g6 8.Bc4,Bg7 is unclear probably even.) 6.d4,Nf6 7.Nf3,e6 8.Bd3,Be7 9.0-0,Nc6 10.Qe2,0-0 was unclear or even in Ivkov-Seirawan, London 1981; 7.Nge2!? with idea: g3, Bg2, Bf4.

6. 5.Bb5+,Nbd7 (5...,Bd7 6.Bc4 is OK for White) 6.Nc3,a6 7.Qa4,Rb8!equalises; 5.Nc3,Nd5 6.Nf3,Nxc3 7.bxc3,g6 8.h4?! (8.d4 is unclear) 8...,Bg7 9.h5,Nc6 10.Rb1.Qc7 11.Ba3?! (11.d4!?) 11...,Bf5 in A.Sokolov-Karpov, Linares, match 1987. Black is better.

7. 7.d4,Bg7 8.Qb3,0-0 9.Bg5,Nb6 10.Bf6,Bxf6 with an unclear position in Larsen-Karpov, Montreal 1979.

8. 10.Qa3,b6 11.0-0,Bb7 12.d4 with slight edge for White in G. Kuzmin-Dolmatov, USSR Championship 1980.

9. 4...,Bh5 5.exd5,cxd5 6.Bb5+,Nc6 7.g4,Bg6 8.Ne5,Rc8 9.d4,e6 is unclear.

10. 5...,e6 6.d4!? (6.Be2,d4 7.Nb1,Nf6 8.d3,c5 9.Qg3,Nc6 10.0-0,h5 11.f4,h4 12.Qf2,Nh5 13.Bxh5,Rxh5 14.Nd2 with an unclear position or slight edge for White in Short-Seirawan, Barcelona World Cup 1989.) 6...,dxe4 7.Nxe4,Qxd4 8.Bd3,Nf6 9.c3,Qd8 10.0-0,Be7 11.Rd1,Nbd7 12.Qg3,Nxe4 13.Bxe4,g6 14.Bf4 and White has the edge.

11. 6.d4!?,dxe4 7.Qe3!,Nbd7 (7...,Qa5!?) 8.Nex4,Nxe4 9.Qxe4 and White is a bit better.

12. 7.Be2,Nbd7 8.Qg3,g6 9.0-0,Bg7 10.Bf4,Qb6 11.Rab1,0-0 12.Bf3,e5! 12.Bd2,dxe4 13.dxe4,a5 even game in Karpov-Portisch, Montreal 1979.

13. 10.Qxe5,d4 11.a3,Ba5 12.Bf3,0-0 even game in Kislov-Timofeev, USSR 1980.

14. 3...,Nf6 4.e5,Ne4 (4..,Nfd7 5.e6!,fxe6 6.d4,e5 7.dxe5,e6 8.Bf4,Be7 9.Ng5,Bxg5 10.Qh5+ with advantage for White says Boleslavsky.) 5.Ne2,Qb6 6.d4,c5 7.dxc5,Nxc5 8.Nf4,e6 9.Be2,Be7 10.0-0,0-0 11.c4,dxc4 12.Bxc4 with a slight advantage for White.

15. 4...,Nf6 5.Nxf6+,gxf6 6.g3,Bf5 (6...,e5 7.Bg2,Be6   8.0-0,Nd7 9.d4 and White has the edge.) 7.Bg2,Qd7 8.0-0,Na6 9.Re1,0-0-0 and White has a slight advantage in Westerinen-Chandler, Bussum 1981.)

16. 10.0-0,Be7 11.c3!,c5 (Tompa-Petkevich, Lodz 1979.) 12.Rd1,0-0 13.d4,cxd4 14.Rxd4 and White is better (Tompa).

The Advance Variation: 2.d4,d5 3.e5,Bf5

(Diagram 3; the most usual answer by Black.)

There has been an explosion of captivating games in recent years that prove that White does not need to fear overextending himself. Like in the Alekhine Defense (**1.e4,Nf6 2.e5,Nd5**) the danger always exists that the pawn(s) pushed onto Black's side of the board (the extended center) become a target, and White ends up defending when he cannot exploit his initial space advantage. Look for games with these initial moves in chess magazines and chess columns. You will not be disappointed!

Diagram 3
After 3..,Bf5

Diagram 4
Note 7: after 10.Nf4!

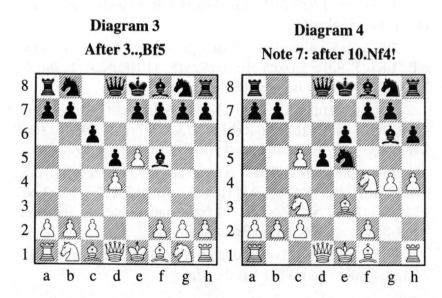

		1.e4,c6 2.d4,d5				
3	**4**	**5**	**6**	**7**	**8**	**9**
e5 [1]	Nc3 [3]	g4	Nge2	h4 [6]	Be3	Qd2
Bf5 [2]	e6 [4]	Bg6	c5 [5]	h6	Qb6 [7]	Nc6 [8] ∞
exd5	c4	Nc3	Qb3 [10]	cxd5	Be2 [11]	Bf3
cxd5	Nf6	g6 [9]	Bg7	0-0	Nbd7	Nb6 [12] ∞/=
--	--	--	Nf3	cxd5 [13]	Bb5+ [14]	Bxd7+
--	--	e6	Be7	exd5	Bd7 [15]	Nbxd7 [16] ±
--	Bd3	c3	Bf4	Nd2	h3	Ngf3
--	Nc6	Nf6	g6 [17]	Bg7	0-0	Bf5 [18] ±

1. 3.f3,e6 4.Nc3,Bb4! 5.Bd3,dxe4 6.Bxe4 with an even game (Kasparov, Shakarov).

2. 3...,c5 4.dxc5,e6 5.Be3!,Ne7 6.c3,Nf5 7.Bd4,Qc7 8.Bd3,Bxc5 9.Bxc5,Qxc5 10.Bxf5,exf5 11.Nf3,Nc6 12.0-0,0-0 13.Nbd2 and White is better (Boleslavsky).

3. 4.Bd3,Bxd3 5.Qxd3,e6 6.Nc3,Qb6 7.Nge2,Qa6 even game; 4.h4!?,h5 5.c4!?.Bxb1?! 6.Rxb1,e6 7.a3,Nd7 8.Nf3 with a small advantage for White as in Spassky-Seirawan, London 1982.

4. 4...,h5 5.Bd3,Bxd3 6.Qxd3,e6 7.Nf3,Qb6 (7...,Nh6.) 8.0-0,Qa6?! (8...,Nd7!?) 9.Qd1,Ne7 10.Ne2,Nd7 11.c3,Nf5 12.Bg5,Be7 12.Ng3!?,Nxg3 14.fxg3! and White has the edge: Short-Seirawan, World Cup Rotterdam 1989.

5. 6...,f6 7.Nf4!?,fxe5 8.dxe5,Bf7 9.h4,Nd7 unclear; 6...,Bb4 7.h4,Be4 8.Rh3 and White has the edge.

6. 7.Be3,Nc6 8.dxc5,Qh4!? 9.Nb5,Be4 10.Nc7+,Kd7 11.Nxa8,Bxh1 12.Ng3,Qxh2 13.b4,Nh6 14.Qe2,Be7 15.b5,Nxe5 and draw agreed in van der Wiel-Sosonko, Amsterdam 1982.

7. 8...,Nc6?! 9.dxc5,Nxe5 10.Nf4! and White had a small advantage in Timman-Karpov, Belfort World Cup 1988.

8. 10.0-0-0!?,h5! unclear or probably even game in A. Sokolov-Karpov, Linares match 1987.

9. 5...,Nc6 6.Bg5,Qa5 7.Bxf6 (7.Bd2,dxc4!? 8.Bxc4,e6 9.d5,exd5 10.Nxd5,Qd8 11.Qe2+,Be6 12.Nf4,Nd4 13.Nxe6,fxe6 equal game in Bronstein-Bagirov, Tallinn 1981.) 7...,exf6 8.cxd5,Bb4 unclear; 6.cxd5,Nxd5 7.Nf3,e6 8.Bd3,Bb4 9.Bd2,0-0 10.0-0,Nf6 11.a3,Be7 12.Be3,b6 13.Re1,Bb7 14.Bc2,Na5?! (14...,a6!?) 15.Ne5,Rc8 16.Qd3 and White has a small advantage as in Dlugi-Oll, Moscow World Cup 1989; 6.Nf3,Bg4 7.cxd5,Nxd5 8.Qb3,Bxf3 9.gxf3,e6 10.Qxb7,Nxd4 11.Bb5+,Nxb5 12.Qc6+,Ke7 13.Qxb5,Qd7 15.Nxd5,Qxd5 15.Qxd5,exd5 16.Be3,Ke6 17.0-0-0,Bb4 equal game in Vaganyan-Dreev, Odessa USSR Championship 1989; 6.Nf3,Be6!? 7.c5,g6 8.Bb5!,Bg7 9.Ne5,Bd7 10.Bxc6,bxc6 11.0-0,0-0 12.Re1,Be8 unclear position in Anand-Miles, Wijk aan Zee 1989.

10. 6.cxd5,Nxd5 7.Qb3,Nb6 (7...,Nxc3 8.Bc4 and White is better.) 8.d5!,Bg7 9.Be3,0-0 10.Rd1,Na6 (10...,Bg4!?) 11.Bxa6,bxa6 12.Nge2 and White is slightly better as in Sveshnikov-S. Garcia, Cienfuegos 1979.)

11. 8.g3,Nbd7 9.Bg2,Nb6 10.Nge2,Bf5 11.Nf4,h6!? unclear.

12. 10.Bg5,Bg4 11.Bxf6,Bxf3 12.Nxf3,exf6! 13.0-0,Qd7 even.

13. 7.Bd3,dxc4 8.Bxc4,0-0 9.0-0,Nc6 10.a3,a6! even game; 7.Bg5,0-0 8.c5,b6 9.b4,a5 unclear position; 7.c5,0-0 8.b4,a5 9.Na4,Nfd7 with an even game.

14. 8.Bd3!?,0-0 9.h3!?,Nc6 10.0-0,Be6 11.Be3 and White had the edge in Vaganyan-van der Wiel, Rotterdam World Cup 1989.

15. 8...,Nc6!? 9.0-0,0-0 10.Ne5,Qb6!? 11.Bg5,Nd8! 12.Qd3,Ne6 13.Be3!,Rd8 14.f4,Nc7 with an unclear position in Adams-Larsen, Cannes 1989.

16. 10.0-0,0-0 11.Qb3,Nb6 12.Bg5 and White has the edge (Botwinnik).

17. 6...,Bg4!? 7.Qb3!?,Qd7!? (7...,Na5?! 8.Qa4+,Bd7 9.Qc2,e6 10.Nf3,Qb6 11.a4! and White had a small advantage in Fischer-Petrosian, Belgrade 1970.) 8.Nd2,e6 9.Ngf3,Bxf3 10.Nxf3,Bd6 11.Bxd6,Qxd6 12.Qxb7,Rb8 13.Qa6,0-0 14.0-0,Rb6 15.Qa3,Qxa3 16.bxa3 even game (Kasparov, Shakarov).

18. 10.Qe2,Rc8 11.0-0,Nh5 12.Bh2 and White had the edge in Benjamin-Santo Roman, Graz 1981).

Variations on the Classical System:

Bent Larsen was one of the first to systematically look at alternatives to **4...,Bf5.** We shall now look at the most logical moves. **4...,Nf6** is not liked by some players, because their pawn-structure gets spoiled after **5.Nxf6+.** Others call this an advantage for tactical counterplay (half open g-line after **5...,gxf6**); or a fortified K-side and open e-line (after **5...,exf6**). The cautious move **4...,Nd7** is a favorite of many GMs including Karpov.

Diagram 5

Main line: 4..,Nd7

Diagram 6

Third line: after 10.h4!

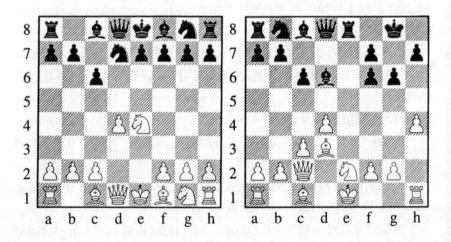

1.e4,c6 2.d4,d5 3.Nc3,dxe4 4.Nxe4

4	5	6	7	8	9	10	11
--	Nf3[1]	Nxf6+[2]	Ne5	Be2	0-0	c3[4]	Nd3!?
Nd7	Ngf6	Nxf6	Be6[3]	g6	Bg7	0-0	Bf5!? ±
--	Bc4	Ng5[5]	Qe2	Bd3[7]	N5f3	dxc5	Ne5[9]
--	Ngf6	e6	Nb6[6]	h6	c5	Bxc5[8]	Nbd7[10] =
--	Nxf6+	c3[11]	Bd3	Qc2	Ne2	h4!	h5
Nf6	exf6	Bd6	0-0[12]	Re8+	g6	Nd7[13]	Nf8[14] ±
--	--	Nf3[15]	Be2	h3	0-0	c4	d5!
--	gxf6	Bg4[16]	Qc7	Bh5	e6[17]	Nd7	0-0-0! ∞

1. 5.Ng5!?,Ngf6 6.Bd3,e6 7.N1f3,Bd6 8.0-0,h6 9.Ne4,Nxe4 10.Bxe4,0-0 11.c3!,e5 12.Bc2,Re8 13.Re1,exd4 14.Rexe8+,Qxe8 15.Qxd4,Qe7 16.Bf4,Bxf4 17.Qxf4,Nf8 18.Re1,Be6 19.Nd4,Rd8 20.h4 and White had a small advantage in Kasparov-Karpov, Amsterdam 1988; 6...,Qc7!? 7.Ne2 (7.N1f3,h6 8.Ne6?!,fxe6 9.Bg6+,Kd8 10.Qe2,Nd5! and Black is better; 7.Qe2,h6 8.N5f3,e6 9.Ne5,Nxe5! 10.dxe5,Nd7 11.Nf3,Nc5 with an even game.) 7...,e6 8.c4,Bb4+ 9.Bd2 (9.Nc3,0-0 10.0-0,e5! with an even game in Gelfand-Dreev, Vilnius 1988.) 9...,Bxd2+ 10.Qxd2,h6 11.Nf3,0-0 12.0-0,e5 13.dxe5,Nxe5 14.Nxe5,Qxe5 15.Ng3,Be6 equalized in Kovalev-Georgadze, Simferopol 1988.)

2. 6.Ng3!?,e6 (6..,c5 7.Bc4!) 7.Bd3,c5 (7...,Be7 8.0-0,0-0 9.Qe2,c5 10.dxc5,Nxc5 11.Bc4,b6 12.Rd1,Qc7 13.Ne5 and White has the edge according to Boleslavsky.; 9...,b6 10.Bf4,Bb7 11.c4 and White had the edge in Tal-Miles, Porz 1981/82.) 8.c3,cxd4 9.Nxd4,Bc5 (9...,Nc5!?) 10.Bc2!,b6 11.Ne4 and White has a slight advantage, Mark Tseilin-Vasyukov 1982.)

3. 7...,Bf5 8.c3,Bg6 (8...,e6 9.g4!,Bg6 10.h4! White is slightly better.) 9.h4,Nd7 10.Nc4,h5 11.Bg5,f6 12.Bf4,b5 13.Bd3 and White had a small advantage, Karpov-Spassky, Bad-Kissingen 1980.)

4. 10.c4,0-0 11.Be3,Qc7 12.Qc1,Rfd8 13.Rd1,Rac8 14.Bf4,Qb6 15.Qe3,a6 16.b3,Qa7 equalizes, Jansa-Bleiman, Sweden 1980.

5. 6.Nxf6+,Nxf6 7.Nf3,Bf5 8.0-0,e6 9.Bg5,Be7 10.Qe2,Bg4 11.Rad1,0-0 12.h3,Bxf3 13.Qxf3,Nd5 14.Be3! with a small advantage (Larsen).

6. 7...,Be7? 8.Nxf7 and White has a decisive advantage.

7. 8.Bb3,h6 9.N5f3,a5 10.a3,a4 11.Ba2,c5 12.c3,Bd7 13.Ne5,cxd4 14.cxd4,Be7 15.Ngf3,0-0 16.0-0,Be8 17.Bd2,Nbd5 18.Rfc1,Qb6 19.Bc4 and White was a bit better in Karpov-Petrosian,Tilburg 1982; 9...,c5 10.Bf4,Nbd5 11.Be5,Qa5+ 12.Nd2,b5 13.c4,bxc4 14.Bxc4,Nb6!? 15.b4!? (15.Bd3,c4!) 15...,Qxb4 (15...,cxb4?! 16.Nb3.) 16.Rb1,Qa5 17.Bb5+,Bd7 18.Bxf6!,gxf6 19.Ngf3,cxd4 20.0-0 unclear position, Short-Speelman, Hastings 1988/89.

8. 10...,Nbd7 11.c6,bxc6 12.Bd2,Be7 13.Nd4,Qb6 14.Ngf3!? and White is a bit better.

9. 11.Bd2!?,Qc7 (11...,Nbd5 12.0-0-0,a6 13.Nh3,b5 14.Nf4!?,Qb6 15.Nxd5,Nxd5 16.Ne5,0-0 17.Rhf1 intebding 18.g4 and a slight edge.) 12.0-0-0,0-0-0 (12...,Nbd7 13.h4,a6 14.Nh3,Bd6 15.Bc3,Nc5 16.g4!?,Bd7 15.g5 and White is slightly better.) 13.Ne5,Nbd7 14.f4,b6 15.Ngf3,Bb7 16.Rhf1,Rac8 17.Kb1 and White had a slight advantage, Chiburdanidze-Ioselani, Telavi, World Championship 1988.

10. 12.Ngf3,Qc7 13.0-0,0-0 even game.

11. 6.g3!?,c5 7.Nf3,Bd6 8.Be3,Qc7 9.dxc5,Bxc5 10.Bxc5,Qxc5 11.Qe2+,Be6? (11...,Kf8! 12.Bg2,Nc6 13.0-0,g6 and White is a bit better.) 12.Bh3 and White had advantage in Tal-Lechtynsky, USSR 1979; 6.Bc4,Qe7 7.Qe2,Be6 8.Bb3,Na6!?

9.Be3,Bxb3 10.axb3,Qe6 11.Nf3,Bd6 12.0-0,0-0 13.Rfd1,Rfe8
14.Qd2,Nb4! 15.c4,a5 equal game, Sznapik-Lechtynsky, Decin
1979; 6...,Bd6 7.Ne2,Qc7! 8.Be3,0-0 9.Qd2,Re8 10.0-0-0,Nd7!
with an even game, Majeric-Mirkovic, Yugoslavia 1988.

12. 7...,Qc7?! 8.Ne2,Bg4?! 9.Be3,Nd7 10.Qd2,Bxe2
11.Qxe2,0-0-0 12.0-0-0,Kb8 13.Kb1,Nb6 14.g3 and White had
advantage, Karpov-Smyslov, Tilburg 1979.

13. 10...,Be6 11.h5,f5 12.hxg6,fxg6 13.Bh6,Nd7 (13...,Qf6!?
Speelman.) 14.g4!?,Bd5 15.0-0-0!,Bxh1 16.Rxh1 and White is
better with compensation for the sacrificed material, in Kudrin-King,
Boyswater 1988.

14. 12.Bh6,Be6 13.0-0-0,Qc7 14.c4! (intending 15.c5.)
14...,c5 15.d5,Bc8 16.hxg6,fxg6 17.Rh4!,f5 18.Rdh1 and White
had advantage in Sznapik-Kostro, Poland 1980.

15. 6.c3,Bf5 7.Bf4,Nd7 8.Bd3,Bg6 9.Ne2,Nb6 10.0-0,e6
11.Bg3,Bd6 12.b4!?,Qc7 13.a4,Nd5 14.Qd2,Rd8 15.Rab1,0-0
16.c4 with a slight edge for White as in Short-Larsen, Hastings
1988/89; 6.Be2,Bf5 7.Nf3,Qc7 8.0-0,Nd7 9.c4,0-0-0 10.d5,e5!?
11.Be3,Qb8 12.Nh4,Bg6 13.f4?!,f5! is unclear, probably a bit better
for Black as in Lyubomirov-Mikhail Tseilin, correspondence game
1988; 6.Ne2!?,Bf5 7.Ng3,Bg6 8.h4,h5! (8...,h6 9.h5,Bh7 10.c3,e6
11.Be3,Nd7 12.Qd2 is a bit better for White.) 9.Be2,Nd7 10.c3,Qa5
even or possibly just a spot better for White.

16. 6...,Bf5 7.Be2,e6 8.0-0,Qc7 9.c4,Be7 10.d5,0-0 11.Nd4!
and White has an edge.

17. 9...,Nd7 10.d5,Rd8 11.c4,Nb6 12.Be3,Bxf3 13.Bxb6,axb6
14.Bxf3,cxd5 15.cxd5,Bh6 and White had a slight advantage in
Smyslov-Pachman, Amsterdam 1964.

And last but not least the **Classical System** (see **Diagram 7**) that
continues to attract Black players who prefer to postpone real combat
until they have secured a solid position. The idea is to chip away at
White's extended boundaries. White needs to know his limits in
aggression, and Black must be prepared for the retribution that such a
provocative stance can entail (in the words of Kasparov himself).

Diagram 7	Diagram 8
3.Nc3,dxe4 4.Nxe4,Bf5	**Fourth line: after 12.c4**

The original theories of H. Caro of Berlin and M. Kann of Vienna who analysed and practised the Defense named after them are continuouly being tested and found to stand up to modern GM practice!

1.e4,c6 2.d4,d5 3.Nc3,dxe4 4.Nxe4,Bf5
5.Ng3 [1],Bg6 6.h4 [2],h6 7.Nf3,Nd7

8	9	10	11	12	13	14	15
h5	Bd3	Qxd3	Bd2 [3]	Qe2	0-0-0	Ne5	Ba5 [5] =
Bh7	Bxd3	Qc7	e6	Ngf6	0-0-0	Nb6 [4]	
--	--	--	--	0-0-0	Ne4 [6]	g3	Qxe4 [7] ∞
--	--	--	--	Ngf6	0-0-0	Nxe4	
--	--	--	Bf4	0-0-0	Kb1 [9]	Ne4	Qxe4 [10] ∞
--	--	e6	Ngf6 [8]	Be7	a5	Nxe4	
Bd3	Qxd3	Bd2	0-0-0	c4 [11]	Bc3	Kb1	Nxd4 =
Bxd3	Qc7	e6	Ngf6	0-0-0 [12]	c5	cxd4	

146

1. 5.Nc5!?,Qb6?! 6.g4!?,Bg6 7.f4,e6 8.Qe2,Be7 9.h4,h5 10.f5!,exf5 11.g5 and White had advantage in Bronstein-Belyavsky, USSR 1974; 5...,b6!? 6.Nb3,Nf6 7.Nf3,e6 8.Be2,h6 9.Bd3,Bxd3 10.Qxd3,Qc7 equalizes, Larsen-Hübner, Tilburg 1979; 5...,Qc7!? 6.Bd3,Bxd3 5.Nxd3,Nd7 8.Nf3,Ngf6 even game, Sigurjonsson-Buerger, Brighton 1981.

2. 6.N1e2,e6 7.Nf4,Bd6 8.Ng6,hxg6 9.Ne4,Be7 even game in Byrne-Kavalek, USA Championship 1981; 6.Bc4,e6 7.N1e2,Nf6 8.0-0,Bd6 9.f4,Qd7! (9...,Qc7 10.f5!) equalized in van der Wiel-Seirawan, Baden 1980.

3. 11.0-0!?,e6 12.c4,0-0-0 13.d5!?,Nc5 14.Qd4,exd4 15.Bf4,dxc4! 16.Qxc4,Bd6 17.Bxd6,Qxd6 18.Rad1,Qxd1 19.Rxd1,Rxd1+ 20.Kh2 and White is a bit better, Vitolinsh-Bagirov, USSR 1980; 11.Rh4,Ngf6 12.Bf4,Qa5+ 13.Bd2,Qb5 14.Qxb5,cxb5 equalized in Sax-Hort, Tilburg 1970.

4. 15...,Nxe5 15.dxe5,Nd7 16.f4,Be7 17.Ne4 is a bit better for White.

5. 15...,Rd5! 16.Bxb6,axb6 17.c4,Rd8 even game.

6. 13.c4,0-0-0 14.Bc3,c5 15.Kb1,cxd4 16.Nxd4,a6 17.Nb3 and White had the edge in Spassky-Portisch, match 1980.

7. 15...,Bd6 16.c4,c5 17.Bc3,cxd4 18.Nxd4,Nc5 19.Qc2,a6 20.Rhe1,Be7 21.Kb1,Bf6 22.f4?! (22.Nb3 even game.) 22...,Rd7 was a bit better for Black in Hjartarson-Timman, Amsterdam 1989; 18.Bxd4,Nf6 19.Qe2,Qa5 20.Kb1 (H_bner-Hjartarson, Barcelona World Cup 1989.) 20...,Qf5+ 21.Ka1,Bc7 22.Bxa7,Rxd1+ 23.Rxd1,Qxh5 with an unclear position (Hübner); 17.d5!?,Nf6 18.Qc2,exd5 19.cxd5,Rhe8 20.Bc3,Kb8 (Tiviakov-Miles, Moscow World Cup 1989.) 21.Kb1!?; 21.Bxf6!?,gxf6 22.Nh4 is a bit better for White (Tiviakov); 15...,Be7 16.Kb1,Rhe8 17.Qe2,Bf8 18.Bc1,Bd6 19.Rhe1,Qa5 20.Nd2! was slightly advantageous for White in Timman-Portisch, match Antwerp 1989.

8. 11...,Qa5+ 12.c3 (12.Bd2,Qc7) 12...,Ngf6 13.a4,c5

14.0-0,Be7! with an even game.

9. 13.Rhe1,a5 14.c4,b5! 15.c5,Nd5 unclear, Tal-Larsen, Tilburg 1980; 13.Ne5,0-0 14.Ne4,Nxe4 15.Qxe4,Nxe5 16.Bxe5,Qd5!

17.Qg4?! (17.Qxd5 gives an even game.) 17...,f6 18.Bf4,Qxa2 19.Bxh6,Rf7 20.c3,a5! was better for Black, in De Firmian-Korchnoi, Lugano 1989.

10. 15...,Nf6 16.Qe2,a4 17.Ne5,Qd5 unclear in Torre-Karpov, Moscow 1981.

11. 12.Rhe1,0-0-0 13.Qb3,c5! 14.Qa4,Kb8 (Zapata-Dorfman, La Habana 1988.) 15.dxc5,Nxc5 16.Bf4,Bd6 17.Rxd6,Nxa4 18.Rxd8+,Rxd8 19.Bxc7+,Kxc7 with an even game (Dorfman).

12. 12...,Bd6 13.Ne4,Bf4 14.g3,Bxd2+ 15.Rxd2,Nxe4 16.Qxe4 and White is slightly better.

* * * *

CHAPTER 2

THE CATALAN SYSTEM

This system has seen an enormous revival of late. A few years ago, a rich Spanish chess sponsor organised a year-long promotion in which GMs worldwide were encouraged to play it and send in their games. We differentiate between the Closed and Open Catalan. The Open Catalan (see below) results in exciting chess in which Black early bids for equality through active counterplay. It has many similarities with the Queen's Gambit Accepted and some of the Botwinnik System (if Black tries to hold onto his extra c-pawn).

The system develops when White chooses to fianchetto his Bf1 via g2. Black must choose between holding the pawn and negotiate its return. By this he will be able to mobilise his forces quickly and force the liberating ...,c5. The games found in the notes give a refreshing reflection of the energetic development in recent tournament games.

1.d4,Nf6 2.c4,e6 3.g3,d5[1] 4.Bg2,dxc4

5	6	7	8	9	10	11
Nf3	0-0	Ne5	Nc3[3]	Nxd5	e4	Qh5
a6	b5[2]	Nd5	Bb7[4]	exd5[5]	dxe4	g6[6] ∞
...	0-0	Qa4[8]	Qxc4	Nxd4	Nc3	Qxd4
c5[7]	Nc6	Bd7[9]	cxd4	Rc8	Nxd4	Bc5[10] ∞
Qa4+	Qxc4	Nf3	Qa4+	Qd1	Nc3	0-0
Bd7	Bc6	Bd5[11]	Qd7	Nc6	Bb4	Bxc3[12] =
...	Qxc4	Qc2[13]	Nf3	Nc3	Bf4	Bxd6
Nbd7	a6	c5!	b5	Qc7	Bd6	Qxd6[14] ±/=

Diagram 9

Open Catalan:

after 4...,dxc4.

Diagram 10

Note 3: 8.e4.

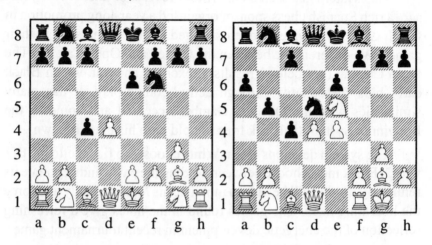

1. 3...,Bb4 4.Bd2,Be7 5.Bg2,d5 6.Nf3,0-0 7.0-0,c6 8.Qc2,Nbd7 9.Bf4,Nh5 10.Bc1,f5 11.b3,Ndf6 12.e3,Bd7 13.Ba3,Bxa3 14.Nxa3 and White had a small advantage in Korchnoi-Chandler, Hastings 1988/89.

2. 6...,Nc6!? 7.e3,Rb8 8.Nfd2,Na7 9.Nc4,b5 10.Ne5,c5 unclear position, Polugayevsky-Portisch, Amsterdam 1981; 7.Na3,Bxa3 8.bxa3,Rb8 9.Bb2,b5 10.Qc2,0-0 11.Rad1,Ne7 12.e4,Rb6! 13.Nh4,Bb7 unclear, Kozul-Davidovic, Liechtenstein 1989.

3. 8.e4,Nf6 9.a4,Bb7 10.axb5,axb5 11.Rxa8,Bxa8 12.Nc3,c6 13.Bg5,Bb7 unclear but probably slightly better for White; 8.a4,Bb7 9.b3!?,cxb3 10.axb5,axb5 11.Rxa8,Bxa8 12.Qb3,c6 13.Nc3!,Be7 14.Nd5,exd5 15.Qa2,Bb7 16.Qa7,Qc7 17.Bf4,Bd6 18.Rc1,Qe7 19.Ra1 and White has advantage with compensation for the sacrificed material, Romanishin-Marjanovic, Erevan 1989.

4. 8...,c6 9.Nxd5,exd5 10.e4,Be6 11.a4 with advantage for White.

5. 9...,Bd5? 10.e4,bb7 11.Qh5,g6 12.Nxg6!,fxg6 13.Qe5 with decisive advantage.

6. 12.Nxg6,fxg6 13.Qe5+,Qe7 14.Qxh8,Nd7 is unclear.

7. 5...,Bd7 6.Ne5,Bc6 7.Nxc6,Nxc6 8.0-0,Qd7 9.e3,Rb8 10.Qe2,b5 11.a4 (11.b3,cxb3 12.axb3,Rb6! 13.Bb2,a6 14.e4,Nxd4! 15.Bxd4,Qxd4 16.Rxa6,Rxa6 17.Qb5+,Nd7 18.Qxa6,Be7 19.Qa8,Bd8 even game in Belyavsky-Karpov, Moscow USSR Championship 1988.) 11...,a6 12.axb5,axb5 13.b3,cxb3 14.Nd2,Be7 15.Nb3,0-0 16.Bd2!,Rfc8 17.Rfc1 with advantage and compensation for the sacrificed material, in Kiril Georgiev-Anand, Wijk aan Zee 1989; 5...Nc6 6.0-0,Rb8 7.a4,a6 8.Bg5,Be7 9.Nc3,0-0 (9...,b5 10.axb5,axb5 11.Nxb5!,Rxb5 12.Qa4 unclear.) 10.e4,b5 11.axb5,axb5 12.Re1 with compensation, Simic-Krasenkov, Ptuj 1989.

8. 7.Ne5,Bd7 8.Nxc6,Bxc6 9.Bxc6,bxc6 10.Qa4,cxd4 11.Qc6,Nd7 unclear but probably even; 8.Nc4!?,cxd4 9.Bf4,Nd5 10.Nd6,Bxd6 11.Bxd6,Nde7 12.Nd2,0-0 13.Qb3,Bc8 14.Nc4,Re8 with an edge for White, Yusupov-A. Sokolov, Moscow USSR Championship 1988; 8.Na3!?,cxd4 (8...,Nd5!? Smagin.) 9.Nac4,Bc5 10.Qb3,0-0 11.Bf4,Qc8 12.Rfd1,Nd5 13.Nd7,Qxd7 14.Ne5,Qe7 15.Nc6,bxc6 16.Be5 and White had a small advantage, Timman-A. Sokolov, Linares 1989.

9. 7...,cxd4 8.Nxd4,Qxd4 9.Bc6,Bd7 10.Rd1,Qxd1! 11.Qxd1,Bc6 12.Qc2,Be7 with compensation in an even game, Polugayevsky-Andersson, Moscow 1981.

10. 12.Qh4,Bc6 13.Rd1,Qa5 unclear but probably better for White.

11. 7...,Nbd7 8.Nc3,Nb6 9.Qd3,Bb4 10.0-0,0-0 11.Rd1,h6 unclear, probably better for White.

12. 12.bxc4,0-0 13.Re1,h6 even game.

13. 7.Nd2,c5 8.dxc5,Bxc5 9.Nb3,Be7 10.Nf3,b5 11.Qd4,Bb7 even game in Smyslov-Karpov, Moscow 1971.

14. 12.dxc4,Qc5 13.Nd2,Rb8 14.Rc1,Bb7 15.Bxb7,Rxb7 even or just a bit better for White.

The **Closed Catalan** (Black's choice) tends to be a bit cramped. It is Black's task to prove that his position is equal. There are again many, many similarities with the Queen's Gambit. Black would do well to study this opening thoroughly at the same time as the Queen's Gambit before embarking on adventures in serious games.

1.d4,Nf6 2.c4,e6 3.g3,d5 4.Bg2,Be7 5.Nf3,0-0 6.0-0

6	7	8	9	10	11	12
...	Qc2	Qxc4	Qc2	Bd2 [1]	Qc1	Bg5
dxc4	a6	b5	Bb7	Be4 [2]	b4	Nbd7 [3] ∞/±
...	...	a4	Qxc4 [5]	Bf4	Nc3	Be5
...	...	Bd7 [4]	Bc6	a5!?	Na6	Nd5 [6] ±
...	Ne5	Nxc6 [7]	Na3 [8]	bxa3	Qa4	Qxc6
...	Nc6!?	bxc6	Bxa3	Nd5 [9]	Nb6	Rb8 [10] =
...	Qc2 [12]	b3	Bb2	Nc3	e4	Nxe4
c6 [11]	Nbd7 [13]	b6	Bb7 [14]	Qc7	dxe4	c5 [15] =

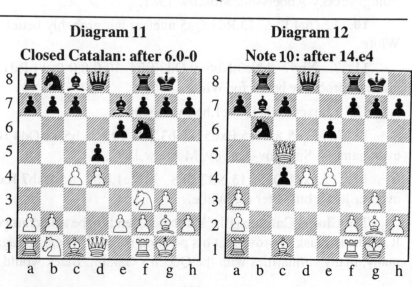

Diagram 11

Closed Catalan: after 6.0-0

Diagram 12

Note 10: after 14.e4

1. 10.Bg5,Nbd7 11.Nbd2 (11.Bxf6,Nxf6 12.Nbd2,Rc8 13.Nb3,Be4 14.Qc3,Nd5 15.Qc1,c5 16.Nxc5,Qb6 17.Qd2,Bxc5 18.dxc5,Rxc5 with an even game, Andersson-Karpov, Moscow 1981.) 11...,c5!? 12.dxc5,Nxc5 13.Bxf6,gxf6 14.Nb3,Rc8 15.Rad1,Qb6 16.Nxc5,Bxc5 (Khalifman-Aseev, Leningrad 1989.) 17.Qd2,Rfd8 18.Qh6,Bxf2+ 19.Kh1,Bxf3 20.Bxf3,Bd4!? 21.g4! with an even game (Aseev).

2. 10...,Nc6 11.e3,Qb8 12.a3,Rc8 13.Re1!,a5 14.Nc3,Nd8 15.e4,b4 16.Na4,Nd7 17.Bf4,Bd6 18.Be3,Bc6 19.d5,b3 20.Qc4,Qb5 21.Qxb5,Bxb5 22.Nc3,Bd3 23.Nd4! and White had advantage in Timman-Hjartarson, Amsterdam 1989.

3. 13.Nbd2,Bd5 14.Ne5!?,Nxe5 15.dxe5,Ng4 16.Bxe7,Qxe7 17.Nf3,c5 18.h3,Nh6 19.Qc2,Rac8 20.e4 and White had the edge in Salov-Short, Amsterdam 1989.

4. 8....Nc6 9.Qxc4,Qd5 10.Nbd2 (10.Qd3,Rd8 11.Nc3,Qh5! is unclear.) 10...,Rd8 11.e3,Qxc4 12.Nxc4 equalizes or is slightly better for White; 8....c5!? 9.dxc5,Nc6 10.Qxc4,e5 11.Be3,Be6! 12.Qc1,Rc8 13.Rd1,Qa5 14.Ng5,Bg4 15.Nc3,Bc5 equalizes, Nicolic-Gligoric, Yugoslavia 1988.

5. 9.Ne5,Bc6 10.Nxc6,Nxc6 11.e3,Na5 12.Nd2,c5 with an even game, Sosonko-Karpov, Tilburg 1980.

6. 13.Qd3,Nab4 14.Qd1,f6 15.Bf4 with a slight edge for White, almost even, Vukic-Gligoric, Yugoslavia 1980.

7. 8.Bc6,bxc6 9.Nxc6,Qe8 10.Nxe7+,Qxe7 11.Qa4,c5 12.Qxc4,cxd4 13.Qxd4,e5 14.Qh4,Qe6!? 15.Nc3,Bb7 16.e4,Rfc8 17.f3,Qb6+ 18.Rf2,h6 with compensation, Gelfand-Aseev, Klaipeda 1988.

8. 9.Qc2,Qxd4! 10.Be3,Qd6 11.Nd2,Nd5 12.Nxc4,Nxe3 13.Nxe3,Ba6 unclear, Larsen-Speelman, London 1980; 9.Bxc6,Rb8 10.Qa4,Rb6 is unclear.

9. 10...,Ba6 11.Bxc6,Rb8 12.Qa4,Rb6 13.Bf3,Nd5 14.Qa5,c3 unclear position in Belyavsky-Geller, Moscow 1981.

10. 13.Qc5,Bb7 14.e4,Qd7 15.Be3,Bc6 with an even game in Hausner-Velimirovic, Banja-Luka 1981.

11. 6...,Nbd7 7.Qc2,dxc4?! 8.Qxc4,c5 9.Rd1!,Qb6 10.Nc3,Qb4 11.Qd3,cxd4 12.Qxd4!,Qxd4 13.Nxd4 and White had advantage in Geller-Milic, Belgrade 1956.

12. 7.Nc3,Nbd7 8.b3,b6 9.Bb2,Ba6!? is unclear.

13. 7...,b6 8.b3.Bb7 9.Nc3,Na6!? 10.Rd1 (10.e4!?) 10...,Rc8 11.e4,c5 12.dxc5,Bxc5 13.e5!,Ng4 14.Ng5,g6 15.Nge4,dxe4! 16.Rxd8,Rfxd8 with compensation for the sacrificed material.

14. 9...,Ba6 10.Nbd2,b5 11.c5,b4 12.Rfe1,Qc7 equalizes in Benkö-Larsen, Long Pain 1981.

15. 13.Nxf6+,Nxf6 14.dxc5,Qxc5 15.Qe2,Rad8 with an even game in Ribli-Spassky, Linares 1981.

* * * *

DUTCH DEFENSE

This Defense is an old favourite of many great players, including ex-world champions Botwinnik and Alekhine, but it is still mistrusted by many players because of the difficulty in completing a harmonious development. Black claims an early stake on e4 by his first f5 move, and will try to advance his K-side pawns if given a chance just like in the King's Indian. The result is weakening of square e6. If White can advance his e-pawn to e4, he can get an advantage. The boldest attempt is the Staunton Gambit 1.d4,f5 2.e4!?,fxe4 3.Nc3 where both players (like in the King's Gambit) need to know the exact theory to hold the balance.

1.d4,f5								
2	3	4	5	6	7	8	9	10
c4 [1]	g3	Bg2	Nf3	0-0	b3 [3]	Bb2	Nbd2	Ne5
e6	Nf6	d5	c6 [2]	Bd6	Qe7	b6	Bb7	0-0 [4] ±
...	...	...	Nf3	0-0	Nc3	b3 [5]	Bb2	e3
...	...	Be7	0-0	d6	Qe8	a5	Na6 [6]	c6 [7] ±
...	Nf3	g3	Bg2	Nc3	0-0 [8]	b3 [10]	Ba3	Qd3
Nf6	g6	Bg7	d6	0-0	Qe8 [9]	Na6 [11]	c6	Rb8 [12] ∞
e4	Nc3	f3 [13]	fxe4	dxe5	Nf3	Bg5	Bh4	Bg3 [14] ∞
fxe4	Nf6	Nc6	e5!	Nxe5	Bd6	h6	Ng6	

Diagram 13

Main line: after 5.Nf3

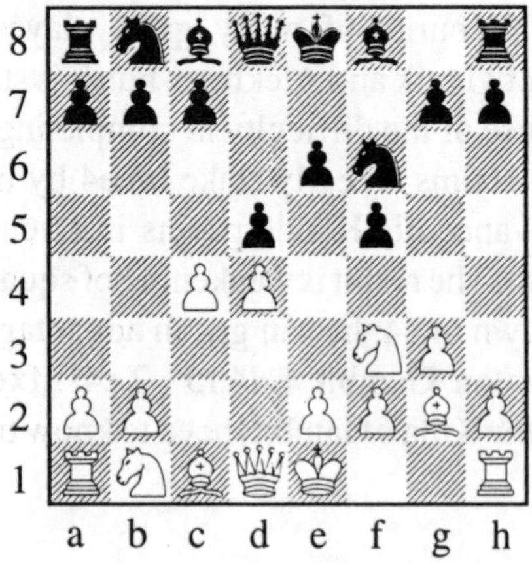

Diagram 14

Staunton Gambit:
after 4.f3

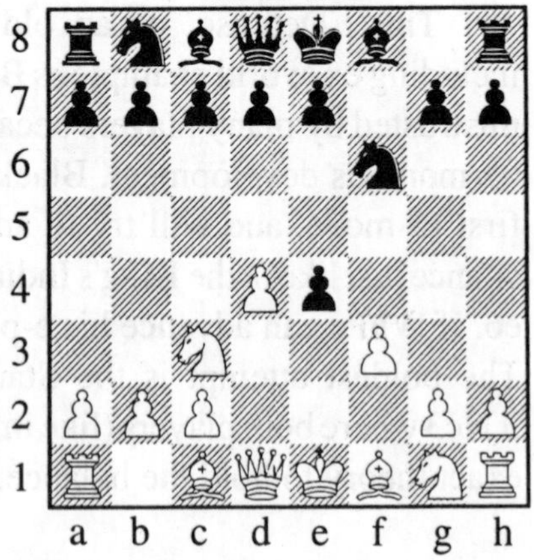

1. 2.g3,Nf6 3.Bg2,g6 4.Nh3!?,Bg7 5.Nf4,d6 6.Nc3,0-0 7.e4,c6 8.0-0,Na6 9.d5,e5 10.dxe6,fxe4 11.Nxe4,Nxe4 12.Bxe4,Re8 13.c3,Nc5 14.Bg2,Ne6 15.Qb3 and White was slightly better, Eingorn-Malaniuk, Odessa USSR Championship 1989.

2. 5...,Be7 6.0-0,0-0 7.Qc2,c6 8.Nbd2,Qe8 9.Ne5,Nbd7 10.Nd3!,Ne4 11.Nf3,Nd6 12.b3 with an edge for White; 7.b3,Nc6 8.Ba3!,Bxa3 9.Nxa3,Bd7 10.Nc2,Be8 11.Ne5,a5 12.Qd3,Ra6 13.Rfd1,Bg6 14.f4 unclear or slightly better for White, Belyavsky-Short, Linares 1989.

3. 7.Bf4!?,Bxf4 8.gxf4,0-0 9.e3,Nbd7 10.Qe2,Kh8 11.Nc3,Qe7 12.Kh1,Rg8 13.cxd5,exd5 (13...,cxd5 14.Rac1 is better for White.) 14.Bh3,Ng4 15.Rg1,Ndf6 16.Rg2,Be6 17.Rag1,Raf8 18.a3!,Bd7 19.b4 unclear but probably better for White in Belyavsky-Yusupov, Linares 1989.

4. 11.Rc1,a5 12.e3,Na6 13.Qe2,Rac8 14.Rfd1,c5 15.cxd5,exd5 16.Qb5!? was a bit better for White in Tukmakov-Haba, Haifa, European Team Championship 1989; 11...,Nbd7 12.cxd5,cxd5 13.Ndc4,Rfc8 14.Nxd6,Qxd6 15.f3 with an edge for White in Tukmakov-Dolmatov, Odessa USSR Championship 1989.

5. 8.Re1,Qg6 9.e4,fxe4! 10.Nxe4,Nxe4 11.Rxe4 with an edge. (11...,Qxe4 12.Nh4!).

6. 9...,c6 10.e3,Qh5 11.Ne1,Qh6 12.Nd3,Nbd7 13.Ba3 with some advantage for White in Ivkov-Maric, Vinkovci 1976.

7. 11.Qc2,Nc7 12.e4!? with an edge for White.

8. 7.d5,c5!? 8.0-0,Na6 9.Ne1,Rb8 10.Nc2,Nc7 11.a4,b6 unclear but probably better for White.

9. 7...,Nc6 8.d5,Ne5!? (8...,Na5 9.Nd2,c5 10.a3,Bd7 11.Qc2,Qc7 12.b3 and White had some advantage, Botwinnik-Matulovic, Belgrade 1970.) 9.Nxe5,dxe5 10.e4,f4 11.b3,g5 12.Ba3,g4 13.Re1,f3 14.Bf1,h5 15.Rc1,h4 16.Rc2,Nh7 17.c5,Qe8 was unclear in Sieglen-Wessijn, Germany 1989; 7...,c6 8.b3,Qc7 9.Ba3,a5 10.Rc1,Na6 11.Qd2!,Bd7 12.Rfe1,Nb4 13.Bb2 with a small advantage for White, Karpov-Yusupov, Linares 1989.

10. 8.d5,Na6 9.Nd4,Bd7 10.e3,c6 11.b3,Nc7 12.Bb2,c5 13.Nde2?!,b5! was unclear in Belyavsky-Malaniuk, USSR 1989.

11. 8...,e5!? 9.dxe5,dxe5 10.e4,Nc6 11.Nd5,Nxd5!? 12.cxd5,fxe4 13.Ng5,Nd4 14.Nxe4,Kh8 15.Bb2,Bf5 unclear but probably even, Gavrikov-Blagoevic, Prague 1988.

12. 11.e4,b5! 12.e5,b4 13.exf6,Bxf6 14.Bb2,bxc3 15.Bxc3,Qf7 16.Rfe1 is unclear, Lerner-Malaniuk, Odessa USSR Championship 1989.

13. 4.Bg5,Nc6 5.d5,Ne5 6.Qd4,Nf7! unclear.

14. 10...,Bxg3 11.hxg3,Qe7 was unclear, Grigoryan-Tal, USSR 1972.

*　　*　　*　　*

ENGLISH OPENING 1.c4

This opening has a lot of adherents today. It possesses a wealth of strategic ideas, and an elastic basic structure that allows a player to hide his intentions and plans for a long time, an important consideration in chess. The move 1.c4 was introduced in the second half of the 19th century. Mostly English masters like Staunton used it; that is how it got its present name. We basically differentiate between the

a) Classical System 1.c4,e5;

b) Symmetrical Systems with 1.c4,c5. Within the context of this book it is impossible to include all variations.

c) Systems with 1.c4,Nf6 2.Nf3;

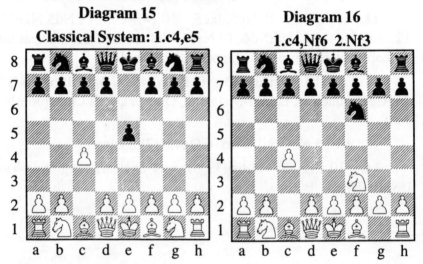

Diagram 15

Classical System: 1.c4,e5

Diagram 16

1.c4,Nf6 2.Nf3

Classical System

Once considered uninspiring, it has reached respectability through a gradual process. White's first move prepares a grip on the d5 square. There is a similarity to the Sicilian with reversed colours; you should be aware of the fact that games can easily transpose into the Queen's Gambit, the King's Indian, the Nimzo-Indian, the Grünfeld and Dutch Defense.

If the games that result from playing with your computer or with friends are to your liking, you should not hesitate to buy a chess monogram on this opening from a reputable GM to expand your knowledge.

1.c4,e5 2.Nc3,Nc6[1]							
3	**4**	**5**	**6**	**7**	**8**	**9**	**10**
g3	Bg2	d3	Nf3 [2]	0-0	Rb1	a3	Nd2
g6	Bg7	d6	Nf6 [3]	0-0	a5	Nd4!?[4]	c6 $\infty/=$
...	...	e3	Nge2	0-0 [5]	Rb1	a3	d3
...	...	d6	Nge7	0-0	a5 [6]	Bf5	Qd7 $\infty/=$
...	...	Nf3	d3	0-0	Rb1	Bd2	Qc1!?
...	...	Nge7	d6	0-0	f5 [7]	a5 [8]	Be6 $\pm/=$
Nf3	d4	Bg5 [9]	Bxe7	Ng1	e3	Nge2	h4
f5	e4	Be7	Qxe7[10]	Nf6 [11]	0-0	d6	Nd8!?[12] ∞

Diagram 17
Main line: after 7..,0-0

Diagram 18
Second line: after 10..,Qd7

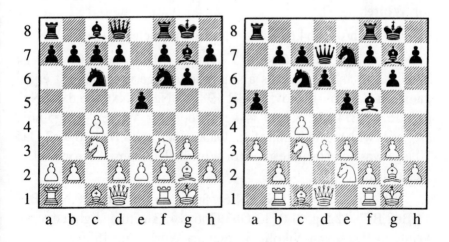

1. 2...,Bb4 3.Qb3 (3.Nd5) 3...,Nc6 4.e3 (4.Nd5!?,Bc5 5.e3,Nf6 6.Ne2,0-0 7.Nec3 unclear but probably a slight advantage for White.) 4...,Nf6 5.Nge2,0-0 6.g3,e4!? 7.Bg2,Re8 8.0-0,Bxc3! 9.Nxc3,d6 unclear, but probably even as in Abatasyan-Razuvaev, Moscow Worldcup 1989.

2. 6.e4,Be6 7.Nge2,Qd7 8.Nd5,Nce7 9.d4,c6 10.Ne3,Bh3 11.0-0,Bxg2 12.Kxg2,exd4 13.Nxd4,h5 14.a4,Nh6 15.Ra3,0-0-0 16.a5,h4 unclear as in Kasparov-Short, Linares 1990; 6.Rb1!?,Bd7 7.b4,Rb8 8.h4,a6 9.a4,a5 10.bxa5,Nxa5 11.Nf3,h6 12.Nd2 unclear or slight advantage for White, Smejkal-Seirawan, Malta Olympiad 1980; 6...,Nge7!? 7.b4,a6! 8.e3 (8.a4,a5!) 8..,0-0 9.Nge2,Bf5 is unclear M. Gurevic - Ye Rongguang, Belgrade 1988.

3. 6...,f5 7.0-0,Nf6 8.Rb1,0-0 9.b4,a6 10.a4,h6 11.b5 with a slight edge for White, Seirawan-Lobron, Bad-Kissingen 1981.

4. 9...,h6 10.b4,axb4 11.axb4,Be6 12.b5,Ne7 13.Bb2!,Nd7 14.Ra1!,c6 15.Rxa8,Qxa8 16.Qc2,d5 17.Ra1 with an edge for White as in Smyslov-Rashkovsky, USSR 1976.

5. 7.d3,0-0 8.0-0,Be6 9.Nd5,Rb8 10.e4,Qd7 11.Be3,b5 12.b3 unclear probably even, Portisch-Ljuboevic, Tilburg 1981.

6. 8...,Be6 9.Nd5,Qd7 10.b4,Nd8 11.d4! is good for White.

7. 8...,a5 9.a3,h6 10.b4,axb4 11.axb4,Be6 12.b5 **is again good for White.**

8. 9...,h6 10.b4,Nd4!? 11.Ne1,g5 is unclear.

9. 5.Ng5,h6!? 6.Nh3,g5 7.Ng1!?,Bg7 8.e3,d6 9.h4,g4 10.Nge2,h5 and White has a slight advantage in an almost equal game, in Bagirov-Ivanov, USSR 1982; 5.Ne5!?,Nxe5 6,dxe5,Ne7 (6...,d6 7.Bf4,g5 8.e3!? is very good for White.) 7.Bg5,h6!? (7...,c6!? with the intention of 8...,Qa5 is unclear.) 8.Bh4,c6 9.e3,Qa5 10.Bg3 was good to quite good for White in Kristiansen-Browne, Las Vegas 1989.

10. 6...,Ncxe7 7.Ng1,Nf6 8.e3,d6 9.h4,c6 10.Nh3,Be6 11.Be2,Bf7 12.Ng5,0-0 13.Qb3,Qb6 14.f3 with a slight edge for White in Vaganyan-Nikolic, Barcelona World Cup 1989.

11. 7...,e3?! 8.f4!,Nf6 9.Nf3,0-0 10.g3,Qb4 11.Qb3 when White had a slight advantage; Tarjan-Speelman, Malta Olympiad

1980.

12. 11.a3,c6 12.Nf4,Nf7 13.Be2,Bd7 was unclear in Kozul-Spassky, Baden 1980.

The **English Four Knights** is at present the most researched variation and occurs after:

			1.c4,e5 2.Nc3,Nf6 3.Nf3,Nc6				
4	**5**	**6**	**7**	**8**	**9**	**10**	**11**
g3	Bg2	0-0	Ng5[3]	bxc3	f3	Nxf3	d4!?[6] ±
Bb4[1]	0-0	e4[2]	Bxc3	Re8	exf3[4]	d5[5]	
...	Nd5	Nh4	Bg2	0-0	d3	Qxd3	Qc2[8] ±
...	e4[7]	Bc5	0-0	Re8	exd3	Ne5	
...	cxd5	Bg2	0-0	d3[9]	a3	b4	Bb2[12]
d5	Nxd5	Nb6	Be7	0-0	Be6[10]	Nd4!?[11]	∞/=
e3[13]	Qc2	Qxc3	a3	b3	d4	Nxd4	Qxd4[16]
Bb4	Bxc3[14]	Qe7	a5[15]	d5	exd4	Nxd4	=

1. 4...Bc5 5.Bg2 (5.Nxe5,Bxf2! is unclear.) 5...,d6 6.0-0,0-0 7.d3,h6 8.a3 and White had a small edge in Tal-Kavalek, Montreal 1979; 4...Nd4 5.Bg2,Nxf3 6.Bxf3,Bb4 7.Qc2,0-0 8.a3,Bxc3 9.Qxc3,d6 10.0-0,Bh3 11.Re1,c6 12.e4,Nd7 13.d4,Qf6 14.dxe5,dxe5 even or slightly better for White, Ivanchuk-Khalifman, Moscow USSR Championship 1988.

Diagram 19

Main line: after 4...,Bb4

Diagram 20

Note 9: after 8.a3!?

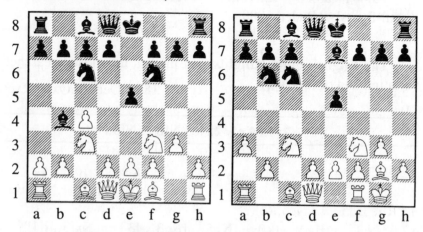

2. 6...,Re8 7.Nd5!,Nxd5 (7...,Bf8 8.d3,h6 9.Nxf6+,Qxf6 10.Nd2! is good for White.) 8.cxd5,Nd4 9.Ne1,c6!? 10.e3,Nb5 with an unclear position.

3. 7.Ne1,Bxc3 8.dxc3,h6 9.Nc2,Re8 (9...,b6 10.Ne3,Bb7 11.Qc2,Ne5 12.h3,Re8 13.Bd2,d6 was unclear in Vasyukov-Gipslis, USSR 1981.) 10.Ne3,d6 11.Qc2,Re5!? 12.Bd2,Ne7 13.f4,exf4 e.p. 14.exf4,Nf5 unclear or slightly better for White in Portisch-Timman, Amsterdam 1981.

4. 9...,e3!? 10.d3!,d5 11.Qb3!,Na5 12.Qa3,c6 13.cxd5,cxd5 14.f4,Nc6 15.Rb1 was unclear in Kasparov-Karpov, Sevilla World Championship match 1987.

5. 10...,Qe7 11.e3,Ne5 12.Nd4,Nd3 13.Qe2,Nxc1 14.Raxc1,d6 15.Rf4,c6 16.Rcf1,Qe5 17.Qd3! with the idea Nf5 and White was better in Kasparov-Karpov, Sevilla World Championship match 1987.

6. 11...,Ne4 (11...,dxc4 12.Bg5 with compensation for the sacrificed material.) 12.Qc2,dxc4 13.Rb1!,f5 14.g4! (Kasparov-Ivanchuk, Moscow USSR Championship 1988; see **Part Two for full score.**) 14...,fxg4 15.Ne5,Nd6!? 16.Nxc6,bxc6 17.e4 with more than adequate compensation: Kasparov.

7. 5...,Bc5 6.d3 (6.Bg2,d6 7.0-0,0-0 8.e3!?,Bg4 9.h3,Bxf3 10.Bxf3 and White is OK.) 6...,Nxd5 7.cxd5,Ne7 8.Nxe5,Bb4+

9.Bd2,Bxd2 10.Qxd2,Nxd5 11.Bg2,Nf6 12.0-0,d6 13.Nf3,0-0
14.Rac1 and White has an edge; Gavrikov-Stefansson, Moscow
World Cup 1989.

8. 11...,c6 12.Be3!? (12.Nxf6+,Qxf6 equalizes.) 12.cxd5
(12...,Bf8 13.Nxf6+,Qxf6 14.Rad1 and White was OK, in
Tal-Gerusel, Köln-Porz 1981/82.) 13.Bxc5,d6 14.Bd4,dxc4
15.Rfd1,Qe7 16.Nf5!?,Bxf5 17.Qxf5,d5 18.a4,Qe6 19.Qxe6,Rxe6
20.a5,h6 21.Kf1,g5 22.Ra4 with a slight edge for White in
Cvetikov-Lerner, Belgrade 1988.

9. 8.a3!?,0-0 9.b4,Be6 (9...,Re8!? 10.d3,a5 11.b5,Nd4
12.Nd2?!,a4! was unclear with a slight edge for Black in
Hjartarson-Ivanchuk, Linares 1989.) 10.Rb1,f6 11.Ne4,Ba2
12.Rb2,Bd5 13.Nc5,Rb8?! 14.e4!,Bf7 15.d3,Nd7 16.Nb3,a5
17.b5,Na7 18.a4 was good for White in Portisch-Timman, Antwerpen
Candidates' match 1989; 8...,Be6 9.b4,Nd4 10.Rb1,Nxf3+
11.Bxf3,c6 12.b5,Rc8 13.a4,0-0 14.a5,Nd5 15.bxc6,bxc6
16.Qa4,Qc7 17.Ba3 when White had a slight advantage in
Portisch-Ljuboevic, Saloniki Olympiad 1988.

10. 9...,Bg4 10.b4,a6 11.Bb2,Kh8 12.Ne4,f5 13.Nc5 equalized
with possibly a slight advantage for White in Timman-Sax, Amsterdam 1981; 9...,a5 10.Be3,Re8 11.Rc1,Bg4 12.Ne4,Nd4
13.Bxd4,exd4 14.Re1 with a small advantage for White,
Suba-Timman, Las Palmas 1982.

11. 10...,f6 11.Be3!?,Qe8?! 12.Bxb6!,axb6 13.d4,exd4
14.Nxd4 was quite good for White in Vanganyan-Psakhis, Erevan
1982.

12. 11...,Nb3?! 12.Rb1,f6 13.Ne4,a5 14.Bxe5! with advantage
for White; 11...,Bb3?! 12.Qc1,c5 13.bxc5,Bxc5 14.Nxd4,Bxd4
15.Bxb7,Rb8 16.Bg2,Qd7 (Kasparov-A. Sokolov, Moscow USSR
Championship 1988.) 17.e3!,Rfc8 18.Qe1!,Bxc3 19.Bxc3,Bd5
20.e4 with advantage for White: Yurkov; 11...,Nxf3+!? 12.Bxf3,c6
13.Ne4,Nd7 14.Qc2,Bd5 15.Nd2,Bxf3 16.Nxf3,Bd6 with an even
game in Kasparov-Salov, Moscow USSR Championship 1988.

13. 4.d4,exd4 5.Nxd4,Bb4 equalizes; 4.e4,Bb4 5.d3,d6
equalizes; 4.a3!?,d6 (4...,d5 5.cxd5,Nxd5 6.Qc2,Be7 7.e3,0-0
8.Nxd5,Qxd5 9.Bd3!?,g6 10.b4 with a small advantage for White,

Vaganyan.) 5.e3,g6 6.b4,Bg7 7.Bb2,0-0 8.b5,Nb8 9.Be2,e4
10.Nd4,c5 11.bxc5e.p.Nxc6 12.Nxc6,bxc6 13.0-0,Qa5 14.Qa4,Qxa4
15.Nxa4,Ba6 16.Rfb1,Rab8 equalizes with a slight edge for White
as in Vaganyan-Eingorn, Odessa USSR Championship 1989.

14. 5...,0-0 6.d3?!,Re8 7.Bd2,Bxc3 8.Bxc3,d5 9.cxd5,Nxd5
10.Be2,Bf5! is unclear with a slight edge for Black in
Ehlvest-Kasparov, Reykjavic World Cup 1989; 6.Nd5!?,Re8 7.a3,Bf8
8.Bd3,g6 9.0-0,Bg7 10.Nxf6+,Qxf6 11.Be4,Qe7 12.b4,Nd8
13.Bb2,d6 14.d3,c6 unclear position, probably even as in
Kortchnoi-Nikolic, Amsterdam 1988.

15. 7...,d5 8.cxd5,Nxd5 9.Qb3,Nb6 10.d3,0-0 11.Be2 with a
small advantage for White in Adorjan-G. Kuzmin, Riga 1979.

16. 11...,c5 12.Qb2,0-0 13.cxd5,Nxd5 14.Be2,Bf5 equalized
in Olafsson-Karpov, Malta Olympiad 1980.

And then there are the **Symmetrical Systems** with **1...,c5** that can
prove much sharper over the board than their reputation. A thorough
preparation may be necessary if your opponent is experienced! The
main lines are given below.

1.c4,c5 2.Nf3,Nf6							
3	**4**	**5**	**6**	**7**	**8**	**9**	**10**
d4	Nxd4	g3	Bg2	Nf3	0-0	e3	exd4
cxd4	e6 [1]	d5 [2]	e5	d4	Nc6	Bc5	exd4 [3] ∞
...	...	Nc3	g3 [5]	Qd3	Nb3 [6]	Bd2!	Qe4
...	...	Bb4 [4]	Ne4	Qa5	Nxc3!? [7]	Ne4!	Bxd2+ [8] ∞
Nc3	d4	Nxd4	g3	Nb3 [10]	e4	Qe2	f4
Nc6	cxd4	e6	Qb6 [9]	Ne5	Bb4	0-0	Nc6 [11] ∞/±
...	g3	Bg2	0-0	d4	Nxd4	Qxd4	Qd3
...	g6 [12]	Bg7	0-0	cxd4	Nxd4 [13]	d6	a6 [14] ±

Diagram 21

Main line: after 3.d4

Diagram 22

Note 7: after 13.Rd1

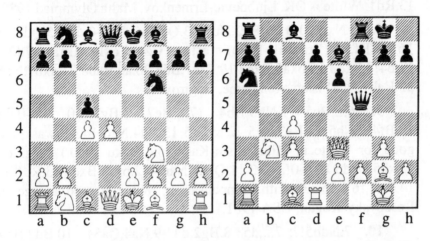

1. 4...,b6 5.Nc3,Bb7 6.f3,d6 7.e4,Nbd7 8.Be3 with a slight advantage for White; 4...,d5 5.cxd5,Nxd5 6.e4,Nb4 7.Ndb5,Qxd1+ 8.Kxd1 and White is OK; 4...,e5 5.Nb5,d5 6.cxd5,Bb4+ 7.Bd2,Bc5 8.d6 and White is OK; 4...,a6 5.Nc3!,d5 6.cxd5,Nxd5 7.Ndb5 and White has again an edge.

2. 5...,Bb4+ 6.Bd2,Qb6 7.Bxb4,Qxb4+ 8.Nc3,0-0 (8...,Qxc4 9.e4 with compensation; 8...,Qb2 9.Ndb5 and White has advantage.) 9.Qb3,Qc5 10.Rd1 and White is a bit better; 5...,Qa5+ 6.Nc3,Ne4 7.Bd2,Nxd2 8.Qxd2,a6 9.Bg2,Be7 10.0-0,0-0 11.Rfd1.Qc7 12.Rac1 and White has an edge; 5...,Qb6 6.Bg2,Bc5 7.e3,Nc6 8.0-0!,Nxd4 9.exd4,Bxd4 10.Nc3,e5 11.Nb5,0-0 12.Nxd4,exd4 13.b3,d5! with compensation, probably even as in Nogueiras-Psakhis, Szirak 1986.

3. 11.Nbd2,0-0 12.Nb3,Qb6 11.Bg5,Ne4 14.Bf4,Re8 15.Re1,Bg4 16.h3,Bh5 17.g4,Bg6 18.Nh4,d3!? 19.Nxc5,Qxc5 (Sveshnikov-Tukmakov, Erevan 1982.) 20.Re3!? unclear, but probably a bit better for White.

4. 5...,d5 6.Bg5,e5 7.Ndb5,a6 8.Qa4 unclear but probably slightly better for White.

5. 6.Bd2,Nc6 7.e3,0-0 8.Nc2,Be7 9.Be2,d5 10.cxd5,exd5 even or a bit better for White, Kupreichik-Gavrikov, USSR Championship 1981.

6. 8.Nc2,Bxc3!+ 9.bxc3,Nc5 is unclear.

7. 8...,Qf5 9.Qe3,Nxc3 10.bxc3,Be7 11.Bg2,Na6 12.0-0,0-0 13.Rd1: White is OK, Ljuboevic-Ermenkov, Malta Olympiad 1980.

8. 11.Nxd2,0-0 12.Bg2,Nc6 13.Qe3,d5 14.0-0,d4 15.Qd3,e5 16.a3,Bf5! (Ftacnik-Prandstetter, Czechoslovakia 1982.) 17.b4!?,Bxd3 18.bxa5,Bxe2 19.Rfe1,Bd3 20.a6,Rab8 21.axb7,Na5 22.Rab1,Nc4! is an even game, Bagirov.

9. 6...,Bc5 7.Nb3,Bb4 (7...,Be7 8.Bg2,0-0 9.0-0,d6 10.Bf4!?,Nh5 11.Be3,Ne5 12.c5!,d5 13.Bd4,Nc6 14.e4! was quite good for White in Mikalchisin-Kasparov, Baku 1980.) 8.Bg2,d5 9.cxd5,Nxd5 10.0-0!,Nxc3 11.Qxd8,Nxd8 12.bxc3,Bxc3 13.Rb1,a5 14.Rd1,f6 15.a3! with compensation; White has advantage in Reshevsky-Kogan, USA 1981.

10. 7.Ndb5!?; 7...,d5 8.Bg2,d4 9.Na4,Qa5+ 10.Bd2,Bb4 11.Nc5! and White had a good game in Kasparov-Vaganyan, Skellefteå World Cup 1989; 7...,Ne5 8.Bg2,a6 9.Qa4!? (9.Na3,Bxa3 10.bxa3,Nxc4 11.Qb3,Qxb3 12.axb3,Na5 13.Rb1,d5 14.Na4,Nd7 with compensation according to Euwe.) 9...,Bc5 10.0-0,Nxc4 11.Qxc4,axb5 12.Qxb5 was quite good for White in Vaganyan-Dvoiris, Odessa USSR Championship 1989; 7...,Bc5!? 8.Nd6,Ke7 9.Nde4,Nxe4 10.Nxe4,Bb4+ 11.Bd2,d5 unclear probably even in Adorjan-Miles, Wijk aan Zee 1984.

11. 11.Be3!?,Qc7 12.Bg2,b6 (12...,Bxc3+!? 13.bxc3,b6 14.e5,Ne8 15.c5,Bb7 is unclear, Gleizerov-Dvoiris, Sverdlovsk 1985.) 13.e5,Ne8 14.Bd2,Bxc3 15.Bxc3,Ba6 16.Nd2 was OK for White in Mikalchisin-S. Garcia, La Habana 1982.

12. 4...,d5 5.cxd5,Nxd5 6.Bg2,g6 7.Ng5!?,e6 8.Nge4,b6 9.d3,Bg7 10.Qa4!?,Bd7 11.Nxd5,exd5 12.Nd6+!,Ke7 13.Nxf7,Ne5 14.Bg5+,Kf7 15.Bxd5,Ke8 16.Qh4 with compensation for the sacrificed material: advantage for White in Dzhindzhikhashvili-Polugaevsky, New York 1989.

13. 8...,d6 9.Nxc6,bxc6 10.Bxc6,Rb8 11.Bg2,Qa5 12.Nb5 is OK for White.

14. 11.Be3,Bf5 12.Qd2,Rb8!? 13.Bd4,b5 14.cxb5,axb5 15.Rfc1,Qd7 16.Bxf6,Bxf6 17.Nd5,Qe6! even or slightly better for

White, Spassky-Tringov, Lugano 1968; <u>11.Bd2!?</u>,Rb8 12.e4,Be6 13.b3,Qd7 14.Rac1,Rfc8 15.Rfe1,b5 16.Nd5 with a small advantage for White in Kochiev-Henao, Manila 1974.

And last but not least the **Anglo-Indian 1.c4,Nf6 2.Nc3** which embraces a number of defenses that are in practice a lot like the Grünfeld, the Nimzo-Indian and the King's Indian except that White leaves **d4** out (for the moment) which give these formations a different look. Especially the so-called **Mikenas Variation 2...,e6 3.e4** often gives White an edge, and does not allow Black any complacency.

1.c4,Nf6 2.Nc3

2	3	4	5	6	7	8	9	10
...	e4	e5	d4[1]	Qxd4	Qe4	Nf3	Nxe5	Nxd7
e6	c5	Ng8	cxd4	Nc6	d6![2]	dxe5[3]	Bd7![4]	Qxd7[5] ±
...	...	e5	exf6	bxc3	d4	Nf3	Bg5	cxd4[8] ±
...	d5	d4[6]	dxc3	Qxf6	c5[7]	cxd4	Qf5	
...	Nf3	Qc2[10]	a3	Qxc3	e3[13]	b4	Bb2	Be2
...	Bb4[9]	0-0[11]	Bxc3	d6[12]	e5[14]	Re8	Nc6	Bg4[15] ∞/=
...	cxd5	Nf3[16]	e4[17]	dxc3	Kxd1	Bf4	Kc2	Nd2
d5	Nxd5	g6	Nxc3	Qxd1+	Nd7[18]	c6	f6	e5[19] ±/=

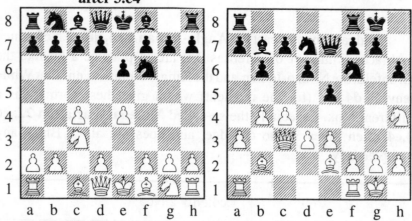

Diagram 23
Mikenas Variation:
after 3.e4

Diagram 24
Note 14: after 13.Nh4

1. 5.Nf3!?,Nc6 6.d4!?,cxd4 7.Nxd4,Nxe5 8.Ndb5 (8.Bf4,Ng6 9.Bg3,e5!? is unclear.) 8...,a6 9.Nd6+,Bxd6 10.Qxd6,f6 11.Be3,Ne7 12.Bb6,Nf5 13.Qc5,d6 14.Qa5,Qe7 15.0-0-0,0-0 16.f4 with compensation for the sacrificed material, e.g. 16...,Nc6 17.Qa3,e5 18.g4!,Nfd4?! (18...,Nh6!? 19.Nd5,Qf7 is unclear according to Bagirov.) 19.Nd5,Qf7 20.f5! with clear compensation as White has advantage, in Kasparov-A. Sokolov, Belfort World Cup 1988.

2. 7...,f5 8.Qe2,a6 9.Bd2,Qc7 10.f4,Nh6 11.Nf3,Nf7 12.g3,d6 13.exd6,Bxd6 14.Bg2 and White is better, Bagirov-Abakarov, Baku 1959.

3. 8...,Qa5?! 9.exd6,Bxd6 10.Qd3!,Be7 11.Bd2 and White has a slight edge in Seirawan-Peters, USA Championship 1980.

4. <u>9...,Nf6</u> 10.Nxc6,Qb6 11.Qf3,bxc6 12.g3,Bb7 12.Bg2 with a small advantage for White; <u>9...,Nxe5</u> 10.Qxe5,Nf6 11.Be2,a6 12.Bf4 with a small edge for White.

5. <u>11.Bg5,Bb4!</u> 12.Be2,Nf6 13.Qe3,Qd4! (Seirawan-Andersson, Mar del Plata 1982.) 14.0-0,Qxe3 15.Bxe3,0-0-0! 16.Nb5,a6 17.a3,Bd2! equalizes; <u>11.Bf4!?</u>,Nf6 12.Qe3,Bb4 13.Rd1,Qe7 14.Be2 and White was OK in Seirawan-Speelman, Hastings 1979/80.

6. 4...,Ne4 5.Nf3,Nc6 6.Be2 (6.cxd5,exd5 7.Bb5,Bc5!

equalizes.) 6...,Be7 7.0-0,0-0 8.d4 with a small advantage for White; 5.Nxe4,dxe4 6.Qg4,Bd7! 7.Qxe4,Bc6 with compensation for the sacrificed material.

7. 7...,e5!? 8,Qe2,Be7 9.dxe5,Qg6 10.Qe3,Nc6 is unclear probably an even game.

8. 10...,Bb4+ 11.Bd2,Nc6 12.Bxb4,Nxb4 13.Rb1!,Qa5 14.Qd2,Nc6 15.Bd3,Qxd2+ 16.Kxd2,b6 17.Rhc1 and White had a very good game in Miles-Sosonko, Tilburg 1977.

9. 3...,b6 4.e4!?,Bb7 5.Bd3,d6 6.Bc2,c5 7.d4,cxd4 8.Nxd4,a6 9.b3,Be7 10.Bb2,Nc6 11.0-0,0-0 12.Nxc6,Bxc6 13.Qd3 and White was OK in Polugaevsky-T. Petrosian, Kislovodsk 1982.

10. 4.a3,Bxc3 5.bxc3,d6 6.g3,e5 7.Bg2,Qe7 8.a4,a5 9.0-0,0-0 unclear probably even; 4.Qb3,c5 5.a3,Ba5 6.g3,0-0 7.Bg2,Nc6 8.0-0,d5 is unclear probably even; 4.g3,0-0 5.Bg2,c5 6.0-0,Nc6 7.d4,Bxc3 8.bxc3,d6 9.Bf4,Nh5 10.Be3,Qe7 unclear probably small advantage for White.

11. 4...,c5 5.a3,Bxc3 6.Qxc3,0-0 7.e3,b6 8.Be2,d5 9.b3,Bb7 10.Bb2,Nc6 11.0-0,Re8 unclear probably even, Kharitonov-Smyslov, Moscow USSR Championship 1988.

12. 6...,b6 7.g3,Bb7 8.Bg2,d5 9.cxd5,exd5 (9...,Nxd5!?) 10.0-0,Re8 and White was OK in Speelman-Seirawan, St. John 1988; 7.b3,Bb7 8.Bb2,d6 9.e3,e5 10.Be2,Nbd7 11.0-0,Qe7 12.d4,Ne4 13.Qc2,Ng5 14.Nxg5,Qxg5 15.d5,Rae8 16.f4! and White had a small advantage in Vyzhmanavin-Rozentalis, Minsk 1983.

13. 7.b4,e5 8.Bb2,Nc6 9.e3,Ne4 10.Qc2,f5 11.Be2 and White is OK; 7.g3,e5 8.Bg2,Nc6 9.b4,Bg4 10.Bb2 (10.h3,Bh5 11.b5,Nb8 12.0-0,Nbd7 13.Bb2,Re8 14.a4 and White has an edge.) 10...,Re8 11.0-0,d5 12.cxd5,Nxd5 13.Qc5 and White was slightly better in Damljanovic-Rohde, St. John 1988.

14. 7...,b6 8,Be2,Bb7 9.b4,Nbd7 10.Bb2,Qe7 11.0-0,e5 12.d3,h6 13.Nh4 with an edge for White in Smyslov-Sunie, Las Palmas 1982.

15. 11.d3,a6 12.0-0,d5 unclear probably even in Timman-B. Larsen, Buenos Aires 1980.

16. 4.e4,Bb4!? 5.d3 (5.Bc4,Be6!) 5...,e5 6.Nf3,Bc5 7.a3,N4c6 unclear probably even; 4.g3,Nxc3 5.bxc3,g6 6.Bg2,Bg7 7.Rb1,Nd7 (7...,0-0? 8.Rb7! and White has advantage.) 8.Nf3,0-0 9.0-0,Rb8 (9...,c5; or 9...,Nb6 are alternatives.) 10.d4,b6 11.e4,e5 12.Re1 unclear probably slightly better for White as in Hübner-Gutman, Germany 1988.

17. 5.Qa4+!?,Bd7 6.Qh4,Nxc3 7.dxc3,Nc6 8.Qg3!? (If 8.e4,e5! equalizes.) 8...,f6 9.h4,e5 10.h5,g5 11.e4,Bc5 12.Be2,Qe7 13.Nh2,Nd8 14.Be3,Bb6! 15.0-0-0,Ne6 16.Bc4,0-0-0 equalized in Mikalchisin-Pribyl, Lvov 1983; 5...,Nc6!? 6.Ne5,Nb4 7.a3,Bg7! 8.axb4,Bxe5 9.b5,Nb8 10.e3,g7 11.d4,0-0 is unclear.

18. 7...,Bg7 8.Kc2,Nd7 9.Bf4,c6 10.Nd2,0-0 11.f3 with an edge for White; 7...,Nc6 8.Be3,e5 9.Bc4,f6 10.Kc2,Nd8 11.a4,Nf7 12.Nd2 and White was OK in Timman-Kozul, Belgrade 1989; 7...,Bg4!? 8.Be2,Nd7.

19. 11.Be3,a5! 12.h4,h5 13.Rh3,Bc5 14.Rd1,Bxe3 15.Rxe3,Nc5 equalizes, in B. Larsen-Tseshkovsky, Riga 1979.

The French Defense 1.e4,e6 is in the words of Kasparov and Keene in Batsford Chess Openings "a defense in the truest sense of the word, appealing to players who are content to endure cramped or passive positions in the hope of emerging with a superior pawn structure or a counterattack."

A formidable weapon especially because of major contributions for Black by ex-world champion Mikhail Botwinnik. There are four main answers open to White:

1) According to GM Predrag Nikolic in his electronic opening book for 'New in Chess', White's best answer is probably (after **2.d4,d5**.) **3.e5** the so-called **Advance Variation** originally proposed by Nimzovitsch, to be studied carefully by anyone wishing to use the French in tournament play.

2) The **Classical Variation** which occurs after **3.Nc3,Nf6.**

3) The **Winawer Variation** which occurs after **3.Nc3,Bb4** leaves White with the Bishops' pair but a fractured pawn structure and an

advantage in space. Popular 20 years ago mostly because of the scintillating games by Fischer, Tal and Spassky.

The **Exchange Variation with 3.exd5,exd5** is also briefly covered to complement the analysis of this important defense.

4) The **Tarrasch Variation 3.Nd2** is less direct but cedes no positional defects. It gives Black more freedom but often results in long-term difficulties in achieving full equality.

Advance Variation

1.e4,e6 2.d4,d5							
3	**4**	**5**	**6**	**7**	**8**	**9**	**10**
e5	c3	Nf3	Bd3	cxd4	0-0	Nxd4	Nc3 [3] ∞
c5	Nc6 [1]	Qb6 [2]	cxd4	Bd7	Nxd4	Qxd4	
...	...	...	Be2	cxd4	b3 [6]	Bb2	Kf1
...	...	...	cxd4 [4]	Nge7 [5]	Nf5	Bb4+	h5 =/∓
...	...	...	a3	g3 [8]	Bh3	Nbd2	0-0
...	...	...	c4 [7]	Bd7	Na5	Ne7	h6 [9] =
exd5	Bd3	c3	Qf3 [10]	h3	Ne2	Bf4	Qxf4 [11] =
exd5	Nc6	Bd6	Nf6	Qe7+	Ne4	Bxf4	

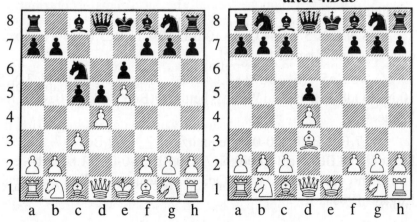

Diagram 25

Main line: after 4..,Nc6

Diagram 26

Exchange Variation: after 4.Bd3

1. 4...,Qb6 5.Nf3,Bd7 6.Be2,Bb5 7.0-0 (7.c4,Bxc4 8.Bxc4,Qb4+! 9.Nbd2,dxc4 10.a3,Qa5 11.0-0,Nc6 12.Nxc4,Qa6 equalizes; 7.dxc5!?,Bxc5 8.0-0,a5 9.Bxb5,Qxb5 10.Na3,Bxa3 11.bxa3,Ne7 12.a4,Qc4 13.Rb1 is OK for White in Gulko-Vitolinsh, Tbilisi 1979.) 7...,Bxe2 8.Qxe2,Qa6 9.Qd1,Nd7 10.dxc5!,Nxc5 11.b4 with an edge for White; 4...,Ne7 5.Nf3,Nec6 6.Bd3 (6.Be3!? Kupreichik.) 6...,b6 7.Bg5,Qd7 8.0-0,Ba6 9.dxc5,bxc5 10.Ba6,Nxa6 11.c4!,h6 12.Bh4,Nc7 13.Nc3,Be7 14.Bxe7,Nxb7 15.Rc1 and White had a small advantage in Sveshnikov-Lputyan, Moscow World Cup 1989.

2. 5...,Bd7 6.a3,c4 7.b4,cxb4e.p. 8.Qxb3,Na5 9.Qc2,Ne7 10.Bd3 when White had a slight advantage in Sveshnikov-Balashov, Moscoe 1976; 6.Be2,Nge7 7.0-0,Nf5 8.Bd3,cxd4 9.Bxf5,exf5 10.Nxd4,Be7 11.Qb3!? and White had an edge in Kupreichnik-Kosten, Tozu 1989.

3. 10...,a6 11.Qe2,Rc8 12.Rd1,Bc5 13.Bc2,Qh4 is unclear but probably better for White; 10...,Qxe5!? 11.Re1,Qb8! 12.Nxd5,Bd6 13.Qg4,Kf8 14.Bd2,h5! 15.Qh3,Bc6 unclear but probably better for Black.

4. 6...,Nge7 7.dxc5! is OK for White; 6...,Nh6 7.Bxh6,gxh6 (7...,Qxb2 8.Bc1,Qxa1 9.Qc2,cxd4 10.0-0,Bd7 is unclear; 8.Be3!?) 8.Qd2,Bg7 9.Na3!? (Alternative is 9.0-0.) 9...,cxd4 10.cxd4,0-0 11.0-0,f6 12.Nc2,Bd7 14.b4 is OK for White as in Lein-Ehlvest, New York 1989.

5. 7...,Bh6 8.Nc3,Nf5 9.Na4,Qa5+ 10.Bd2,Bb4 11.Bc3,b5 equalizes.

6. 8.Nc3,Nf5 9.Na4,Qa5+ 10.Bd2,Bb4 11.Bc3,Bxc3+ 12.Nxc3 even or slightly better for Black.

7. 6...,a5 (6...,Bd7? 7.b4,cxd4 8.cxd4,Nge7 9.Nc3,Nf5 10.Na4,Qd8 11.Bb2 and White is better.) 7.Bd3,Bd7 8.0-0 is OK for White.

8. 7.Be2,Bd7 8.0-0,f6! equalizes; 7.Nbd2,Bd7 (7...,Nge7? 8.Bxc4!) 8.Be2,Na5 9.0-0,Ne7 10.Rb1,0-0-0 11.b4,cxb4 e.p. 12.Bb2,h6 13.c4,Ba4 14.c5,Qc7 is unclear as in Zinn-Hamman, Lugano 1968.

9. 11.Nh4,0-0-0 12.Ng2,g6!? 13.Ne3,h5 14.Rb1,Bh6 even game, Platonov-Ree, Kiev 1978.

10. 6.Ne2,Qh4!? 7.Nd2,Bg4 8.Qc2 (8.Qb3,0-0-0 9.Qxd5,Nf6 is slightly better for Black.) 8...,0-0-0 9.Nf1,g6 10.Be3,Nge7 11.0-0-0,Bf5 with an even game, Winter-Alekhine, Nottingham 1936.

11. 10...,g5 11.Qe3,f5 12.f4,h6 even game as in Böhm-Farago, Amsterdam 1976.

The **Classical Variation** has that name for an obvious reason. It must be studied in order to understand the main concepts and the origins of the approaches for both White and Black.

It really will help your game if you play it a number of times against the computer and a few friends. If you intend to play in a club at a later stage, you will be lost sooner or later, unless you have gained some experience over the board with it.

It has lost popularity on the master level, since most complications have been solved and there is little surprise left. Players who play for a win have to work harder.

			1.e4,e6 2.d4,d5 3.Nc3						
3	**4**	**5**	**6**	**7**	**8**	**9**	**10**	**11**	
...	Nxe4	Nf3	Nxf6+	Bd3	0-0[2]	Bg5	dxc5	Qe2	±
dxe4	Nd7[1]	Ngf6	Nxf6	Be7	0-0	c5	Bxc5		
...	...	...	...	Bg5	Bb5[3]+	Bxd7+	Bxf6	c3	±
...	...	...	...	c5	Bd7	Qxd7	gxf6		
...	...	Nc3[4]	Nf3	Bd3	0-0!	bxc3	Rb1	Rb5[5]	≡
...	Qd5	Bb4	Nf6	Ne4	Nxc3	Bxc3	Nc6		
...	e5	f4	Nf3	Be3	Nxd4	Qd2	0-0-0	Kb1[7]	∞
Nf6	Nfd7	c5	Nc6	cxd4[6]	Bc5	0-0	a6		

Diagram 27
Fourth line:
after 4...,Nfd7

Diagram 28
Note 5: after 13.Ng5!

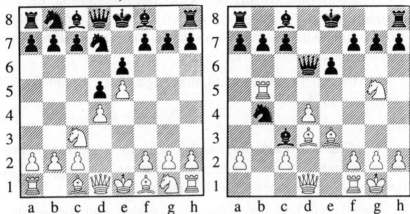

1. 4...,Be7 5.Bc4,Nf6 6.Nxf6+,Bxf6 7.Nf3,0-0 8.0-0,b6 9.Qe2 and White is slightly better.

2. 8.Qe2,0-0 9.Bg5,c5 10.0-0-0,Qa5 11.Kb1,cxd4 12.h4,Bd7! 13.Nxd4,Bc6 14.Nxc6,bxc6 15.Bd2 and White was OK in Nunn-Skembris, Paris 1983.

3. 8.Bc4,cxd4 9.0-0,Be7 10.Qe2,0-0! 11.Rad1,Nd5 with an even game or slightly better for White.

4. 5.Bd3,Nf6 6.Nxf6+,gxf6 7.Nf3,Rg8 8.0-0 and White was OK in Keres-Katalymov, Moscow 1965.

5. 11...,Qd6 12.Be3,Nb4 13.Ng5!,c6 14.Ne4,Qd8 15.Qg4,Kf8 16.Rg5. White had advantage in Kotkov-Bukhman, Krasnodar 1966.

6. <u>7....Qb6</u> 8.Na4!,Qa5+ 9.c3,cxd4 (9...,c4!? 10.b4,Qc7 11.Be2,Be7 12.0-0,0-0 13.Qb1,b5 14.Nc5,a5 15.a3,Nxc5 16.bxc5,Rb8 17.Ng5,g6 18.Qe1,f6 is unclear, in Oll-Vaganyan, Odessa USSR Championship 1989.) 10.b4,Nxb4 11.cxb4,Bxb4+ 12.Bd2,Bxd2+ 13.Nxd2,b6 14.Qb3,g5!? unclear in Ehlvest-Ivancuk, Tallinn 1986; <u>7....a6</u> 8.Qd2,b5 9.dxc5,Bxc5 10.Bxc5,Nxc5 11.Qf2,Qb6 12.Bd3,b4 13.Ne2,a5 14.0-0,Ba6 15.Kh1,Bxd3 16.cxd3,Rb8 17.f5 was unclear in Nunn-Nogueiras, Rotterdam World Cup 1989.

7. 11...,Nxd4 12.Bxd4,b5 13.Bxc5,Nxc5 14.Qf2,Qc7

15.Bd3,Bb7 16.Qh4,Ne4 17.Ne2,b4 18.Rhe1,Rac8 19.Rc1,f6 20.exf6,Rxf6 was unclear in Nunn-Timman, Rotterdam 1989.

The continuation with **3...,Nf6 4.Bg5** requires special attention, although it is seen less and less at the GM level. Since the complications are less than in the **Winawer** it has a lot of appeal to players with a more moderate Elo rating.

1.e4,e6 2.d4,d5 3.Nc3,Nf6 4.Bg5								
4	**5**	**6**	**7**	**8**	**9**	**10**	**11**	**12**
...	e5	Bxe7[1]	f4	Nf3	dxc5[2]	Bd3	exf6	g3 ±
Be7	Nfd7	Qxe7	0-0	c5	f6	Nc6	Qxf6	
...	Nxe4	Bxf6	Nf3	Qd2	0-0-0	Qf4	Bd3	h4[3] ∞
dxe4	Be7	Bxf6	0-0	b6	Bb7	Nd7	Be7	
...	...	...	Bc4[4]	Ng3!?	Nf3	Qe2	Bb3	0-0-0[6] ±
...	...	gxf6	f5[5]	Rg8	Nd7	Nb6	Nd5	
...	e5	Bd2[7]	bxc3	Qg4	Bd3	Kxd2	Rb1[9]	Nf3 ∞/±
Bb4	h6	Bxc3	Ne4	g6![8]	Nxd2	c5	Nc6	

Diagram 29	**Diagram 30**
Note 1: after 6.h4	**Third line: after 10.Qe2**

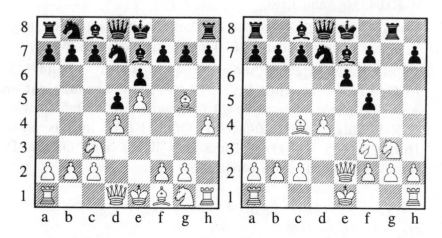

1. 6.h4,Bxg5!? 7.hxg5,Qxg5 8.Nh3,Qe7 9.Nf4,g6!? 10.Qg4,Nc6 11.0-0-0,Nb6 is unclear; 6...,c5 7.Bxe7,Kxe7!? 8.Nf3!? (Alternative is 8.f4.) 8...,cxd4 9.Qxd4,Nc6 10.Qf4,Qc7 11.0-0-0,Ndxe5 12.Kb1,Qb8 13.Bb5 and White was OK in Kovalev-Dreev, Simferopol 1989.

2. 9.Qd2,Nc6 10.dxc5 (If 10.0-0-0,c4! with the idea b5-b4 then an unclear position results.) 10...,Nxc5 11.g3,f6 and White is slightly better or just about even; 9.Nb5,cxd4 10.Nc7,Ne5! 11.Nxa8,Qb4 with compensation; White is slightly better.

3. 12.Kb1,Nf6 13.c4,Qb8!? 14.d5,c5! 15.d6,Bxe4 16.Bxe4,Bxd6 17.Bxh7+,Kxh7 18.Ng5+ draw agreed in A.Sokolov-Vaganyan, Odessa USSR Championship 1989; 12.h4,Nf6 13.Neg5,Qd6! 14.Ne5,Rad8 15.Rh3,c5! 16.Rg3,Qxd4 17.Bxh7+,,Nxh7 18.Rxd4,Rxd4 19.Qe3,Nxg5 20.hxg5,Re4 and Black had the advantage in Sax-Ehlvest, Rotterdam World Cup 1989.

4. 7.Nf3,b6 8.Bc4,Bb7 9.Qe2,Nd7 10.0-0-0,c6 11.Rhe1,Qc7 12.Kb1,0-0-0 13.Ba6 with a slight advantage for White.

5. 7...,a6 8.a4,b6 9.Nf3,Bb7 10.Qe2,c6 11.0-0,Nd7 12.Rad1,Qc7 13.Rfe1,0-0 14.Qe3,Kh8 15.Ng3 and White was OK in Ehlvest-Korchnoi, Skelleftea, World Cup 1989.

6. Minasyan-Savchenko, Belgorod 1989; 12...,Nf4?! 13.Qd2,Nxg2? 14.Rhg1,Nh4 15.Nxh4,Bxh4 16.Nxf5! with a winning advantage for White: Glek and Piskov.

7. 6.exf6,hxg5 7.fxg7,Rg8 8.h4,gxh4 9.Qg4,Qf6! 10.Rxh4,Qxg7 equalizes.

8. 8...,Kf8 9.Bd3,Nxd2 10.Kxd2,c5 (10...,Qg5+ 11.Qxg5,hxg5 12.f4 and White is better.) 11.h4 with a slight edge for White.

9. 11.Nf3,Qc7 12.h4,cxd4 13.cxd4,Nc6 14.Qf4?!,f5! 15.Qg3,Ne7 16.Rhc1,Bd7 17.Ke2,Bc6 was unclear in Aseev-Dolmatov, Odessa USSR Championship 1989; 12...,Nc6 13.Rab1,Bd7 14.dxc5,0-0-0 15.Qf4,g5! (The idea is ...g4.) 16.hxg5,hxg5 17.Qxg5,Rhg8 and Black was OK in D. Ivanovic-Kalinichenko, Sibenik 1989.

The **Winawer Variation** is the most logical outflow from the Classical Variation, and we therefore will analyse it first.

The complications that result can be dazzling and one has to keep a clear eye on the possibility that the opponent will want to simplify towards the endgame. White's resulting pawn structure leaves him vulnerable with less pieces on the board, particularly if he loses the advantage of the Bishops' pair. **3...,Bb4** is a move first used by Nimzovitsch.

			1.e4,e6 2.d4,d5 3.Nc3,Bb4					
4	**5**	**6**	**7**	**8**	**9**	**10**	**11**	
e5	a3[2]	f4	Nf3	Bd3	0-0	Bxa6	Qd3 ±	
b6[1]	Bf8	Ne7	Nf5	h5	Ba6	Nxa6		
...	a3[3]	b4[4]	Qg4[6]	bxa5	Qxg7	Qxh7	f4	
c5	Ba5	cxd4[5]	Ne7	dxc3	Rg8	Nbc6	Qxa5[7]	∞
a3	bxc3	Qg4	Qxg7	Qh6	Ne2	Bg5		
Bxc3+	dxe4	Nf6	Rg8	Nbd7!	b6	Qe7[8] ∓		
Bd3[9]	Bxe4	Bf3	Ne2	a3	bxc3	Bg5 =		
dxe4[10]	Nf6	c5	Nc6	Bc3	e5			

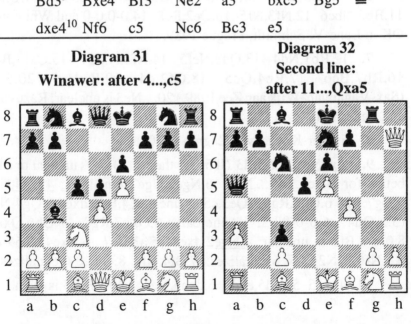

Diagram 31
Winawer: after 4...,c5

Diagram 32
Second line:
after 11...,Qxa5

1. 4...,Qd7 5.a3 (5.Qg4,f5 6.Qg3,b6 7.a3,Bf8 and White is OK.) 5...,Bxc3+ 6.bxc3,b6 7.Qg4,f5 8.Qg3 with a slight advantage for White.

2. 5.Qg4,Bf8 6.Bg5,Qd7 7.0-0-0,h6! 8.Be3,Ba6 9.Nge2,h5! is unclear probably even; 5.Nh3!?,Qd7 6.Nf4 and White is OK.

3. 5.Bd2,Nc6! 6.Nb5,Bxd2+ 7.Qxd2,Nxd4 8.Nxd4,cxd4 9.Nf3,Ne7 10.Qxd4,0-0 equalizes; 5.Qg4!?,Ne7 6.dxc5,Nbc6 7.Bd2,0-0 8.Nf3,f5 with an unclear position.

4. 6.Qg4!?,Ne7 7.dxc5!?,Bxc3+ 8.bxc3,Qa5 9.Bd2,Ng6 10.Nf3,Nd7 11.c4,Qa4 12.h4!?,Qxc2!? 13.cxd5,Qxb2! 14.Rc1!,Ngxe5 15.Nxe5,Qxe5+ 16.Be2,h5 17.Qg5!?,exd5 18.Rh3!?,0-0 19.Rd3,d4! (If 19...,Re8? then 20.Re3 gives White a winning advantage.) 20.Bf4,Qxg5 21.hxg5,b6! equalized in Short-Vaganyan, Rotterdam World Cup 1989; 6.dxc5,Bxc3+ 7.bxc3,Qc7!? 8.Nf3,Nd7 9.Bb5,Qxc5 10.a4,a6 11.Bxd7+,Bxd7 12.0-0.Qxc3 13.Bd2,Qc4!? 14.Rb1,Qc7! 15.c4!?,Ne7 16.Bb4,Bc6 unclear but probably better for Black as in Short-Vaganyan, Barcelona World Cup 1989.

5. 6...,cxb4? 7.Nb5,bxa3 8.c3 and White has advantage.

6. 7.Nb5,Bc7 8.f4,Ne7 9.Bd3,Bd7 10.Nxc7+!,Qxc7 11.Bb2,Nbc6 12.Nf3,Nf5 13.Qe2,Rc8 14.0-0,0-0 and White was OK in Lanc-V. Schmidt, Prague 1989.

7. 12.Rb1,Nd4 13.Qd3,Nef5 14.Nf3,Nxf3+ 15.Qxf3,Bd7 16.Rb7,Bc6 17.Rb4,Qc5 18.Qf2,d4 19.Rg1,a5 20.Rb1 (Sax-Vaganyan, Wijk aan Zee 1989.) 20...,Ne3 is unclear: Razuvaev and Lepeshkin.

8. Fischer-Kovacevic, Zagreb 1970.

9. 4.exd5,exd5 5.Bd3 (If 5.Qf3 then 5..,Qe7! is unclear or a bit better for Black.) 5...,Nc6 6.Nge2,Nge7 equalizes; 4.Qg4,Nf6 5.Qg7,Rg8 6.Qh6,Rg6 7.Qe3,c5! is unclear; 4.Bd2,dxe4 5.Qg4,Nf6 (5...,Qd4 6.0-0-0,h5! is unclear.) 6.Qxg7,Rg8 7.Qh6,Qxd4 8.0-0-0,Bf8 is unclear; 4.Nge2,dxe4 5.a3,Be7 6.Nxe4,Nc6 (If 6...,Nf6 7.N2g3,Nc6 equalizes.) 7.Bf4,Nf6 8.Qd3,0-0 equalizes.

10. 4...,c5 5.exd5,exd5 6.dxc5,Nc6 7.Nf3,Bxc5 is even.

1.e4,e6 2.d4,d5 3.Nc3,Bb4 4.e5,c5 5.a3,Bxc3+ 6.bxc3

6	7	8	9	10	11	12	13	
...	a4	Nf3	Bd2[1]	Be2	0-0[2]	exf6	Nh4	
Ne7	Nbc6	Qa5	Bd7	c4	f6	gxf6	0-0-0[3]	∞
...	Qg4[4]	Qxg7	Qxh7	Ne2[6]	f4	Qd3	Nxc3[8]	
...	Qc7[5]	Rg8	cxd4	Nbc6	Bd7[7]	dxc3	a6[9]	∞
...	...	Bd3	Qh5[11]	Bxh6!	Qxh6	Bxf5	Nh3	
...	0-0	Nbc6[10]	h6	gxh6	Nf5	exf5	f6[12]	±
...	Nf3[13]	a4	Bb5	Bd3	0-0	Be2	Ba3	
Qc7	Ne7	b6[14]	Bd7	Nbc6	c4?![15]	f6	fxe5[16]	⩲

Diagram 33
Second line: after 7.Qg4

Diagram 34
Note 3: after 14...,Ng6!

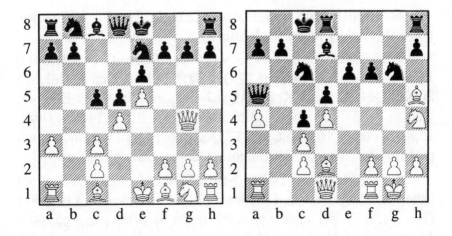

1. 9.Qd2,Bd7 10.Bd3,c4 11.Be2,f6 12.Ba3,0-0-0 13.0-0,h5 with an even game or slightly better for White.

2. 11.Ng5,h6 (11...,0-0 12.0-0,f6 13.exf6,Rxf6 14.Bg4 with an edge for White.) 12.Nh3,Nc8 13.Nf4,Nb6 14.Nh5 with a small advantage for White.

3. 14.Bh5,Ng6! 15.Bxg6,hxg6 16.Nxg6,Rh7 (Or 16.Rhg8.) with compensation for the sacrificed material.

4. 7.Nf3,Nd7 (7...,Qa5 8.Bd2,Nbc6 9.Be2,cxd4 10.cxd4,Qa4 11.Rb1!?,Nxd4 12.Bd3,Ndc6 13.Rb3,Nf5 14.0-0,Nfd4 15.Nxd4,Qxd4 16.Re1,Qh4 17.Bb5 with compensation; White is better in Dolmatov-Oll, Odessa USSR Championship 1989.) 8.h4 (Or 8.Bd3,c4 9.Be2,Ba4.) 8...,Ba4 9.h5,h6 10.Rb1,Qc7 11.Bd3,Nd7 12.0-0,a6 13.Re1,Rc8 14.Rb2,Bb5!? 15.Bxb5,axb5 16.Qe2,b6 17.Qxb5,0-0 18.Qd3,Ra8 19.Rb1,Rfc8 20.Re2,cxd4 21.cxd4,Qc4 with compensation in Ehlvest-Nogueiras, Rotterdam World Cup 1989; 7.h4,Qc7 8.Nf3,b6 9.h5,h6 10.a4,Ba6 11.Bb5,Bxb5 12.axb5,Nd7 13.Qd3,0-0 14.Bd2,f6! remained unclear in Ljuboevic-Short, Rotterdam World Cup 1989.

5. 7...,Nf5 8.Bd3,h5 9.Qf4,Nc6 (Or 9...,cxd4 10.cxd4,Qh4 11.Qxh4,Nxh4 12.Bg5!,Nf5 13.Ne2 is OK for White.) 10.Nf3,Qc7 11.0-0,Nce7 12.a4,c4 13.Be2,Bd7 14.a5,0-0-0 15.Qg5,Rdf8 16.Ba3,f6 17.Qc1,Rf7 18.Bc5,Nc6 19.Qa3 with advantage for White in Kruppa-Rozentalis, Podolsk 1989.

6. 10.Kd1,Nbc6 11.Nf3,dxc3 12.Ng5!?,Nxe5 is unclear but probably slightly better for White.

7. 11...,dxc3 12.Qd3,d4 13.Ng3 (Or 13.Rb1,Bd7 14.Rg1,0-0-0 15.Nxd4,Nxd4 16.Qxd4,Bb5 17.Qa7,Bxf1 18.Kxf1,Qc6 19.Be3,Nf5 20.Kf2,Qe4 21.Qc5+,Kb8 22.Qxa7+ was even in Aseev-Eingorn, Odessa USSR Championship 1989.) 13...,Bd7 14.Ne4,0-0-0 15.Rb1,Nxe5!? 16.fxe5,Qxe5 17.Qe2,Bc6 18.Ng3 was unclear but probably for White in Oll-Eingorn, Odessa Championship 1989.

8. 13.Qxc3,Rc8 14.Rb1,Nf5 15.Bd2,a6 16.Rg1,b5 17.g4 (Short-Kosten, Hastings 1988/89.) 17...,d4 is unclear; 13.Rb1,Nf5 (13...,d4!?) 14.g4! unclear probably better for White; 13.Ng3,0-0-0 14.Be2,Nf5 15.Nxf5,exf5 16.0-0,d4 equalizes in Sveshnikov-Webb,

Hastings 1977/78.

9. 14.Ne2,Nf5 (The alternative is: 14...,Rc8 like in Short-Nogueiras, Barcelona World Cup 1989 which continued 15.Bd2,Nf5 16.h3,Qd8 17.Rb1,b5 18.Rg1,Qb6 19.g4,Nfd4 20.Rg3 and White had a small advantage.) 15.h3 (Or 15.Rb1.) 15...,Na5 16.g4!?,Bb5 17.Qxc3,Qxc3 18.Nxc3,Bxf1 19.Rxf1,Nd4 20.Ra2,Rc8! (20...,Rh8 21.Be3 with advantage for White.) 21.Bd2,Rh8 22.Ne2,Rxc2! 23.Rxc2,Nxc2+ 24.Kd1,Nxa3 25.Ba5,Nc4 26.Bd2,Rxh3 with compensation for the sacrificed material; an even game in Timman-Short, Rotterdam World Cup 1989.

10. 8...,Nd7!? 9.Nf3,f5 10.Qh3! (Not 10.exf6?!e.p.,Nxf6 11.Qh4,c4 12.Be2,Nf5 which is just a bit better for Black.) 10...,Nb6 11.a4!? (11.dxc5,Na4!? is unclear.) 11...,c4 12.Be2,a5 13.Rg1,Qe8 14.g4! was unclear probably a bit better for White in Ehlvest-Vaganyan, Skellefteå World Cup 1989; 14...,Nxa4? 15.gxf5,Nxf5 16.Ng5,h6 17.Bh5,Qc6 16.Bg6 with a clear advantage for White in Sax-Dolmatov, Clermont-Ferrand 1989.

11. 9.Nf3,f5 10.exf5e.p.,Rxf6 11.Bg5,Rf7 is an even game.

12. 14.Qg6+,Kh8 15.Qh6+,Kg8 16.Qg6,Kh8 17.0-0-0!,fxe5 18.Qh6+,Kg8 19.Qg6+,Kh8 20.Rd3,f4 21.Rg3!! with decisive advantage for White in Oll-Ulybin, Tbilisi 1989.

13. 7.Qg4,f5 (Interesting is also 7...,f6.) 8.Qg3,cxd4 9.cxd4,Ne7 10.Bd2,0-0 11.Bd3 with an even game or slightly better for White.

14. 8...,Nbc6 9.Be2,Bd7 10.0-0,b6 11.Bd3,h6 12.Ba3 with a small advantage for White in Hartston-Portisch, Nice 1974.

15. 11...,Na5!? gives an unclear position.

16. 14.dxe5,Nxe5 15.Re1!,N7c6 16.Nxe5,Nxe5 17.Bg4 with a good game for White in Fischer-Darga, West-Germany 1960.

We come now to the ever popular **Tarrasch Variation which occurs after 3.Nd2**. Named after the famed Russian GM who lived around the turn of the century, who initiated a lot of new ideas in openings, the **Tarrasch** is much more double-edged than its harmless reputation for Black. The finer points of attacks that White can start have been demonstrated time and again by Kasparov who has won an extraordinary number of excellent games with it.

	3	4	5	6	7	8	9	10	
		c3	Bd3	e5	Ne2	0-0	f4	Nf3	
	b6[1]	Bb7	c5	Nc6	Qd7	0-0-0	f5	c4[2] ±	
		Ngf3[3]	e5	Be2[5]	exf6	Nf1	Ne3	Nd5	
	Nc6	Nf6	Nd7[4]	f6	Qxf6[6]	e5[7]	e4	Qd6[8] ±	
		e5	c3	Ndf3	cxd4	Bd3	Ne2	0-0[10] ∞/±	
	a6	c5[9]	Nc6	cxd4	Nge7	Nf5	Be7		
		exd5	Ngf3	Bc4	0-0	Nb3	Nbxd4	Nxd4[12] ±	
	c5	Qxd5	cxd4	Qd6[11]	Nf6	Nc6	Nxd4		

1.e4,e6 2.d4,d5 3.Nd2

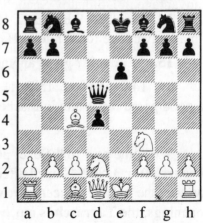

Diagram 35
Main line: after 7.Ne2

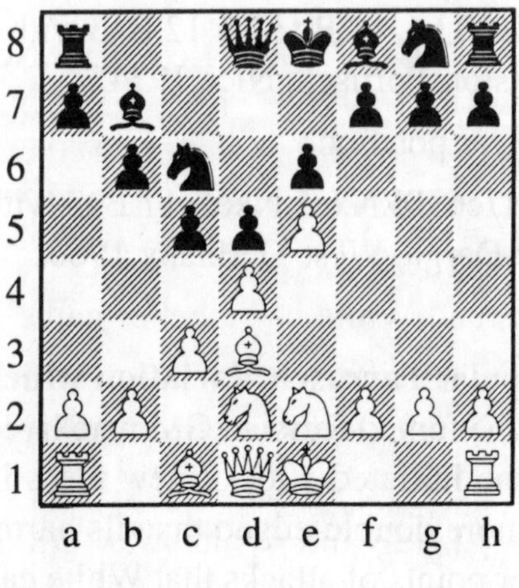

Diagram 36
Fourth line: after 6.Bc4

1. 3...,f5 4.exf5,exf5 5.Ndf3,Nf6 6.Bg5 (Or 6.Bd3 with the idea Ne2 and 0-0 is OK for White.) 6...,Be7 7.Bd3,Ne4 8.Bxe7,Qxe7 9.Ne2,Qb4+?! (9...0-0 is better.) 10.c3,Qb2 11.0-0,0-0 12.c4 was very good for White in Karpov-Enevoldsen, Scopje 1972.

2. 11.Bc2,Nh6 12.b3 with a slight edge for White in Aseev-Gulko, Moscow 1982.

3. 4.c3,e5 5.exd5,Qxd5 6.Ngf3,exd4 (Not 6...,Bg4? 7.Bc4,Bxf3 8.Qb3! and White had the advantage in Keres-Botwinnik, USSR Championship 1955.) 7.Bc4,Qh5!? 8.cxd4,Nf6 9.0-0,Be7 10.Ne5,Qxd1 11.Rxd1,Nd8!? equalizes.

4. 5...,Ne4?! 6.c3,Nxd2 (6...,f5 7.exf6e.p.,Nxf6 8.Bb5+,Bd7 9.0-0,Bd7 10.Re1 is quite good for White.) 7.Bd2,b6 8.Bd3 is OK for White.

5. 6.Nb3,Be7 7.Bb5,a5 (Not 7...,0-0 8.0-0,Nb6 9.Re1,Bd7 10.Bf1 with an edge for White.) 8.a4,Na7 9.Bd3,b6 10.0-0,Bb7 equalizes; 6.Bd3,f6 7.Ng5,Nde5! 8.dxe5,fxg5 9.Qh5+,g6 10.Bxg6,Kd7! is unclear but probably even.

6. 7...,Nxf6!? 8.0-0,Bd6 9.c4,0-0 10.b3,Bd7 11.Bb2,Ne4 12.g3 is OK for White.

7. 8...,Bd6 9.Ne3,0-0 10.0-0,Nb6 11.Ng4,Qg6 12.h3! with a small advantage for White.

8. 11.Bc4!,exf3 12.Bf4,Qg6 13.Nxc7+,Kd8 14.Qxf3,Nb6 15.Bd3,Bg4 16.Qg3,Bf5 17.Qxg6,hxg6 18.Nxa8 and White had the advantage in Dolmatov-Sisniega, Graz 1978.

9. 4...,Bd7!? 5.c3,Bb5 6.Ndf3,Bxf1 7.Kxf1,c5 8.g3,Nc6 9.Kg2,cxd4 10.cxd4,Nge7 11.Ne2,Qb6 12.Bd2,h5 13.Bc3,Nf5 14.h3,Be7 15.g4,Nh4 16.Nxh4,Bxh4 17.f4,f6 18.Qd3,0-0-0 was unclear in Dvoiris-Eingorn, Odessa USSR Championship 1989.

10. 10...,Qb6 11.a3,Bd7 12.Bc2,Rc8 13.b4,a5 14.bxa5,Nxa5 15.Bxf5,exf5 16.Nf4,Qc6 17.e6! and White has a better game in Dvoiris-Dolmatov, Odessa USSR Championship 1989.

11. 6...,Qd8 7.0-0,Nc6 8.Nb3,Nf6 9.Qe2,a6 10.Rd1 and White was a little better in Sax-Andersson, Hilversum 1973.

12. 10...,Be7 11.c3,Bd7 12.Re1 and White was OK in

Balasov-Spassky, Munich 1979; <u>10...,a6</u> 11.Bb3,Be7 12.c3,0-0 13.Qf3 and White had advantage in Jansa-Petrosian, Moscow 1977; <u>10...,Bd7</u> 11.c3,Qc7 12.Qe2,Bd6 13.Nb5,Bxb5 14.Bxb5+,Ke7 15.g3 with a small advantage for White in A. Sokolov-Andersson, Clermont-Ferrand 1989.

Besides the moves **4...,Qxd5 (After 1.e4,e6 2.d4,d5 3.Nd2,c5 4.exd5)** Black has the solid alternative: **4...,exd5.** The Black d-pawn may become a target later on, but this is balanced by the fact that the problem Bc8 now is free to travel.

The other main variation in the **Tarrasch** that deserves study for both White and Black occurs after: **1.e4,e6 2.d4,d5 3.Nd2,Nf6 4.e5,Nfd7.**

* * * *

THE KING'S GAMBIT

1.e4,e5 2.f4

This Gambit is as old as (and probably even older than) the Two Knights' Defense which we shall cover in the Italian Game. By his second move **2.f4**, White begins to fight for the centre in the sharpest possible way. He wants to get rid of pawn e5 and he wants to build up a formidable tandem in the center by combining pawns e4 and d4! What about the White King? Well, the center is more important.

A wonderful weapon in the hands of the great attacking masters of the 19th century, it has lost some of its teeth since Black discovered that he can reach almost certain equality by giving back the pawn at the right moment. If Black is not greedy and holds on to the pawn without trying to get more, and if White cannot capitalize on his chances, the endgame tends to be better for Black. When Black rejects the Gambit, he normally uses the cautious **2...,Bc5** or the **Falkbeer Counter-Gambit   2...,d5**. The first choice leads to positional confrontations resulting in a struggle for the superiority in development. The counter-gambit is somewhat analogous to the Two Knights' Defense (1.e4,e5   2.Nf3,Nc6 3.Bc4,Nf6!? 4.Ng5) in which Black sacrifices a pawn for the sake of free play and initiative. After **3.exd5** Black plays **3...,e4!** and White has difficulties in development.

Leading masters in recent years like Keres, Bronstein, Fischer and Spassky have not been afraid to use it when they were in the mood. Most chess magazines can render wonderful games at regular intervals from GM tournaments testifying to the enduring attraction and basic correctness of this 16th century invention that proves that as long as you have two or three tempi advantage in development, sacrifice of a pawn is worth it.

Readers who have just started to study chess are advised to try and play it as White; there are few openings that will expose them better to tactics that can occur over the board in open games.

	2	3	4	5	6	7	8	9
1.e4,e5 2.f4								
	...	Nf3	Nc3[1]	Bc4	d3	h3[2]	Qxf3	Qg3
	Bc5	d6	Nf6	Nc6	Bg4!?	Bxf3	Nd4	Qe7[3] ±
	...	exd5	d3	dxe4[5]	Nf3	Qe2	Nc3	Be3
	d5	e4[4]	Nf6	Nxe4	Bc5[6]	Bf5	Qe7[7]	Bxe3[8] ±
	...	...	Nc3[9]	d3[10]	Bd2	Bxe3	Bd2	Be2
	...	...	Nf6	Bb4	e3!?	Nxd5	0-0!	Bxc3[11] ∞/∓
	...	Bc4[12]	Nc3[14]	Bb3[15]	exd5	d4	Nge2	0-0
	exf4	Nf6[13]	c6!	d5	cxd5	Bd6	0-0	g5 ∞

Diagram 37

Main line: after 3.Nf3

Diagram 38

Note 5: after 9...,Bg4!

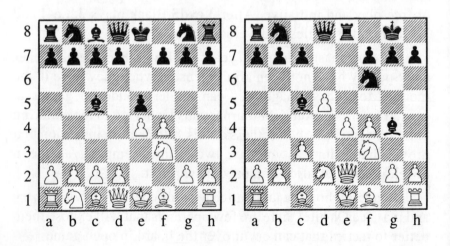

1. 4.c3!?,Nf6 5.fxe5,dxe5 6.d4,exd4 7.cxd4,Bb4+ 8.Bd2,Bxd2+ 9.Nbxd2,0-0 with an even game or a slight advantage for White.

2. 7.Na4,Nd4!? 8.Nxc5,dxc5 9.c3,Nxf3+ 10.gxf3,Bh5 with a slightly better game for White in an unclear position.

3. 9...,Nxc2+? 10.Kd1,Nxa1 11.Qxg7; 9...,Qe7 10.fxe5,dxe5 11.Kd1 and White has a small advantage.

4. 3...,Bc5 4.Nc3! and White has the advantage; 3...,Qxd5 4.Nc3,Qe6 5.fxe5 and White is better; 3...,c6!? 4.Nc3!,exf4 5.Nf3,Bd6 6.Bc4,Ne7 7.dxc6,Nbxc6 8.d4,0-0 9.0-0,Bg4 10.Ne4,Bc7 11.c3 was unclear in Illescas-Nunn, Dubai Olympiad 1986.

5. 5.Qe2,Bb4+!? 6.c3 (6.Bd2?!,Bg4! 7.Nf3,0-0 8.Bxb4,Re8 and Black is better.) 6...,Bc5 7.dxe4,0-0 8.Nf3,Re8 9.Nbd2 (Kuindzi-Sukhanov, Moscow 1970.) 9...,Bg4! with a sharp unclear position where Black tends to hold the advantage; 5.Nd2,exd3 6.Bxd3,Nxd5 7.Qe2+,Be7 is unclear but probably slightly better for Black.

6. 6...,Bf5 7.Be3!,c6 8.Bc4,b5 9.Bb3,c5 10.d6! and White had a small edge in Alekhine-Tarrasch, St. Petersburg 1914.

7. 8...,0-0? 9.Nxe4,Re8 10.Ne5,Bxe4 11.Qxe4,f6 12.d6!,Qxd6 13.Be3! and White had a winning advantage in Blackburn-Marco, Berlin 1987.

8. 10.Qxe3,Nxc3 11.Qxe7+,Kxe7 12.bxc3 and White has an edge.

9. 4.Bb5+,c6 5.dxc6,Nxc6 6.d3,Nf6 7.Nc3,Bb4 with compensation for the sacrificed material.

10. 5.Qe2,Bg4! 6.Qe3,Bf5 7.Bb5+,c6 8.dxc6,Nxc6 9.d3,Bb4 again with sufficient compensation.

11. 10.bxc3,Qf6 11.Qc1?,Re8 12.c4,Nc3 13.Qb2,Nxe2 and Black had a decisive advantage in Gruzman-Kimelfeld, Moscow 1966.

12. 3.Nc3,Qh4+ 4.Ke2,d5!? 5.Nxd5,Bg4+ 6.Nf3,Bd6 7.d4,Nc6 is unclear.

13. 3...,Qh4+ 4.Kf1,d5!? 5.Bxd5,Bd6 6.Nc3,Ne7 7.d4,f6 is unclear or slightly better for White; 3...,d6?! 4.Nc3,Be6 5.Bxe6,fxe6

(Hjartarson-Belyavsky, Reykjavic 1988.) 6.Nf3!?,Nc6 7.d4,e5 8.0-0,Be7 9.d5,Nb8 10.Nxe5! with attack (Belyavsky).

14. 4.d3,d5 5.exd5,Nxd5 6.Nf3,Nb6 7.Bb3,Bd6 8.Qe2+,Qe7 9.Nc3,Bg4 10.Qxe7+,Kxe7 11.Ne4 and White had a small advantage in Judit Polgar-Flear, Hastings 1988/89.

15. 5.d4,d5 6.exd5,Nxd5 7.Bxd5,cxd5 8.Nf3 equalizes; 5.e5,d5 is slightly better for Black.

The continuation **2...,exf4 3.Nf3** is known as the King's Knight Gambit and contains some of the most dangerous and double-edged variations for both White and Black. Many of these were already analysed in the last century, and may lead to a forced draw. If you are unfamiliar with them, however, a loss is the logical outcome. All readers should study and play them at least once or twice because of the richness and the tactical depth of ideas underlying the analysis.

1.e4,e5 2.f4,exf4 3.Nf3							
3	4	5	6	7	8	9	10
...	e5	d4	Qe2!?	c4	cxd5	Nc3	Bd2!
Nf6	Nh5	d6[1]	d5[2]	Be6	Bxd5	Nc6	Bb4[3] ∞
...	...	Be2[4]	0-0	d4	Qd3	Nh4	Bxh5
...	...	g5[5]	Rg8	d5	Rg6	Rh6	Rxh5[6] ∞
...	Bc4	e5[9]	Nc3[10]	d4	Kf1	Bxe3	Qd3
Be7[7]	Nf6[8]	Ng4	d6!	Bh4+	Ne3+	fxe3	Bg5 ∞/=
...	Nc3	Ke2	d4	Bxf4	Qd3	Kd2	gxf3
...	Bh4+[11]	d6	Bg4	Nc6	Nge7	Bxf3	Qd7[12] ∞

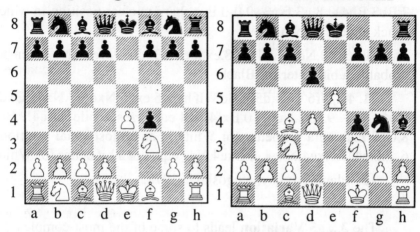

Diagram 39

King's Knight Gambit

Diagram 40

Third line: after 8.Kf1

1. 5...,d5 6.c4,Nc6 7.cxd5,Qxd5 8.Nc3,Bb4 9.Kf2,Bxc3 10.bxc3,Bg4 11.Be2,0-0 12.h3!,Bc8 13.Re1 and White is better according to Keres.

2. 6...,dxe5 7.Qxe5+,Qe7 8.Be2! and White has an edge.

3. 11.Nxd5,Qxd5 12.0-0-0!?,0-0-0!? 13.Qc4 with an unclear position in which White is slightly better.

4. Qe2,Be7 6.d4,0-0 7.g4,fxg3e.p. 8.Qg2 (Or 8.Nc3,d5 9.Qg2,Bxg4 10.hxg4,Nc6 equalizes.) 8...,d6 9.hxg3,Bg4 10.Nh2,Nxg3! is unclear or slightly better for Black.

5. 5...,d6!? 6.0-0,dxe5 7.Nxe5,Bc5+ 8.Kh1,Nf6 is unclear, probably slightly better for White; 5...,g6!? is a valid alternative but not played very often in tournament practice.

6. 11.Nf5!?,Qd7 12.g4 is an unclear position, but definitely better for White.

7. 3...,d6 4.d4,g5 5.Bc4,g4 6.Bxf4!? (Only alternative is 6.Ng1.) 6...,gxf3 7.Qxf3,Nf6 (Interesting play develops after 7...,Be6 according to Glazkov.) 8.Bg5,Be7 9.0-0,Nbd7 10.Nc3,c6 11.Rf2,Qa5 12.e5,dxe5 13.Ne4 with a strong attack for White in Alekhine-Velikanov, Odessa 1916.

8. 4...,Bh4+ 5.Kf1,d5 6.Bxd5,Nf6 7.Bb3!?,Nxe4? 8.Qe2! and

White has a winning advantage (Glazkov).

9. 5.Nc3,Nxe4! 6.Ne5 (6.Nxe4,d5 is OK for Black.) 6...,Nd6 7.Bb3,Bh4+ 8.g3,fxg3 9.0-0 is a sharp unclear position in which Black should be better.

10. 6.0-0,Nc6 7.d4,d5 8.exd6e.p.,Bxd6 9.Re1+,Ne7 even but probably a bit better for Black.

11. 4...,Nf6 5.d4,d5 6.Bd3 (If here 6.exd5,Nxd5 7.Nxd5,Qxd5 8.c4,Qa5+ 9.Kf2,Nc6 10.Bxf4,Bg4 equalizes; while 7.Bc4!?,Be6 8.Qe2 may be a bit better for White in an almost equal position.) 6...,dxe4 7.Nxe4,Nxe4 8.Bxe4,Nd7 equal or a bit better for White.

12. Planinc-Ivkov, Yugoslavia 1978.

The **3...,g5 Variation** leads to some of the most complex positions in the open games where a piece sacrifice is often the norm. The analysis given below is a good guide-line.

		1.e4,e5 2.f4,exf4 3.Nf3					
3	**4**	**5**	**6**	**7**	**8**	**9**	**10**
...	exd5	Bb5+[2]	dxc6	d4	0-0	Nbd2!?[4]	c3[5] $\pm$
d5[1]	Nf6	c6!	Nxc6[3]	Bd6	0-0	Bg4	
...	h4![6]	Ne5[7]	d4[9]	Nd3	Bxf4	Qe2	c3[11] $\overline{\infty}/\pm$
g5	g4	Nf6[8]	d6	Nxe4	Qe7[10]	Bg7	
...	Bc4	0-0	d4	c3	g3	gxf4	Rf2[14] ∞
...	Bg7[12]	h6	d6	Nc6	Bh3![13]	Qd7	
...	d4	Nc3	Bc4	0-0	Be6	e5	exd6[16] ∞
...	h6[15]	Bg7	d6	Be6	fxe6	Nc6!	

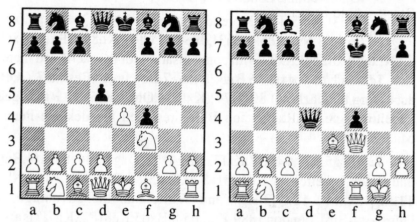

Diagram 41

Main line: after 3...,d5

Diagram 42

Note 12: after 10.Be3!

1. 3...,h6 4.d4,g5! 5.Nc3 (If 5.h4,Bg7 6.g3,g4 7.Nh2,fxg3 8.Nxg4,d6 equalizes.) 5...,d6 6.g3!?,fxg3 (Better than 6...,Bg7 7.gxf4,g4 8.Ng1,Qh4+ 9.Ke2,g3 10.Nf3,Bg4 11.Be3!,gxh2 12.Kd2 and White is doing fine.) 7.h4,g4 8.Ng1,g2 9.Bxg2,Be7 10.h5 with compensation.

2. 5.Nc3,Nxd5 6.Nxd5 (Slightly better proved for White 6.Bc4!?,Be6 7.Qe2,Be7 8.d4,c6 9.0-0,0-0 10.Nxd5,cxd5 11.Bd3,Nc6 in Spassky-Pytel, Nice Olympiad 1974; although Black could then have played the better 6...,Nxc3!? 7.bxc3,Bd6 which gives an even game.) 6...,Qxd5 7.d4,Be7 8.c4,Qe4+ 9.Be2 (Or 9.Kf2,Bf5 10.c5,Nc6 11.Bb5,Qd5! 12.Bxf4,0-0-0 and Black is OK; or 12.Re1,Be4 is again OK for Black in an almost even game.) 9...,Nc6 10.0-0,Bf5 11.Re1,0-0-0 12.Bf1,Qc2 13.Qxc2,Bxc2 14.Bxf4 equalized in Spielmann-Milner-Berry, Margate 1938; 5.c4?!,c6 6.d4,Bb4+ (6...,cxd5 7.c5! and White has a small advantage.) 7.Nc3,cxd5 8.Bxf4,0-0 9.Bd3,dxc4 10.Bxc4,Re8+ 11.Be5,Nc6 12.0-0,Nxe5 13.Nxe5,Be6 and an even game with a slight edge for Black.

3. 6...,bxc6 7.Bc4,Nd5 8.Nc3,Be6 (8...,Nxc3 9.dxc3!,Bd6 10.Qd4,0-0 11.Bxf4,Qe7+ 12.Kd2!?,Rd8 13.Bd3 and White had the advantage in Krustali-Endre, correspondence game 1970.) 9.Qe2,Be7 10.0-0,0-0 11.d4,Nxc3 12.bxc3,Bxc4 13.Qxc4,Bd6 14.Ne5 and White has a small advantage.

4. 9.c4!?,Bg4 10.Nc3,Rc8 is unclear (Muchnik); 9.Nc3,Qb6! equalizes.

5. Kinley-Nunn, London 1977.

6. 4.Nc3!?,g4 5.d4!? (More adventurous is 5.Ne5,Qh4+ 6.g3,fxg3 7.Qxg4,Qxg4 8.Nxg4,d5 9.Bh3!,dxe4 10.Nf6+,Kd8 11.Bxc8,Kxc8 12.Nfxe4,gxh2 13.Rxh2 with compensation for the sacrificed material: Schmidt.) 5...,gxf3 6.Bxf4!,Nc6 7.Bc4,fxg2 (Best is 7...,Qf6 according to Glazkov.) 8.Bxf7+!,Kxf7 9.Qh5+,Kg7 10.Rg1,Nge7 11.Bh6+,Kg8 12.Rxg2+ and Black resigned in Alekhine-Peres, Madrid 1943.

7. 5.Ng5,h6! 6.Nxf7,Kxf7 7.Bc4+ (7.Qxg4,Nf6 8.Qxf4,Bd6 and Black is better; or 7.d4,f3! 8.gxf3,d5! 9.Bf4,Nf6 10.e5,Nh5 11.fxg4,Nxf4 12.Qf3,Kg7 and White had the advantage in Gunsberg-Bird, London 1889.) 7...,d5 8.Bxd5,Ke8 (8...,Kg7!? is also worth consideration.) 9.d4,Nf6 10.Nc3,Bb4 unclear but probably better for Black.

8. 5...,h5?! 6.Bc4,Rh7 7.d4,d6 8.Nd3 (Possible is also 8.Nxf7!?) 8...,f3 9.gxf3,Be7 10.Be3,Bxh4+ 11.Kd2,Bg5 12.f4,Bh6 13.Nc3 with advantage for White and compensation for the sacrificed material (analysis by Fischer.)

9. 6.Bc4,d5 7.exd5,Bd6 (7...,Bg7 is best says Fischer.) 8.d4,Nh5 9.0-0,Qxh4 10.Qe1,Qxe1 11.Rxe1,0-0 12.Bd3 equalizes; 6.Nxg4?!,Ne4 7.d3,Ng3 8.Bxf4,Nxh1 9.Qe2 (9.Bg5,Be7 10.Qe2,h5 11.Qe5,f6! 12.Nxf6+,Kf7 and Black has the advantage according to Steinitz.) 9...,Qe7 10.Nxf6+,Kd8 11.Bxc7+,Qxc7 12.Nd5+,Kd8 13.Nxe7,Bxe7 and Black was better in Morphy-Andersen, Paris 1858.)

10. 8...,Bg7 9.c3! (9.Not as good is: 9.Nc3?!,Nxc3 10.bxc3,c5! 11.Be2,cxd4 12.0-0,Nc6 and Black had advantage in Spassky-Fischer, Mar del Plata 1960.) 9...,0-0 (Better is 9...,Qe7!? 10.Qe2,Bf5 with an unclear position according to Fischer.) 10.Nd2,Re8 11.Nxe4,Rxe4+ 12.Kf2 and White is OK.

11. 10...,Nc6 11.Nd2,Nxd2 12.Kxd2,Qxe2+ 13.Bxe2,h5 14.Rhe1 and White has a small advantage; 10...,h5 11.Nd2,Nxd2 12.Kxd2,Qxe2+ 13.Bxe2,Bf5 14.Rhf1 and White is again just a bit better.

12. The most important line that <u>must</u> be studied is: 4...,g4!? 5.0-0!? (Unclear and probably better for Black is: 5.Ne5,Qh4+ 6.Kf1,Nh6 7.d4,f3 8.Nc3,d6; alternatives for Black are 6...,f3!? and 6...,Nc6.) 5...,gxf3 6.Qxf3,Qf6 7.e5,Qxe5 8.d3,Bh6 9.Nc3,Ne7 10.Bd2,Nbc6 11.Rae1,Qf5 12.Nd5,Kd8 13.Qe2,Qe6! 14.Bc3,Qxe2 15.Rxe2,Rg8!? 16.Nxf4,d6 17.Bxf7 with compensation for the sacrificed material. A valid alternative still being tried out at the GM level is (instead of 8.d3) 8.Bxf7+!?,Kxf7 9.d4,Qxd4+ 10.Be3,Qf6 11.Bxf4,Ne7 12.Nc3,Qf5 (Not 12...,Nf5 13.Nd5!) 13.Qe2,Ke8 14.Be5,Qe6 15.Rf6,Qg8 16.Qh5+,Kd8 17.Raf1,d6! (And not: 17...,Bg7? 18.Rf7,Be5 19.Qxe5,Nbc6 10.Qxh8! with a winning advantage in Glazkov-Muratov, Moscow 1973.) 18.Rxf8,Qxf8 19.Rxf8+,Rxf8 20.Bg7,Rf5 21.Qxh7 with the idea 22.Ne4 and White has a small advantage; or 22.Qh8+ with a slight advantage for White: analysis by Glazkov.)

13. 8...,g4 9.Nh4,f3 10.Nd2,Bf6 11.Ndxf3!,gxf3 12.Qxf3 with sufficient compensation.

14. 10...,Nf6 11.Qe1,0-0-0 is unclear, probably a bit better for Black (Glazkov.)

15. 4...,g4 5.Bxf4!?,gxf4 6.Qxf3 with compensation, e.g.: 6...,d6 7.Nc3,Qh4+ 8.Bg3,Qg4 9.Qf2,Bh6 10.Be2,Qg5 11.Nd5,Qd2+ 12.Kf1 and White was better in Khmelnitsky-Mukhametov, Chelyabinsk 1987.

16. 10...,Qxd6 11.Nb5,Qd7 12.d5,0-0-0 13.Bxf4!?,Qxd5 (13...,gxf4 14.dxc6,bxc6 15.Qxd7+,Rxd7 16.Nc3 with compensation.) 14.Qxd5,Rxd5 15.c4,Rd7 16.Be5! with compensation for the sacrificed material (an analysis by Glazkov).

One comment: some of these detailed analyses may look awkward and the compensation may not seem adequate. If you have a chess computer, input the ultimate position and you will see quickly how, through a few tactical moves, the compensation and/or advantage claimed is indeed fully justified. If

you are painstaking in following these interesting moves and manage
to incorporate the ideas into your own game, especially lesser skilled
players you choose as your opponents will be continuously outplayed.

* * * *

KING'S INDIAN DEFENSE
Four Pawn Attack and Sämisch

We come now to another complex opening of a completely different nature belonging to the Closed Opening Systems. **The King's Indian Defense.** GM Eduard Gufeld, who has played this defense throughout his career with a passion, now even calls it the **King's Indian Attack!** The reason for proposing this new name was the stupendous wins that World Ladies' Champion Xie Jun of China booked with it as Black in her 1993 title match against Nana Ioselani of Georgia. She won quite convincingly in all games that the **King's Indian** appeared on the board.

Together with the **Sicilian Defense** (Open games that occurs after 1.e4,c5), the King's Indian is one of the most varied and widely played systems in modern day GM play. It is impossible to discuss even one quarter in the scope of this volume, but the main lines that appear in the following pages will allow the reader together with his computer to understand the basic ideas connected with this defense.

Leading players that utilise it are among others: Kasparov, Fischer and former challenger David Bronstein. Black allows White to establish a broad front in the center of **e4** together with the **d4 and c4** (normally White's first two moves) then usually starts to attack it, or tries to work around it. As soon as one of the players 'locks' the center, both start to work on their own wings. That is usually: Black on the King-side and White on the Queen-side. Another feature of this defense is that Black invariably plays **Nf6, g6 and Bg7** and almost always **d6.**

The **Fianchetto Variation** in which White too develops his King's Bishop along the long diagonal is discussed first. Positional players are able to excel here, as the game tends to be quiet at first: White keeps Bg2 aimed at the center hoping to exploit his spatial advantage. Black does not need to worry unduly, since his position is quite solid. He can vary his approach depending on his own style and the moves chosen by his opponent.

1.d4,Nf6 2.c4,g6 3.Nf3,Bg7 4.g3,d6 5.Bg2,0-0 6.0-0

6	7	8	9	10	11	12	13
...	Nc3	h3[1]	e4	Nxd4	Nb3	Be3	e5[3] ±
c6	Qa5	e5[2]	exd4	Qc5	Qb4!	a5	
...	...	...	d5!?	Nd4	cxd5	Be3	Nb3[4] ±
...	...	Be6	cxd5	Bd7	Rc8	Na6	
...	Nc3[5]	dxc5	Bf4	Be5	Qxd8	Bc7	Ne5[8] ±
c5	Nc6	dxc5	Nd4[6]	Nc6!	Rxd8	Rf8[7]	
...	...	...	Be3	Bd2	Nd5	Nh4	h3[10] ±
...	...	...	Qa5[9]	Bf5	Qd8	Bg4	

Diagram 43

Main line: after 6.0-0

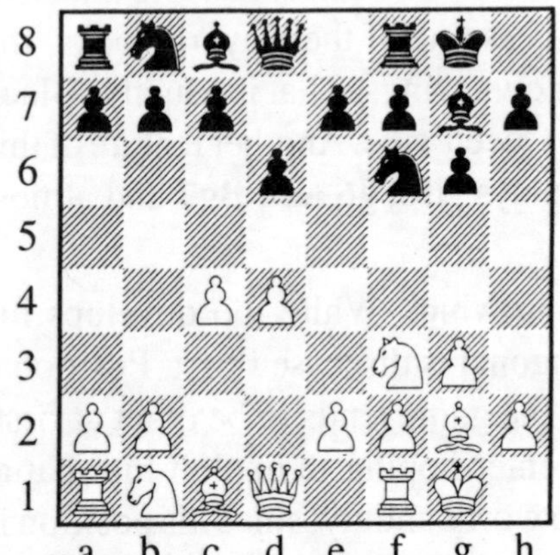

Diagram 44

Note 6: after 11.Qa4

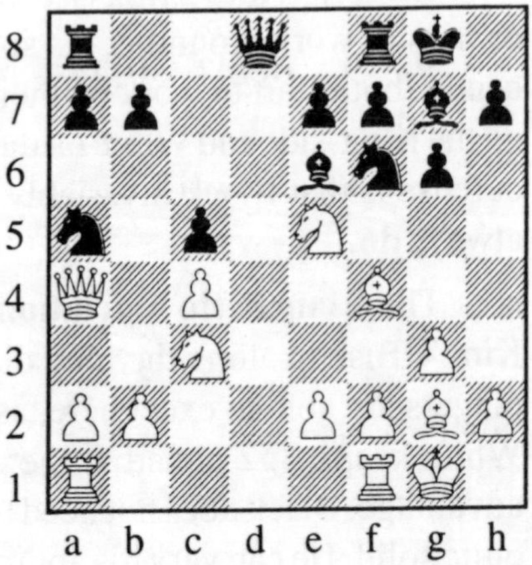

1. 8.e4,e5 9.d5,cxd5 10.cxd5,b5! 11.Re1,Na6 12.a3,b4 13.Na4,Bd7 14.b3,Rfb8 is unclear in Makarov-Demetiev, Erevan 1981.

2. 8...,Qh5? 9.Ng5! and White has the advantage; 8...,Bf5 9.Nd2,e5 10.d5 and White has an edge; 8...,Qa6 9.b3,b5 10.a4! and White has a small advantage.

3. 13...,dxe5 14.Bc5,Qxc4 15.Bxf8,Bxf8 16.Nxa5!,Qe6 (If 16...,Rxa5 17.Qd8 etc.) 17.Nb3,Nbd7 18.Re1 and White was OK in Podgaets-Padchenko, USSR 1981.

4. 13...,Qd8 14.Bd4 (14.Qd2,Be8 15.Rac1,Nd7 16.Bh6,Bh8! with an unclear position in Nikolic-Vukic, Yugoslavia Championship 1981.) 14...,Be8 15.e4,Nd7 16.Bxg7,Kxg7 17.f4!,Qb6+ 18.Kh2! and White had a small advantage in Janosevic-Vukic, Yugoslavia Championship 1975.

5. 7.d5,Na6 (Interesting too is 7...,e5.) 8.Nc3,Nc7 9.a4,Rb8 10.e4 (Or 10.Bf4!?) 10...,a6 11.a5,Nd7 is unclear probably even.

6. 9...,Be6 10.Ne5,Na5 11.Qa4 and White is OK; 9...,Nh5!? 10.Be3,Nd4 11.Qd2,Bg4 12.Rad1,Bxf3 13.exf3,e6 14.Ne4 and White had a slight advantage in Larsen-Ribli, Riga 1979.

7. 12...,Rd7 13.Bf4 is a bit better for White.

8. 13...,Nd4 14.Nd3,Nd7 15.Rfd1 was OK for White in Ribli-Gligoric, Linares 1981.

9. 9...,Be6!? 10.Qa4,Nd4 11.Bxd4,cxd4 12.Nb5,Bd7 13.Qb3,Ne4 is unclear.

10. 13...,Bd7 14.Bc3,e5 15.e3 is a bit better for White.

The **Panno Variation** when Black plays **6...,Nc6** is Black's sharpest approach and is now increasingly popular. White has to thread carefully not to overextend himself.

1.d4,Nf6 2.c4,g6 3.Nf3,Bg7 4.g3,d6 5.Bg2,0-0 6.Nc3,Nc6 7.0-0

7	8	9	10	11	12	13	14	
...	d5	c5[1]	cxb5e.p.[3]	e4	Bd2	Qc2	Nh4[4]	‘±
e5	Ne7	b5!?[2]	axb5	h6	Nd7	Kh7		
...	d5[5]	Nd4	b3	dxc5e.p.	Bb2	Rb1	Nc2[6]	
Bf5	Na5	Bd7	c5!	bxc5!?	Rb8	c5		
...	d5	b3[8]	Bb2	Nd2	Qc2	Rfe1	Nd1	±
Bg4	Na5[7]	c5	a6	Rb8	b5	Qc7		
...	b3	Bb2[9]	cxb5	Rc1	Nb1	Ne1!	Nd3[11]	±
a6	Rb8	b5	axb5	b4[10]	Na5	c6		

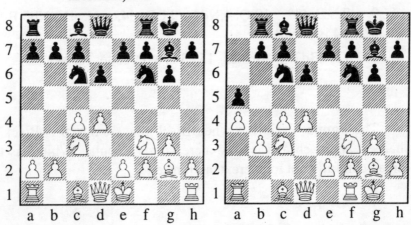

Diagram 45
Panno Variation:
after 6...,Nc6

Diagram 46
Note 9: after 9...,a5!

1. 9.e4,Ne8 10.b4,h6 (10...,f5 11.Ng5,h6 12.Ne6,Bxe6 13.dxe6,c6 14.b5!,Qc8 15.bxc6,bxc6 16.c5,Qxe6 17.Ba3 and White had a slight advantage in Mortensen-Kupreichik, Esbjerg 1988.) 11.Bb2,f5 12.exf5,gxf5 13.Nh4! with a small advantage for White (Uhlmann).

2. 9...,dxc5 10.Nxe5,Nfxd5 11.Nxd5,Bxe5 12.Bg5,f6 13.Nxf6+! with a small advantage for White; 9...,e4 10.Ng5,dxc5 11.Ngxe4,Nexd5 12.Nxd5,Nxd5 13.Bg5 and White is a bit better; 9...,Ne8 10.cxd5,cxd5 11.a4,h6 12.Nd2,f5 13.Nc4,g5 14.Bd2!,f4 15.Ne4,Nf5 16.e3!,Nf6 17.Bb4,Nxe4 18.Bxe4 and White was slightly better in Romanishin-Grünberg, Dresden 1988.

3. 10.Nxb5,Nexd5 11.e4,Ba6 12.Qa4,Bxb5 13.Qxb5,Rb8 14.Qe2 and White had some advantage in Vaganian-Zaitsev, Moscow 1982.

4. 14...,Ba6 15.Rfd1 with a small advantage for White in Romanishin-Zaitsev, USSR 1982.

5. 8.Ne1,Qc8 9.e4,Bh3 10.Nc2 with an edge for White; 8.h3,Ne4 9.Nd5,Bd7 10.Be3 with an unclear position.

6. 14...,Nc6 15.Nd5,Nh5! 16.Bxg7,Nxg7 equalizes in Antonishin-Gulko, Moscow 1982.

7. 8...,Bxf3 9.exf3!,Na5 10.Qe2,c5 11.f4 with an edge for White.

8. 9.Nd2,c5 10.h3,Bd7 11.Qc2,e5! 12.dxe6e.p.,Bxe6 equalized in Schmidt-S.Garcia, Wijk aan Zee 1972.

9. 9.a4,a5! 10.h3,Bf5 11.Nh4,Bd7 12.e4,Qc8 is unclear, probably just a bit better for White.

10. 11...,Na5?! 15.Qc2,b4 13.Nb1,c6 14.e4,Ne8 15.Nbd2 with an edge for White in Romanishin-Tseshkovsky, Erevan 1982.

11. 14...,Ba6 15.Qc2,Nd7 16.Rfd1!?,Qb6 17.Nf4 and White was a bit better in Romanishin-Keene, Dortmund 1982.

Other answers than 8.b3 by White (after 6.Nc3[1],Nc6 7.0-0,a6)

8	9	10	11	12	13	14	15	
h3	e4	e5!?	dxe5	Rxd1	e6	cxb5	Ng5[3]	⊞
Rb8	b5	dxe5[2]	Qxd1	Nd7	fxe6	axb5		
...	Be3	Nd2	Rc1	dxe5	b3	Nd5	Nxf6+[6]	=
...	b5	Bd7[4]	e5[5]	Nxe5	Re8!?	bxc4		
d5	Nd2	Qc2[7]	b3	Bb2	Rab1[9]	e4	Rfe1[10]	±
Na5	c5	Rb8[8]	b5	e6	Re8	Bd7		
...	...	...	...	...	f4	bxc4	Rae1[12]	∞/±
...	...	...	...	Bh6[11]	bxc4	e5		

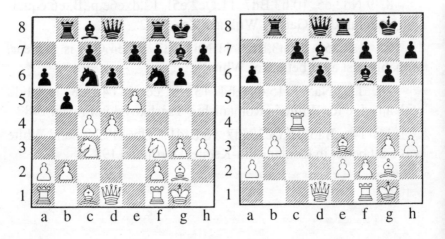

Diagram 47
Main line: after 10.e5!?

Diagram 48
Note 6: after 17.Rxc4

1. 6.0-0,Nc6 7.d5,Na5 8.Nbd2,c5 9.Ne1,b5!? 10.cxb5,Rb8 11.Nc2,Rxb5 12.Rb1,Ba6 13.Re1,c4 14.e4,Nd7 15.b4,cxb4e.p. 16.Nxb3,Nxb3 17.axb3 (Dorfman-Smejkal, Moscow World Cup 1989.) 17...,Nc5! gives an even game (says Dorfman).

2. 10...,Nd7 11.cxb5,axb5 12.Ng5,dxe5 13.Bxc6,exd4 14.Nxb5,Rb6 15.Na7 and White has some advantage. In the game Geller-Gufeld, USSR 1981 (instead of 11.cxb5) play continued: 11.e6,fxe6 12.d5,exd5 13.cxd5,Na5 14.Nd4,Ne5 15.b4,Nac4 16.f4,c5! with an unclear position.

3. 15...,Nd4 16.Be3,c5 17.Nce4,e5 18.Bd4,cxd4 19.Rac1 with compensation for the sacrificed material.

4. 10...,Bb7 11.Rc1,Na5 12.cxb5,axb5 13.b4! and White is doing OK; 10...,Na5 11.cxb5,axb5 12.b4,Nc4 13.Nxc4,bxc4 14.b5 and White has a very good game.

5. 11...,Na5!? 12.cxb5,axb5 13.b4,Nc4 14.Nxc4,bxc4 15.b5,d5! is unclear in Saidy-Georgiu, Las Palmas 1973.

6. 15...,Bxf6 16.Nxc4,Nxc4 17.Rxc4 equalizes.

7. 10.Rb1!?,e5 11.dxe6e.p.,Bxe6 12.Nde4,Nxe4 13.Nxe4,Nxc4 14.b3,Ne5 15.Bg5,f6 16.Bf4 and White had an edge in A. Petrosian-Korzubov, USSR 1982.

8. 10...,e6!? 11.b3,exd5 12.cxd5,b5 13.Bb2,Re8 14.e4,Bd7 15.h3,Rc8 16.Kh2 (Interesting is too 16.Rae1.) 16...,h5 (Worth considering was 16...,Re5!? with the idea ...Rh5.) 17.Rae1,Qc7 18.Nd1,h4 19.g4,c4 with an unclear position in Shirov-Tseshkovsky, Moscow World Cup 1989.

9. 13.dxe6,fxe6 (Not 13...,Bxe6?! 14.cxb5,axb5 15.Nce4,Nxe4 16.Nxe4,Bxb2 17.Qxb2 and White is slightly better.) 14.cxb5,axb5 15.Nce4,Bb7 16.Rad1,Qe7 equalizes.

10. 15...,Bh6?! 16.dxe6!,Bxe6 17.Nd5 and White has the advantage; 15...,bxc4!? 16.bxc4,Ng4 17.Nd1 and White is just a bit better according to Spassky.

11. 12...,e5 13.Rae1,Nh5 14.Nd1,Bh6 15.e3,Bf5 16.Ne4 with a good game for White; 13.Rac1,Ng4 14.h3,Nh6 15.e4,f5

16.exf5,gxf5 17.Nd1,f4 18.g4,Nf7 19.f3,Qh4 is unclear; <u>12....,bxc4</u> 13.bxc4,Bh6 14.Ncb1!,Bd7 15.Bc3,Qc7 16.Nb3!,Nxb3 17.axb3,Bc8 18.e4,Bg7   19.Nd2 with a small edge for White in Goldin-Oll, Yaroslavl 1983; 14...,e5 15.Bc3,Bd7 16.Na3,Rb4!? 17.Bxb4,cxb4 18.Nab1,Qc7 19.c5!,Qxc5! 20.Qb2,Ng4 21.Ne4,Qb6 22.Bf3! and White had a small advantage in Kurajica-Filipowitz, Banja-Luka 1983.

12. 15...,exf5 16.gxf5,Nh5 17.e3,Bg7!? 18.Nd1,Bf5 is unclear but probably a bit better for White (Kasparov).

Black's main other continuation (which is a bit tamer) in this line is to play **6....,Nbd7** (instead of 6....,Nc6). Play then usually continues: **7.0-0,e5 8.e4,c6 9.h3.** However, there are many variations possible on moves 7 and 8.

This brings us to the **Classical Line**: White plays **e4** early and develops Bf1-e2 and Ng1-f3. Black normally quickly plays e7-e5 after which the centre either is opened by exd5 or White locks the centre by d5. If Black plays 6.c5, Benoni-type positions may appear on the board. After the advance d5, White tries to attack on the Queen-side. Modern theory has sharpened Black's chances on the other wing to at least equal chances. Any good chess magazine contains at least one of these games.

1.d4,Nf6 2.c4,g6 3.Nc3,Bg7 4.e4,d6 5.Nf3,0-0 6.Be2							
6	**7**	**8**	**9**	**10**	**11**	**12**	**13**
...	Be3[1]	Rc1[2]	d5	a3	Rb1	b4	Qc1!? $\pm$
Bg4	Nfd7	e5[3]	a5	Na6	f5	Bf6	
...	d5[4]	dxe6[5]	Bf4	Bd6	0-0	a3[6]	b4[7] ∞
c5	e6	Bxe6	Nc6	Re8	Qa5	Red8	
...	dxe5	Qxd8	Bg5	Nd5[9]	cxd5	Bc4	Bxd5[10] =
e5	dxe5	Rxd8	Re8[8]	Nxd5	c6	cxd5	
...	d5[11]	Bg5	Bh4	Nd2	0-0	a3	
...	a5[12]	h6	Na6	Qe8 [13]Nh7		Bd7[14] ∞	

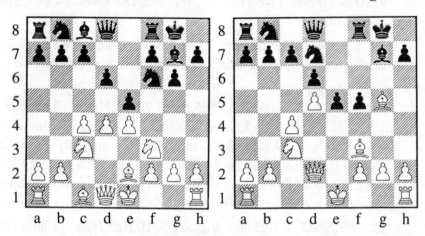

Diagram 49

Classical line: after 6...,e5

Diagram 50

Note 2: after 12.Bg5

1. 7.Bg5,Bxf3!? 8.Bxf3,Nc6 9.Ne2,Re8 10.Qd2,e5 11.d5,Nd4 12.Nxd4,exd4 equalized: Krasenkov-Muratov, Blagoveshchensk 1988.

2. <u>8.Qd2</u>,e5 9.d5,Bxf3 10.Bxf3,f5 11.exf5,gxf5 12.Bg5,Nf6 is unclear; <u>8.0-0</u>,Nc6 (Better than 8...,e5 9.d5,a5 10.a3,Na6 11.Rb1 and White has the edge.) 9.d5,Bxf3 10.Bxf3,Na5 11.Be2,Bxc3!? 12.bxc3,e5 is unclear; <u>8.Ng1!?</u>,Bxe2 9.Ngxe2,e5 10.0-0,a5 11.Qd2,Nc6 12.f3 and White was just a bit better in Kasparov-Bukic, Banja-Luka 1979.

3. 8...,c5 9.d5,Na6 10.0-0,Nc7 11.h3,Bxf3 12.Bxf3,Qb8 13.Be2,e5 14.dxe6e.p.,Nxe6 15.Rc2,a6 16.Rd2 and White had advantage in Andersson-Vaganian, Skellefteå World Cup 1989.

4. 7.0-0 with options for Black: 7...,Nc6 8.d5,Na5 9.Bd2,Bg4 10.b3,a6 11.Rc1,Rb8 12.Qe1! and White was a bit better in Eingorn-Balashov, Uzhgorod 1988; 7...,Na6 8.Be3,Ng4 9.Bg5,h6 10.Bf4,cxd4 11.Nxd4 and White is OK; 7...,Bg4 8.d5!,Na6 9.Bf4,Nc7 10.h3 and White keeps a small advantage.

5. 8.0-0,Re8 9.Nd2,Na6 10.Kh1,Nc7 11.a4,Rb8 12.f3,b6 equalizes.

6. 12.Nd2!?,Rad8! 13.e5,Nd7 14.f4,Nd4 is unclear.

7. 13...,cxb4 14.axb4,Qxa1!? 15.Qxa1,Nxe4! is unclear.

8. 9...,c6 10.Nxe5,Re8 11.f4,Nh5! 12.Bxh5,gxh5 13.Bh4,Nd7 with compensation for the sacrificed material.

9. 10.0-0-0,Na6 11.Ne1,c6 12.Nc2,Nc5 13.f3,Ne6 14.Be3,Bf8 is an even game.

10. 13...,Nd7 14.Nd2,Nb6 15.Bb3,Be6 16.Ke2,Bf8 equalizes in Andersson-Byrne, Sao Paulo 1979. An interesting alternative is 13...,Na6.

11. 7.Be3,Qe7 8.d5 (If 8.dxe5,dxe5 9.Nd5,Nxd5 10.cxd5,c6 equalizes.) 8...,Ng4 9.Bg5,f6 10.Bh4,h5 11.Nd2,a5 is unclear; 7...,Ng4 8.Bg5,f6 9.Bh4,Nc6 11.d5,Ne7 is unclear; 7...,h6!? 8.0-0,Ng4 9.Bc1,Nc6 10.d5,Ne7 11.Nd2,f5 12.Bxg4,fxg4 13.b4,b6 14.Nb3,g5 15.a4,Ng6 16.a5,Bd7 was unclear as well in Kasparov-Nunn, Reykjavic World Cup 1988.

12. 7...,Nbd7 8.Bg5!,h6 9.Bh4,g5 10.Bg3,Nh5 11.h4,g4!? 12.Nd2,Nxg3 13.fxg3,h5 and White is doing OK.

13. 10...,h5!? 11.Bg5 (Or 11.0-0,Bh6.) 11...,Qe8 12.a3,Bd7 13.b3,Nh7 14.Be3,h4! is unclear but probably better for Black in Lerner-Uhlmann, Berlin 1989.

14. 13.b3,f5 14.exf5,gxf5!? 15.Bh5,Qc8 16.Be7,Re8! 17.Bxe8,Qxe8 18.Bh4,e4 with sufficient compensation for Black as in Yusupov-Kasparov, Barcelona World Cup 1989; 13.Rb1,h5! 14.f3,a4 15.Nb5,Bh6 16.b4,axb4e.p. 17.Nxb3,f5 and Black is slightly better (Magerramov); 13.Nb5!?,h5 14.f3,Bh6 15.Kh1,Be3 16.Rb1,a4 17.Be1! and White had the edge in Litinskaya-Popova, Moscow 1990.

As above and including the moves: 6.Be2,e5 7.0-0,Nbd7[1]						
8	**9**	**10**	**11**	**12**	**13**	**14**
Be3	Qc2	Bg5	Bd2	Rad1[3]	Rfe1	Bc1
c6[2]	Ng4	f6	Qc7	Nh6	Nf7	Re8 ∞
d5	Qc2	Bg5	Be3	Nd2	Bxg4	a3
Nc5	a5	h6	b6[4]	Ng4!?	Bxg4	a4!?[5] ∞
Re1	Bf1	Rb1[6]	d5	b3	dxc6	Qc2
c6	a5	Re8	Nc5	Bd7	Bxc6	Rc8 ∞
...	...	Nxd4	h3	Qxg4!?[7]	Qe2	Bh6
...	exd4	Ng4	Qb6!?	Bxd4[8]	Nc5	Re8[9] ±

Diagram 51
Main line: after 10.Bg5

Diagram 52
Note 7: after 16.Rad1

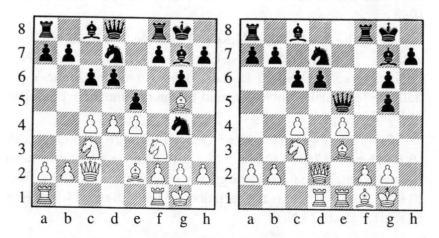

1. <u>7....exd4</u> 8.Nxd4,Re8 (8...,c6 9.f3,Nbd7 10.Kh1,Re8 11.Bg5,a5 12.Qd2,a4 13.Rfd1,Qa5 14.Nc2 Cebalo-Todorcevic, Yugoslavia 1989.) 9.f3,c6 10.Kh1,d5 11.cxd5,cxd5 12.Bg5,dxe4 13.fxe4,Nbd7 14.Ndb5 and White had the edge in Tal-Spassky, Montreal 1979; <u>7....c6</u> 8.dxe5,dxe5 9.Qxd8,Rxd8 10.Nxe5,Nxe4 11.Nxe4,Bxe5 12.Bg5,Re8 13.Bf3,Be6 14.Rae1!,Nd7 15.b3,Bf5 16.Rd1,Bxe4 17.Rxd7 with some advantage for White in Skembris-Kramling, Geneva 1989; <u>7....Qe8!?</u> 8.dxe5,dxe5 9.Be3,b6 10.Nd5,Na6 11.Nd2!?,Nd7!? 12.Qa4,Bb7 13.Qa3 was unclear in Dreev-Gelfand, Arnhem 1988/89; 8.d5,Nh5 9.g3,f5 10.exf5,gxf5 11.Nxe5,Nxg3+ 12.fxg3,Qxe5 13.Qc2,Na6 14.Bf4,Qf6 15.Rf2 with a small advantage for White in Chernin-Cvitan, Moscow World Cup 1989.

2. <u>8....Ng4</u> 9.Bg5,f6 10.Bd2,Nh6 is unclear; probably better is: 10.Bh4,g5 11.Bg3,Nh6 which is not clear but more likely an even game; <u>8....h6</u> 9.dxe5,Ng4 10.Bd2,dxe5 11.Qc1,h5 12.h3,Ngf6 13.Be3,c6 14.c5 is slightly better for White in I. Belov-Strikovic, Pula 1989; 10...,exd5!?,Nxe3 11.dxc7,Qxc7 12.fxe3 is also a bit better for White.

3. 12.d5,f5 13.Ne1,Ndf6 14.f3,Nh6 15.Nd3,c5 was unclear in Bukic-Hausner, Banja-Luka 1981.

4. 11...,Nh5!? 12.g3,Bh3 13.Rfe1,b6 was unclear in Antoshin-Martinovic, Baku 1980.

5. 15.Bxc5,bxc5 16.Nxa4,h5 17.Nc3,Bh6 18.Nb3,h4 with compensation for the sacrificed material in Yusupov-Geller,USSR 1982.

6. <u>10.h3</u>,exd4 11.Nxd4,Re8 12.Bf4,Nc5 13.Qc2,Nh5!? is unclear; <u>10.dxe5</u>,dxe5 11.Na4,Re8 12.Qc2,Qe7!? 13.h3,Nc5 14.Nxc5,Qxc5 15.Be3,Qe7 16.Rad1,Be6 was unclear in Malic-Vogt, Halle 1978; equally unclear would be the continuation 13.c5,Bf8 14.Be3,Nh5.

7. 12.hxg4,Qxd4 13.g5,Qe5 14.Be3,f6 15.Qd2,fxg5 16.Rad1,g4 17.Bd4,Qxd4 18.Qxd4,Bxd4 19.Rxd4 as in Ftacnik-Vogt, Tallinn 1981; the game would be even after: 19...,Rf6! 20.Red1,Ne5. Unclear is the variation: 13.Qxd4,Bxd4 14.Bh6,Re8 15.Rad1,Be5 16.f3,Nc5.

8. 12...,Qd4?! 13.Rd1,Qc5 14.Qg3,Be5 15.Qd3,Qb6 16.Qc2 and White is slightly better.

9. 15.Qd2,Be5 16.Kh1,f5 17.Rad1!,Nxe4 18.Nxe4,fxe4 19.Rxe4,Bf5 20.Re2 and White had a small advantage in Lerner-Vogt, Berlin 1989.

Black can almost force White to advance his pawn to d5 by **7...,Nc6.** Games with this manoeuvre can be found in most GM tournaments today, and the last word has not been said about this, especially after the already discussed Ladies' title match. This line has been very much analysed of late. World Champion Kasparov plays it eagerly as Black, and is not averse from playing it as White, a clear indication that it is a very playable variation where results depend mainly on one's skill.

As above with moves: 6.Be2,e5 7.0-0,Nc6 8.d5,Ne7							
9	**10**	**11**	**12**	**13**	**14**	**15**	**16**
Ne1	Nd3[1]	Bd2[2]	f3	c5	cxd6	Rc1[6]	Nb5
Nd7	f5	Nf6[3]	f4[4]	g5[5]	cxd6	Ng6	Rf7[7] ±
...	f3	g4[8]	Nd3[9]	Nf2	Bd2	a3	Rb1
...	f5	Nf6	c6	Kh8	a5	Bd7	Qb8[10] ∞
Nd2	a3	Rb1	b4	f3[13]	Qc2[15]	Nb5	exf5
a5[11]	Nd7[12]	f5	Kh8	Ng8[14]	Ngf6	b6	gxf5[16] ±
b4[17]	Nd2	c5!	f3	Nc4	a4	Ba3	b5
Ne8[18]	f5	Nf6	f4	g5	Ng6	Rf7	Bf8[19] ∞/±

Diagram 53

Main line: after 9.Ne1

Diagram 54

Note 13: after 16.c5

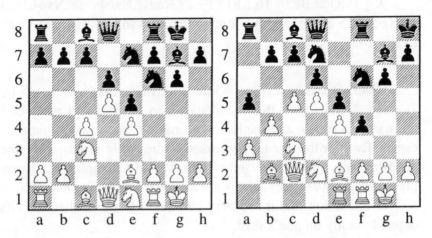

1. 10.Be3,f5 11.f3,f4 12.Bf2,g5 13.b4,Nf6 14.c5,Ng6 15.cxd6,cxd6 16.Rc1,Rf7 17.a4,Bf8!? 18.a5,Bd7! is unclear, e.g.: 19.Nb5,g4! 20.Nc7,g3! 21.Nxa8?,Nh5! 22.Kh1,gxf2 23.Rxf2,Ng3+! 24.Kg1,Qxa8 and Black had a decisive advantage in Piket-Kasparov, Tilburg 1989; however, White could have improved his chances by: 21.hxg3,fxg3! 22.Bxg3,Bh6! 23.Nxa8!,Nh5 24.Bf2,Ngf4 which is still unclear but likely better for Black (Kasparov).

2. 11.exf5,Nxf5 12.f3,Nf6 13.Nf2,Nd4 14.Nfe4,Nxe4 15.Nxe4,Bf5 16.Bd3,c6! is unclear.

3. 11...,Kh8 12.b4,Nf6 13.f3,Neg8 (13...,c6 14.a4,f4 15.g4,h5 16.g5,Nh7 17.h4,Nxg5!? 18.hxg5,Nxd5 was unclear in Bareev-A.Kuzmin, Moscow 1989.) 14.c5,Bh6 15.Rc1,Bxd2 16.Qxd2,f4 17.Nf2,g5 18.g4,h5 19.h3,Rf7 20.Rc2,Rh7 21.a4,hxg4 22.hxg4,Qf8 23.Kg2 with a small edge for White in Malaniuk-Gelfand, Odessa USSR Championship 1989.

4. 12...,Kh8 13.Rc1,c5 14.g4,a6 15.Nf2,h6 16.h4,fxg4 17.fxg4,Neg8 18.Kg2,Nh7 19.Rh1,Bf6 20.g5,hxg5 21.h5 was unclear but proved slightly better for White in Gelfand-Kasparov, Linares 1990.

5. <u>13...,dxc5</u> 14.Nxc5,c6 15.Be1,cxd5 16.Nd5 was OK for White in Ermolinsky-Mochalov, USSR 1980; <u>13...,c6</u> 14.cxd6,Qxd6

15.dxc6,Nxc6 16.Nb5,Qe7 17.Nb4 which was OK for White in Ftacnik-Gufeld, Tallinn 1981.

6. 15.Nf2,Ng6 16.Qc2,Rf7 17.Rfc1,h5 18.h3,a6 19.a4,g4!? in Spasov-Danilov, Pamporovo 1981.

7. 17.Qc2,Ne8 18.a4,h5 19.Nf2,Bf8 20.h3,Rg7!? 21.a5 (Even more interesting was 21.Qd3!?) 21...,Bd7 22.Qb3,Nh4 23.Be1 and White was slightly better in Polugayevsky-Tal, USSR 1980.

8. 11.Be3,f4! 12.Bf2,g5 13.Nd3,Nf6! 14.c5,Ng6 15.cxd6,cxd6 remains unclear.

9. 12.Ng2,c6! 13.Be3,cxd5 14.cxd5,Bd7 15.h3!,Rc8 is unclear.

10. Taimanov-Kavalek, Montilla 1977.

11. 9...,c5 10.dxc6e.p.,bxc6 11.b4,d5 12.Ba3,a6 (Or 12...,Be6 13.Re1,Re8 14.Bf3 is OK for White.) 13.Re1,Be6 14.Bf1,Re8 15.Bb2,Qc7 16.exd5,cxd5 17.cxd5,Nfxd5 18.Nxd5,Nxd5 19.Rc1 and White had a small advantage in Gavrikov-Efimov, Beltsy 1979. The alternative at move 10 for White was: 10.Rb1,Ne8 11.b4,b6 12.bxc5,bxc5 13.Nb3,f5 14.Bd2,Nf6 15.f3,Nh5! which is unclear.

12. 10...,Bd7 11.b3,c5 12.Rb1,Ne8 13.b4,axb4 14.axb4,b6 15.bxc5,bxc5 16.Nb3,f5 17.f3,Nf6 18.Bd2,f4 19.Nb5,Nc8 was unclear in Vaganian-Gelfand, Odessa USSR Championship 1989.

13. 13.Qc2,Ng8 14.Bb2,Ngf6 15.Rbe1,f4 16.c5,dxc5 17.bxc5,Nxc5 18.Nb5,Nfd7 19.Nf3,b6 20.a4,Ba6 21.Ba3 with compensation for the sacrificed material as played in Salov-Short Skellefteå World Cup 1989. In the game Gavrikov-Kasparov, Moscow USSR Championship 1988, Black tried (after 13.Qc2) 13...,b6 14.Nb3,axb4 15.axb4,fxe4 16.Nxe4,Nf6 17.Bd3,Nxe4 18.Bxe4,Nf5 19.Qd3,Qh4 20.g3,Qf6 21.f3,Bd7 with an unclear position.

14. 13...,f4 14.Na4,axb4 15.axb4,c6! (Not 15...,g5 16.c5 which gives White the advantage.) 16.c5!?,cxd5 17.cxd6,Nc6 18,exd5,Nd4 which was unclear in Salov-Nunn, Rotterdam World Cup 1989.

15. 14.Nb3?!,axb4 15.axb4,Ndf6! 16.Bd2 (Interesting is also 16.Be3.) 16...,Nh5! 17.g3,Nhf6 with a double-edged position but better for Black in Karpov-Kasparov, Skellefteå World Cup 1989.

16. 7.f4! was good for White in Lerner-Smirin, Odessa USSR Championship 1989.

17. 9.Bd2,Nh5 10.g3,f5 11.exf5,Nxf5 12.Ne4,Nf6 13.Bg5,h6 14.Bxf6,Bxf6 equalizes.

18. 9...,Nh5 10.c5!,Nf4 11.Bxf4,exf4 12.Rc1,h6 13.Nd2,g5 14.Nc4,a6 15.Na4,Ng6 16.cxd6,cxd6 17.Nab6,Rb8 18.Bg4 was OK for White in Goodman-Carrion, Mexico 1980; 9...,Nd7!? 10.Nd2,f5 11.c5,Nf6 12.Ba3,Bh6! 13.exf5,gxf5 14.b5,Ng6 15.Nc4,Ne8 16.g3,b6 17.cxd6,Nxd6 18.Qb3 with an unclear position in Shpilker-Kuksov, Leningrad 1977.

19. 17.a5 (Also good is 17.b6!?) 17...,b6 18.cxb6,cxb6 19.axb6,axb6 20.Na2!,g4 21.Nb4 and White has a small advantage.

The other two main variations that White normally chooses are the **Four Pawn Attack** and the **Sämisch with f3**. The latter is considered the most solid, and allows White to combine aggression with a good defense.

The Four Pawn Attack gives Black plenty of chances to undermine White's intentions. Games tend to be very violent and if White plays well, his chances can be considered better than average. We give a table of the Four Pawn Attack with just a few variations to demonstrate this, followed by a more extensive commentary for the Sämisch as it will be more instructive and of more immediate use to the average reader.

THE FOUR PAWN ATTACK

1.d4,Nf6 2.c4,g6 3.Nc3,Bg7 4.e4,d6 5.f4

5	6	7	8	9	10	11	12	
...	d5	Bd3	dxe6[2]	Nge2	0-0	Ng3	Be3	
c5	0-0	e6[1]	fxe6	Nc6	Nd4[3]	Bd7	Bc6[4]	∞/±
...	Nf3	d5	Be2	cxd5	e5	fxe5	Bg5	
0-0	c5[5]	e6	exd5	Re8	dxe5	Ng4	Qb6	±
...	...	...	...	...	0-0	Nd2	Qxe2	
...	...	...	...	Bg4	Nbd7	Bxe2	Re8	±
...	...	...	...	exd5	0-0	bxc3	Be3	∞/±
...	...	...	...	Nh5	Bxc3!?f5			

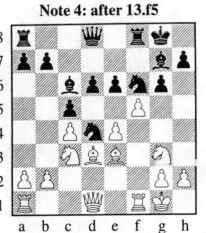

Diagram 55

Four Pawn Attack:5.f4

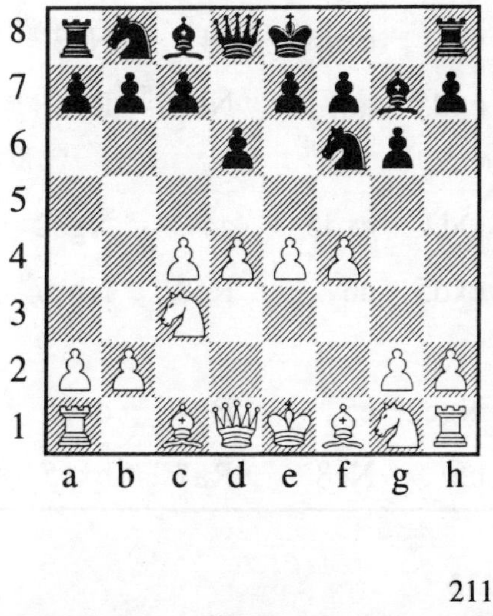

Diagram 56

Note 4: after 13.f5

1. 7...,a6!? 8.Nge2,b5 9.cxb5,axb5 10.Nxb5,Ba6 (Hernandez-Kasparov, Banja-Luka 1979.) 11.Nbc3 is unclear.

2. 8.Nge2!?,exd5 9.cxd5,Bg4 (Not 9...,Nh5 which gives White at once a small advantage after 10.0-0.) 10.0-0,Nh5 11.h3,Bd4+ 12.Kh2,Re8 13.Bd2 when White was just a bit better in Cherepkov-Mochalov, Minsk 1981.

3. 10...,Qe7 11.Ng3,Bd7 12.f5!,Ne5 13.Bg5 and White had a small edge in Antoshin-Suetin, Sochi 1979.

4. <u>13.f5</u>,Nd7 14.fxe6,Rxf1+ 15.Bxf1,Ne5 16.Nd5,Qh4 with an unclear position; <u>13.Rb1</u>,Nd7 14.Kh1,a6 15.Qg4 and White is a bit better.

5. 6...,Na6 7.e5,Nd7 8.c5!?,dxc5 9.d5 with compensation for the sacrificed material in Semkov-Hebden, Villaneuve Tolosane 1989.

THE SÄMISCH

1.d4,Nf6 2.c4,g6 3.Nc3,Bg7 4.e4,d6 5.f3

5	6	7	8	9	10	11	
...	Be3	Bd3[1]	Nge2[2]	cxb5	b4	0-0	
c6	a6	b5	Nbd7	axb5	0-0	Bb7	∞/=
...	Bg5	d5	Qd2	cxd5[4]	a4	Nh3	
0-0[3]	c5	e6	exd5	a6	Nbd7[5]	Re8[6]	=
...	Be3	d5[8]	Qd2	cxd5	a4	Nge2	
...	c5!?[7]	e6	exd5	a6	Re8	Nbd7[9]	∞
...	...	Bd3[10]	Nge2	e5	Be4	dxc5	
...	b6	a6[11]	c5	Ne8	Ra7	bxc5	∞

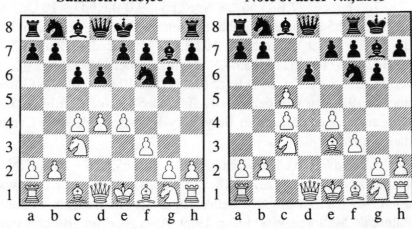

Diagram 57
Sämisch: 5.f3,c6

Diagram 58
Note 8: after 7...,dxc5

1. 7.Qd2,b5 8.0-0-0,Qa5 9.Kb1,Nbd7 with an unclear position; or 9.e5,b4! 10.exf6,bxc3 11.fxg7,cxd2+ 12.Bxd2,Qxd2+ 13.Rxd2,Rg8 with equality in Balashov-Byrne, Bugojno 1978; 7.c5,b5 8.cxd6,exd6 9.Bd3,Nbd7 10.Nge2,0-0 11.0-0 with equality in Bronstein-Podgaets, USSR 1974. The game Larsen-Byrne, Leningrad 1973 gave White a small advantage after: 7.c5,0-0 8.Nge2,Nbd7 9.Nc1,b5 10.Be2,dxc5 11.dxc5,Ne5 12.Qc2.

2. 8.e5,Nfd7 9.f4,0-0 10.Nf3,Nb6 11.b3,N8d7 12.a4,bxc4! 13.bxc4,c5! with an unclear position in Portisch-Kavalek, Wijk aan Zee 1975.

3. 5....c5 6.dxc5,dxc5 7.Qxd8+,Kxd8 8.Bg5,Nfd7 9.f4,Nc6 10.Nf3,Nd4 11.0-0-0 and White was slightly better; in Petrosian-Kyarner, Tallinn 1983; 5....b6 6.Bg5,Nbd7 7.Qd2,e5 8.Nge2 and White had an edge in Yusupov-Kyarner, Moscow 1981; 5....e5 6.d5,Nh5 7.Be3,Na6 (Slightly better for Black but still good for White is: 7...,f5 8.Qd2,f4 9.Bf2,Bf6 10.Nge2,Bh4 11.g3!) 8.Qd2,Qh4+ 9.g3,Nxg3 10.Qf2,Nxf1 11.Qxh4,Nxe3 12.Ke2!,Nxc4 13.Rc1 and White had the advantage in S. Garcia-Marosi, Zamardi 1980.

4. 9.Nxd5,Be6 10.Ne2,Bxd5 11.cxd5,Nbd7 12.Nc3,a6 with equality.

5. 10...,Re8 11.Nge2,Nbd7 12.Ng3,Qc7 13.Be2 with equality.

6. 12.Nf2,Qc7 13.Be2 equalizes.

7. 6...,c6 7.Bd3,a6 8.Nge2,b5 9.0-0,Nbd7 10.Qd2,e5 11.cxb5,axb5 is unclear, probably even; in Timman-Petrosian, Rio de Janeiro 1979 White tried: 10.b3,e5 11.d5,cxd5 12.cxd5,Nc5 13.Bc2,Nh5 14.Qd2,f5 15.b4,Nd7 with an unclear position; 6...,a6 7.Bd3,c5!? 8.dxc5,dxc5 9.Bxc5 (9.e5,Nfd7 10.f4,Nc6 11.Nf3,f6 is unclear.) 9...,Nc6 10.Nge2,Nd7 11.Bf2,Nde5 12.Nc1,Bh6 13.Nd5,e6 with an unclear position in Belyavsky-Kasparov, Moscow Candidates' match 1983.

8. 7.dxc5,dxc5 8.Qxd8,Rxd8 9.Bxc5,Nc6 10.Nd5,Nd7 11.Bex7,Nxe7 12.Nxe7+,Kf8 13.Nd5,Bxb2 14.Rb1,Bg7 was double-egded but slightly better for Black in Georgiu-Gelfand, Palma de Mallorca World Cup 1989. Also good for Black would have been (instead of 13.Nd5): 13.Nxc8,Bxb2 14.Rb1,Bc3+ 15.Kf2,Bd4+! 16.Ke1,Raxc8.

9. 12.Ng3,h5!? 13.Be2,h4 14.Nf1,Ne5 15.Bg5,h3 16.g4,Qa5 17.Ng3,b5 18.0-0,b4 19.Nd1,c4! with an unclear position in Timman-Speelman, London Candidates' match 1989.

10. 7.Qd2,c5 8.d5,e6 9.0-0-0,exd5 10.exd5,a6 (with the intention of playing next b5) leaves an unclear position.

11. 10...,c5?? 8.e5!,dxe5 9.dxe5,Nfd7 10.Be4 gives a winning advantage to White; 7...,Bb7 8.Nh3!?,c5 9.d5,e6 10.Qd2,exd5 11.cxd5,Re8 12.Nf2 is OK for White; not much better for Black is: 8...,e5 9.d5,Bc8 10.Ng1!

* * * *

CHAPTER 7

OPEN GAMES

ITALIAN AND HUNGARIAN GAMES AND TWO KNIGHTS' DEFENSE

These openings are related in that they all start with the moves **1.e4,e5 2.Nf3,Nc6 3.Bc4.** What complications will then arise depends mainly on Black's answer, but it may be safely said that if Black knows the existing theory, he will be able to reach equality. **3...,Bc5** is called the Giuoco Piano or Italian Opening and dates over 400 years back: it was already played by Greco. The center and the King-side are the two main places on the board where the action takes place. This opening is not devoid of tactical finesses. Both Bc4 and Bc5 aim at the weakest squares on the board respectively f7 and f2, only protected in the initial position by the King. The romantic 19th century gave us many spectacular games in this opening. Since then opening theory has been conducted on a more scientific basis. This means that there are today few surprises left for the initiated. If Black chooses **3...,Be7,** we call the opening the Hungarian Game after a correspondence match between Paris and Budapest in 1842-45. Black remains a bit passive, and often follows this up by playing **4...,d6** where it easily transposes into the Philidor Defense already discussed in Parts One and Two. The move **3...,Nf6** brings a new gambit element into the opening. The final verdict has not been issued: the bulk of modern theory about Black's chances comes from correspondence games, although it is also played at the master level. At the club level, the Italian Game is seen almost as often as the Spanish Opening (3.Bb5 instead of 3.Bc4), a clear indication that it is a logical opening in which good play is rewarded with at least a draw. The symmetry also appeals to many players allowing to reach equality early in the game. These three openings are quite essential for understanding the basic ideas underlying the Open Games (starting with 1.e4,e5). The beginner and occassional player who wants to advance rapidly will find great benefit in studying and trying out the main lines against a programmable computer and a few friends. The inherent tactics will be just as exciting today when they occur as they were for the romantics who loved to play the Italian 150 years ago!

1.e4,e5 2.Nf3,Nc6 3.Bc4

3	4	5	6	7	8	9	10	11	
...	c3[1]	d4[2]	cxd4	Nc3	0-0	d5[4]	Re1	Rxe4	
Bc5	Nf6	exd4	Bb4+	Nxe4	Bxc3![3]	Bf6!	Ne7	d6[5]	∓
...	...	...	...	Bd2	Nbxd2	exd5	Qb3	0-0	
...	...	...	...	Bxd2+[6]	d5!	Nxd5	Nce7	0-0[7]	=
...	d3	Nc3	Bg5	Bxf6	Nd5	c3	Ne3[10]		
...	Nf6	d6	h6[8]	Qxf6	Qd8	Ne7[9]	0-0[11]		=
...	d4	dxe5[13]	Bd5!?	Ng5	c3	Bb3	g3	h3	
Be7	d6[12]	dxe5	Bd6	Nh6	Ne7	Ng6	Qe7	Bd7[14]	±

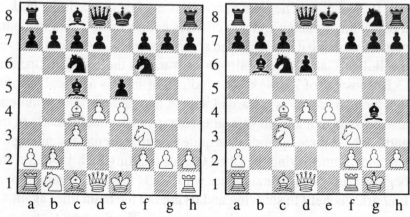

Diagram 59
Main line: after 5.d4

Diagram 60
Evans Gambit:
after 9...,Bg4!?

1. The Evans Gambit (named after a master mariner who invented it) occurs after: 4.b4,Bxb4 5.c3,Bc5 6.d4,exd4 7.0-0,d6 (If here 7...,dxc3 8.Bxf7+,Kxf7 9.Qd5+ and White is better; or 7...,d3 8.Ng5,Nh6 9.Nxf7! is also good for White.) 8.cxd4,Bb6 9.Nc3 (Not 9.h3,Nf6 10.Re1,h6 11.Ba3,0-0 in Mariotti-Gligoric, Venice 1971 and Black had the edge.) 9...,Bg4!? 10.Bb5,Kf8! 11.Be3,Nge7 with an even game slightly favouring Black. If Black plays 5...,Ba5 White does well after both: 6.d4,exd4 7.0-0,d6!? 8.cxd4,Bb6; or 7...,Nge7 8.cxd4,d5 9.exd5,Nxd5 10.Qb3.

2. 5.b4,Bb6 6.d3,d6 7.a4,a6 8.Ndb2,0-0 9.0-0,Ne7 10.Bb3,Ng6 11.Nc4,Ba7 12.Be3,Be6 13.Bxa7,Rxa7 14.Re1,Ra8 with equality or slightly better for White in Ljuboevic-Hjartarson, Linares 1989. If White plays instead 8.0-0,0-0 9.Bg5.h6 10.Bh4,g5 11.Bg3,Bg4 12.a5,Ba7 13.h3,Bh5 14.Nbd2,Bg6 15.Qb3,Nh5 16.Bh2,Nf4 as in Yudasin-Mikhail Tseitlin, Moscow 1989, Black should be favoured in this unclear position.

3. 8...,Nxc3 9.bxc3,d5!? 10.cxb4,dxc4 11.Re1+,Ne7 12.Bg5,f6 13.Qe2 and White is a bit better; if 9...,Bxc3? then 10.Ba3! and White has advantage.

4. 9.bxc3,d5! and Black is a bit better.

5. 12.Bg5,Bxg5 13.Nxg5,h6 (Not 13...,0-0? 14.Nxh7.) 14.Bb5+,Bd7 15.Qe2,Bxb5 16.Qxb5+,Qd7 17.Qe2,Kf8! 18.Nxf7,Kxf7 19.Re1,Ng8! with advantage for Black in Barcza-Portisch, Bucharest 1969.

6. 7...,Nxe4 8.Bxb4,Nxb4 9.Bxf7+,Kxf7 10.Qb3+,d5 11.Ne5+,Ke6! 12.Qxb4,c5 13.Qa3! and White has the edge.

7. 12.Rfe1,c6 13.a4,Qb6! with equality.

8. 6...,Na5 7.Bb3,Nxb3 8.axb3,Be6 9.Na4!?,h6 10.Bh4,Bg4 11.Nxc5,dxc5 12.h3 with a good game for White in Hug-Barle, Paris 1975; 6...,Be6!? 7.Nd5,Bxd5 8.Bxd5,h6! with equality.

9. 9...,a6 10.d4,Ba7 11.dxe5,dxe5 (Interesting is 11...,Nxe5.) 12.Qe2 with a slight advantage for White in Kotronias-J. Arnason, Reykjavic 1988.

10. 10.d4,Nxd5!? 11.dxc5,Nf4 12.0-0,Qf6 13.cxd6,cxd6 14.Bb5+,Ke7 15.Re1,h5! 16.Re3,h4 17.Qd2,Rh6 with an unclear

The Art of Mastering Chess

position in Tisdall-Hjartarson, Akureiri 1988.

11. 10...,c6?! 11.d4,exd4 12.Nxd4 with a small advantage for White in Barle-Ivkov, Bled-Portoroz 1979.

12. 4...,exd4 5.Nxd4,Nf6 6.Nc3,0-0 7.0-0,d6 8.Re1,Bg4!? 9.Be2 (Or 9.f3,Bd7.) 9...,Nxd4 10.Qxd4,Bxe2 11.Rxe2,Re8 with equality in Sariego-Djuric, Holguin 1989.

13. 5.d5,Nb8 6.Bd3,Nf6 7.c4,0-0 8.h3,Nbd7 9.Nc3,Ne8 10.0-0 with a good game for White; 5.Nc3,Nf6 6.h3,0-0 7.0-0 and White was OK in Tal-Miskolz 1963.

14. 12.Qe2,0-0-0 13.Nf3 and White had a small advantage in Bronstein-Reshevsky, Petropolis Interzonal Tournament 1973.

We come now to the most exciting part: The Two Knights' Defense in which Black allows White to threaten f7 immediately but where the sacrificed pawn gives him space and a few tempi.

			1.e4,e5	2.Nf3,Nc6	3.Bc4,Nf6	4.Ng5		
4	5	6	7	8	9	10	11	12
...	exd5	c3	Bf1!	Ne4[1]	Ng3	f3	cxd4	Bxb5+[4] ±/±
d5	Nd4	b5	Nxd5	Qh4[2]	Bg4[3]	e4	Bd6	
...	...	Bb5+[6]	dxc6	Be2	Nf3[7]	Ne5	d4[9]	Nxd3[10] ±/
...	Na5[5]	c6	bxc6	h6	e4	Bd6[8]	exd3e.p.	
...	Bxf7+	Bd5	Nf3	c3	0-0	d4	Bxc6	cxd6
Bc5	Ke7	Rf8[11]	Qe8[12]	Qh5	d6	exd4	bxc6	Bb6 ±
...	Nxf7[13]	Kf1	Nxh8	exd5	h3[14]	c3	Qa4+	Bb5
...	Bxf2+!	Qe7	d5!	Nd4	Bg3	Nf5	Bd7	Qc5[15] ∞

Diagram 61

Two Knights' Defense:

4.Ng5

Diagram 62

Note 1: after 10...,Nf6!

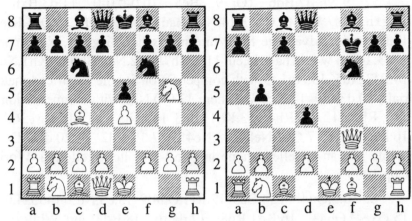

1. 8.cxd4,Qxg5 9.Bxb5+,Kd8 10.0-0 (If 10.Qf3,Bb7 11.Nc3,exd4 12.0-0,Qf4 13.Qh3,Nf6 14.Ne2,Qe5 with equality.) 10...,Bb7 11.Qf3,Rb8 12.Nc3,exd4 13.Ne4,Qe5 with an unclear position (Paoli); 8.Nxf7,Kxf7 9.cxd4,exd4 10.Bxb5 (If here 10.Qf3+,Nf6! 11.Qxa8,Bc5 12.Bb5+,Re8! and Black has advantage.) 10...,Qe7+ 11.Qe2,Qxe2+ 12.Bxe2,Nb4 13.Bc4+,Be6 14.Bxe6+,Kxe6 with compensation for the sacrificed material in Suetin-Ravinsky, Leningrad 1949; 8.h4,h6 9.Nxf7,Kxf7 10.cxd4,exd4 11.Bxb5,Bc5 is unclear but probably a bit better for Black.

2. 8...,Ne6 9.Bxb5+,Bd7 10.Bxd7+,Qxd7 11.0-0,Be7 12.d4,exd4 13.cxd4,0-0 14.Nbc3 and White is a shade better.

3. 9...,Bb7 10.cxd4,0-0-0 11.d3,Nf4 12.Bxf4,exf4 13.Qh5! and White has a very good game.

4. 12...,Kd8 13.0-0,exf3 14.Qb3!,Nf4 (If 14...,fxg2 15.Rf2,Nf4 16.Rxg2.) 15.Rxf3,Rb8 16.Rf4,Rxb5 17.Qxb5,Bxf4 18.Qd5+,Bd7 19.Nf1 and White had advantage in Estrin-Nilsen, correspondence game 1965/66.

5. 5...,Nxd5 6.d4!,Bb4+ (Not 6...,exd4 7.0-0,Be7 8.Nxf7!,Kxf7 9.Qf3+ with a winning attack.) 7.c3,Be7 8.Nxf7!,Kxf7 9.Qf3+,Ke6 10.Qe4 with a winning attack; 5...,b5 6.Bxb5 (Or 6.Bf1!,Nd4.) 6...,Qxd5 7.Bxc6+,Qxc6 8.Qf3 with equality or a slight edge for

White.

6. 6.d3,h6 7.Nf3,e4 8.Qe2,Nxc4 9.dxc4,Bc5 10.Nfd2,0-0 with compensation and advantage for Black.

7. 9.Nh3!?,Bd6 (Or 9...,Bc5 10.0-0,0-0 11.d3,Bxh3?! 12.gxh3,Qd7 13.Bf3,Qxh3 14.Nd2,Rad8 15.Bg2,Qf5 16.Qe1,Rfe8 17.Ne4 with advantage for White in Fischer-Bisguier, New York 1963; better would have been: 11...,Nb7!? 12.Nc3,Bb6 13.Kh1,Nc5 14.Bf3,Nd5 15.Ng1,f5 with compensation for the sacrificed material.) 10.d3,0-0 11.Nc3!? (If here 11.0-0,Nd5 with compensation.) 11...,Rb8 12.0-0,Rb4 13.Kh1!,Bh3 14.gxh3,Rh4 15.Rg1,Rxh3 16.Rg3!,Rh4 17.Qg1,Ne8?! 18.Ne4!,Bc7 19.Nd2!,e4 20.dxe4! and White had an excellent game in Short-Nikolic, Skellefteå World Cup 1989.

8. 10...,Qd4 11.f4,Bc5 12.Rf1,Qd8!? 13.c3,Nd5 14.Qa4,0-0 15.Qxe4!,Qh4+ 16.Kd1,Rd8 17.d4,f6 18.Bd3 and White had advantage in Nesterenko-Mosin, Moscow 1963.

9. 11.f4,Qc7 12.0-0,0-0 13.Nc3,Bf5!? 14.a3,Nd5 with compensation in Timman-Gligoric, Bad Lauterberg 1977.

10. 12...,Qc7 13.b3,0-0 14.Bb2,Nd5 15.Nc3,Nf4 16.Nxf4,Bxf4 17.g3,Rd8 18.Bd3,Re8+ 19.Ne2,Bg5 with compensation in Honfi-Tal, Sarajevo 1966.

11. 6...,d6 7.c3!,Qe8 8.d4,exd4 9.cxd4 (If here 9.Bxc6!?,Qxc6 10.0-0,dxc4 11.Nc3 and White was OK in Paoli-Shneider 1976.) 9...,Nxd4 10.Nc3,Qh5 11.Qd3,Rf8 (Karpov-Belyavsky, Moscow 1983.) 12.e5!,dxe5 13.0-0 is unclear but likely better for White (Estrin).

12. 7...,d6 8.c3,Bg4 9.Bc6,bxc6 10.d4,Bb6 11.Qd3 and White is OK.

13. 5.d4 (If 5.b4 then 5...,d5! 6.exd5,Nb4 with equality.) 5...,d5! (Not 5...,exd4 6.Nxf7,Qe7 7.Nxh8 and White has advantage.) 6.Bxd5 (Or 6.exd5,Nxd4 7.c3,Nf5 with equality; or 6.dxc5,dxc4 7.Qxd8+,Nxd8 with equality.) 6...,Nxd4! 7.Nxf7,Qe7 8.Nxh8,Bg4 9.f3,Nxd5 10.fxg4 (If 10.exd5,Bf5!) 10...,Nb4! 11.Na3,Qh4+ 12.g3,Qh3 13.c3,Qxg2 and White resigned in Lihtanen-Ostroverkhov, correspondence 1968/69.

14. 9.c3,Bg4 10.Qa4+,Nd7 11.Kxf2,Qh4+! is excellent for Black; 9.d6,cxd6 10.c3,Bg4 with compensation.

15. 13.Bxd7+,Nxd7 14.d4,Nxd4! with compensation in Polser-Meier, correspondence 1977.

Since accepting Black's challenge is so dangerous, White indeed also often declines to commit himself to the above complications. This is either done by opening up the position by 4.d4 or by defending pawn e4 with the quiet 4.d3.

The Scotch Opening which occurs after **1.e4,e5 2.Nf3,Nc6 3.d4,exd4** has a lot in common with the Italian Game if followed by **4.Bc4**. The Vienna Opening **1.e4,e5 2.Nc3** easily can transpose into these two openings or even the already discussed King's Gambit. We shall cover them in the next few pages. We shall then proceed to a few more of the Half-Open and Closed Openings.

		1.e4,e5	2.Nf3,Nc6	3.d4,exd4				
4	**5**	**6**	**7**	**8**	**9**	**10**	**11**	
c3[1]	exd5	cxd4	Nc3	Be2	Bd2	bxc3	Qxd2	
d5[2]	Qxd5	Bb4+[3]	Nf6	Ne4	Bxc3	Nxd2	0-0[4]	=
Nxd4	Nc3	Nxc6	Bd3	exd5[5]	0-0	Bg5	Qf3[7]	
Nf6	Bb4	bxc6	d5	cxd5	0-0	Be6[6]	Be7[8]	=
...	Nc6	e5	Qe2	c4[10]	Nd2	Nf3	a3	
...	bxc6	Qe7[9]	Nd5	Ba6	Nb4[11]	c5	Nc6	=
...	Be3[12]	c3[14]	Nc2[15]	Nd2	Bxc5	Ne3	b3	
Bc5	Qf6[13]	Nge7	b6	Qg6	bxc5	Rb8	0-0[16]	=

Diagram 63
Main line: 4.c3

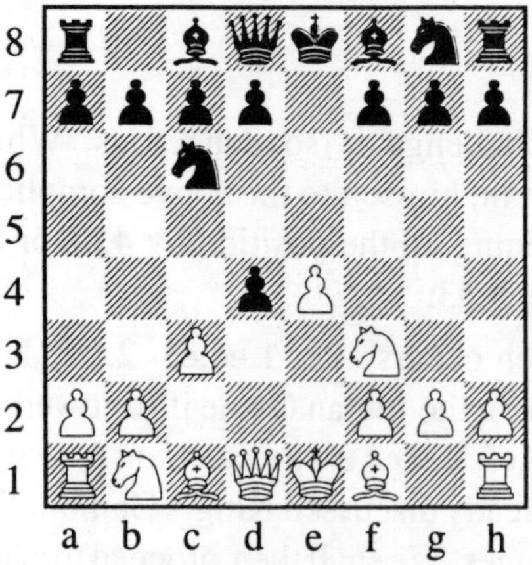

Diagram 64
Danish Gambit (note 2)
5.Bc4

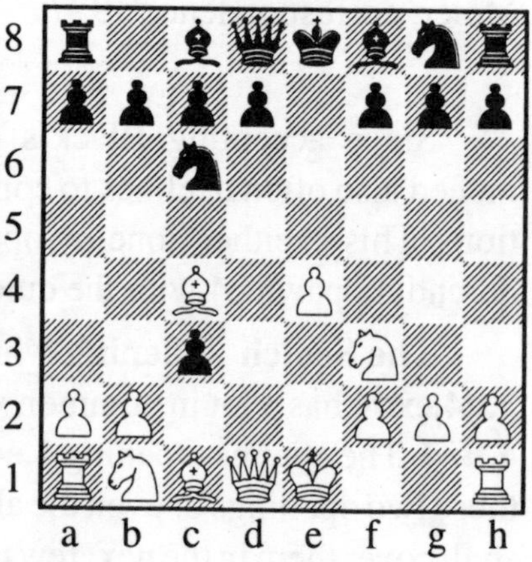

1. 4.Bc4,Bc5 (4...,Bb4 5.c3,dxc3 6.0-0 with compensation for the sascrificed material; White has the advantage.) 5.c3,d3!? 4.b4,Bb6 7.Qb3,Qf6 8.0-0 is unclear.

2. <u>4...,dxc3</u> 5.Bc4 (The Danish Gambit; probably better is 5.Nxc3!?) 5...,Nf6 (Or 5...,cxb2 6.Bxb2,Bb4+ 7.Nc3,Nf6 8.e5,d5! with terrible, often violent complications especially for Black in a difficult and unclear position.) 6.Nxc3,Bb4 7.0-0,Bxc3 8.bxc3,d6 9.e5,Nxe5 (If 9...,dxe5 10.Ng5,Be6!? 11.Bxe6,fxe6 12.Qb3,Qd5 12.Nxe6,Qxb3 14.axb3 with equality.) 10.Nxe5,dxe5 11.Qb3,Qe7 is unclear; <u>4...,d3</u> 5.Bxd3,d6 6.0-0,Nf6 7.Nbd2,Be7 8.Nd4,0-0 9.f4,Ne5 10.fxe5,dxe5 11.N2f3,exd4 12.cxd4 and White is better (Ravinsky).

3. 6...,Bg4!? 7.Be2,Bb4+ 8.Nc3,Bxf3 9.Bxf3,Qc4! 10.Qb3 (10.Be3,Bxc3+ 11.bxc3,Qxc3+ 12.Kf1,Qc4+ 13.Kg1,Nge7 14.Rc1,Qa2 15.Ra1 and draw agreed in Marshall-Capablanca, Lake Hopatcong 1926.) 10...,Qxb3 11.axb3,Nge7 12.0-0,a6 13.Ra4,Bd6 with equality in Ljuboevic-Ree, Amsterdam 1972.

4. 12.0-0,Bf5! with equality.

5. 8.e5?!,Ng4 9.0-0,0-0 10.Bf4,f6! with at least equality for Black but probably a bit of advantage.

6. <u>10...,c6</u> 11.Qf3 (11.Ne2,Re8 12.Nd4,Qd6 13.Bh4,Ne4

14.c3,Bc5   15.f3,Qh6 with equality in Nimzovitsch-Teichmann, Hamburg 1910; 11.Na4!?,Be7 12.Bh4,Qc7 is unclear according to Khavsky.) 11...,Be7   12.Rae1,h6   13.Bxh6!?,gxh6   14.Qe3,d4 15.Qh6,Qd6! is unclear, an analysis by Euwe; 10...,Be7 11.Bxf6,Bxf6 12.Qh5!,g6 13.Qxd5,Qxd5 14.Nxd5,Bxb2 15.Rab1 and White has a small advantage in Lutikov-Tarve, Pyarnu 1971.

7.   11.Nb5!?,c5   12.a3,Ba5   13.b4,cxb4   14.Qe1 is unclear, probably a bit better for White (Bastrikov).

8.   12.Rae1,Rb8 13.Nd1,c5 14.Bf5,Rb6 with equality.

9. 6...,Nd5 7.Bd3,Bc5 8.Qg4!,g6 9.Bh6,d6 10.Qa4 and White has an edge (Estrin); 6...,Ne4 7.Qf3,Qh4 8.g3,Ng5 9.Qe2 and White is doing OK.

10.   8.h4!?,d6   9.c4,Nb6   10.exd6,cxd6   11.Bg5,Qxe2+ 12.Bxe2,Be6 13.Nd2,h6 14.Bf4,Be7 15.0-0,0-0 and White was just a bit better in vander Wiel-van der Sterren, Budel 1987; 8...,f6!? 9.c4,Ba6   10.Rh3!?,fxe5   11.Ra3,Nb4   12.Nc3,Qxh4 13.g3,Qd4 14.Rxa6,Nxa6 15.Bf4,0-0-0 16.Be3,Qd6 is unclear in van der Wiel-Timman, Amsterdam 1987.

11.   9...,Nf4 10.Qe4,Ng6 11.f4,0-0-0 12.g3,d5 13.cxd5,Bxf1 14.Rxf1,cxd5   15.Qa4 and White is a bit better (Lepeshkin).

12.   5.Nb3,Bb6   6.a4,a6   (6...,a5?!   7.Nc3,d6   8.Nd5,Ba7 9.Bb5,Bd7 10.0-0,Ne5 11.Bd2!,Nf6 12.Ba5,Nxd5 13.exd5 and White was better in van der Wiel-Gulko, Amsterdam 1987.) 7.Nc3,Nf6 (If 7...,Qf6   8.Qe2,Nge7   9.Nd5,Nxd5   10.exd5,Ne7 11.a5,Ba7 12.h4,h6 13.Ra4!,0-0 14.g4 with a dangerous attack for White.) 8.Bg5,d6 9.Qe2,h6 10.Bh4,Nd4 11.Nxd4,Bxd4 with equality.

13. 5...,Bxd4?! 6.Bxd4,Nf6 7.Nc3,0-0 8.Bxf6!?,Qxf6 9.Qd2 (with the intention of playing 0-0-0) 9...,d5!? 10.exd5,Re8 11.Be2,Nd4 12.0-0 with a slightly better game for White in Sveshnikov-B. Ivanovic, Yugoslavia 1987; 5...,Bb6 6.Nc3,Nge7 7.g3 (Or 7.Bc4.) 7...,0-0 (7...,d5!?)   8.Bg2,d6   9.0-0,Nxd4 10.Bxd4,Nc6   (10...,Bxd4 11.Qxd4,Bd7 with the idea Qc8 and White has a small advantage, analysis by Sveshnikov.) 11.Bxb6,axb6 12.Nd5,Be6 13.c4 and White is a bit better in Sveshnikov-Kharitonov, Sochi 1987.

14. 6.Nb5?!,Bxe3 7.fxe3,Qh4! 8.g3,Qxe4 9.Nc7+,Kd8 10.Nxa8,Qxh1 11.Qd6,Nf6 12.Nc3,Qf3 and Black has a slight advantage (Keres).

15. 7.g3,d5! 8.Bg2,dxe5 9.Nb5,Bxe3 10.Nc7+,Kf8 11.0-0,Rb8 12.fxe5,Qxe5 13.Qb3,f5 14.Nb5 and a draw was agreed in Sveshnikov-Geller, Sochi 1976.

16. Blackburn-Lasker, St. Petersburg 1914.

VIENNA GAME

A close cousin and an equally neglected opening with many interesting twists in which it can transpose is the Bishop's Opening which occurs after 1.e4,e5 2.Bc4.

1.e4,e5 2.Nc3							
2	3	4	5	6	7	8	9
...	f4	fxe5	Nf3[1]	d4[2]	Bd3	exf5e.p.	0-0
Nf6	d5!	Nxe4	Be7!	0-0	f5!	Bf6	Nc6 =
...	Bc4	Qh5	Bb3[3]	Nb5[5]	Qf3	Qd5	Nxc7+
...	Nxe4	Nd6	Nc6[4]	g6	f5[6]	Qe7	Kd8[7] ∞
...	g3	exd5	Bg2	bxc3	Nf3	0-0	d3[10]
...	d5!?[8]	Nxd5	Nc3[9]	Bd6	0-0	Nd7	Rb8 =
...	Bc4[12]	d3	Bg5	Bf6	bxc3	Ne2	0-0 =
Nc6[11]	Nf6	Bb4	h6	Bc3	Qf6	d6	g5

Diagram 65

Main line: after 3...,d5!

Diagram 66

Note 7: after 12.h4

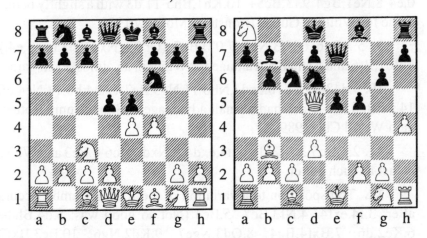

1. <u>5.Qf3,f5!?</u> 6.d3,Nc3 7.bxc3,d4 8.Qg3 (8.Bd2?!,dxc3 9.Bxc3,Bb4! with advantage for Black.) 8...,Nc6 9.Be2,Be6 10.Bf3,Qd7 11.Ne2,0-0-0 12.0-0,Bc5 with initiative for Black in Vorotnikov-Kapengut, USSR 1975; <u>5.d3</u>,Qh4+ (Unclear is 5...,Nxc3!? 6.bxc3,d4!) 6.g3,Nxg3 7.Nf3,Qh5 8.Nxd5,Bg4!? 9.Bg2,Nh1 10.Nxc7+,Kd7 11.Nxa8,Nc6 12.Be3 (with the idea of playing d4.) with initiative and a better game for White.

2. 6.Qe2!?,f5! 7.d3,Nc5 8.g3,d4 9.Nd1,Ne6 10.Bg2,0-0 remains unclear.

3. 6.Qxe5+,Qe7 6.Qxe7+,Bxe7 7.Bb3,Nf5! 8.Nd5,Bd8 with equality in Suttles-Tarjan, Venice 1974.

4. 5...,Be7?! 6.Nf3,0-0 7.h4! (with the idea 8.Ng5) is better for White.

5. 6.Nf3,Be7 7.d3 (Or 7.Nxe5,0-0! is unclear.) 7...,g6 8.Qh3,Nf5 is unclear probably even.

6. 7...,Nf5 8.Qd5,Nh6 9.d4,d6 10.Bxh6,Be6 11.Bg5!? is unclear but likely slightly better for White.

7. 10.Nxa8,b6 11.d3 (11.Nxb6,axb6 12.Qf3,Bb7 13.d3,Nd4 14.Qh3,f4 with a better game for Black and compensation for the sacrificed material.) 11...,Bb7 12.h4 is unclear.

8. <u>3...,Bc5</u> 4.Bg2,d6 5.Nf3 (5.Nge2,Nc6 6.0-0,h5!? in

Augustin-Kan, Moscow 1977.) 5...,Nc6 6.d3,Bg4 7.Na4,Nd7 8.h3,Bh5 with equality; 3...,c6 4.Bg2,d5 5.exd5,cxd5 6.Nf3,Nc6 7.0-0,e4 8.Ne1,Bg4 9.f3,Bc5+ 10.Kh1,Bh5 11.d3 with a slightly better game for White in Gulko-Bronstein, Moscow 1978.

9. 5...,Be6 6.Nf3,Nc6 7.0-0,Be7 (Or 7...,Nxc3!? 8.bxc3,e4.) 8.Re1,Bf6 and a small advantage for White in an almost even game.

10. 9.d4?!,exd4 10.cxd4,Nb6 11.Ng5,Be7 12.h4,h6 13.Ne4,c6 14.a4,Be6 and Black had a small advantage in Short-Nunn, Rotterdam World Cup 1989.

11. 2...,Bc5 3.Nf3,d6 4.d4,exd4 5.Nxd4,Nc6 6.Be3 and White is just a touch better.

12. Transposition to a variation of the King's Gambit occurs after: 3.f4,exf4 4.Nf3,Be7 5.Bc4 (Not so good was: 5.d4,Bh4+ 6.Ke2,d6 7.Bxf4,Bg4 8.Qd3,Nge7 9.Kd2,Ng6 10.Be3,Bxf3 11.gxf3,Bg5!? with a slight advantage for White in Hector-Feingold, Budapest 1989.) 5...,d6 6.d4,Bh4+ 7.Kf1,Bg4 8.Bxf4,Nge7 is unclear but probably just a bit better for Black in Hector-Skembris, Genova 1989.

PIRC-UFIMTSEV DEFENSE

This opening/defense was already played in the 19th century, but thought to be incorrect. That is why most opening books until the 1930s listed them under the irregular openings. Its parentage is therefore mixed. In general, the Yugoslav GM Pirc has won out in the West, while in the Soviet block the Russian master Ufimtsev played it consistently and was thus seen as its main proponent. In this book, however, we let them share the honours. Only since 1960 have universally respected GMs started to play it. Its ideas are now much better understood. It has a lot in common with the Modern Defense (which will be covered in this book and which occurs after 1.e4,g6 2.d4,d6 or 2...,Bg7.). The Soviets considered it part of the Ufimtsev system. The aim of Black is ideally to undermine or even blow up White's center and to establish the effectiveness and latent power of the so-called 'fianchettoed' Bishop (i.e. placed on the long diagonal g7-a1). As in most defenses that tie in with the Hypermodern ideas,

White is initially allowed superiority in space, which he has to prove and maintain.

	1.e4,d6 2.d4,Nf6 3.Nc3,g6					
4	**5**	**6**	**7**	**8**	**9**	**10**
f3	Be3	Qd2	Bd3[2]	Nge2	a4	0-0
Bg7	c6[1]	b5	Nbd7	a6	Bb7	0-0 ∞
Bg5	Qd2[4]	f4	Nf3	Bd3	f5	Ne2
Bg7[3]	c6	0-0	b5	Bg4[5]	b4	Nbd7 ∞
g3	Bg2	Nge2	0-0[6]	h3	Be3[7]	g4
Bg7	0-0	e5	Nbd7	Re8	Qe7	exd4[8] ±
Bc4[9]	Qe2	e5	Nf3	Bb3	h3	
Bg7	Nc6[10]	Nd7[11]	Nb6	0-0	Na5 ±	

<table>
</table>

Diagram 67

Main line Pirc: after 6...,b5

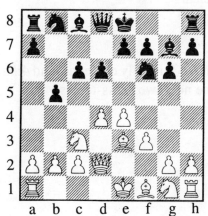

Diagram 68

Note 8: after 11.Bxd4!

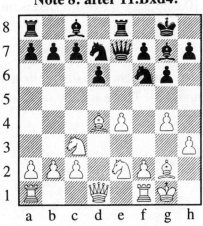

1. 5...,Nc6 6.h4,a6 7.Qd2,b5 8.a4! with a slightly better game for White.

2. 7.0-0-0,Qa5 8.Kb1,Nbd7 9.Bh6,Bxh6 10.Qxh6,Nb6 is unclear.

3. 4...,c6!? 5.Qd2,Bg7 6.Bh6,Bxh6 7.Qxh6,Qa5 8.Bd3,Na6 9.Nge2,Nb4 10.0-0,Qh5 11.Qd2,Nxd3 12.cxd3,0-0 13.f4 with a good game for White in van der Wiel-Ftacnik, Haninge 1989.

4. 5.e5!?,dxe5 6.dxe5,Qxd1?! 7.Rd1,Ng4?! 8.h3!,f6 9.Bc1,Nxe5 10.Nd5 and White had advantage in Kotkov-Korsunsky, Moscow 1989.

5. 8...,Nbd7 9.0-0,Nb6 10.e5,b4 11.Ne2,Nfd5 12.f5! and White is doing fine in Soltis-Botteril, Graz 1972.

6. 7.h3,Nc6 8.Be3,exd4 9.Nxd4,Bd7 10.0-0,Re8 11.Re1,Qc8 12.Kh2,Re5!? is unclear (Voigt-Zaichik, Berlin 1989) 13.g4,Bxg4 14.hxg4,Nxg4+ 15.Kg1,Nxe3 16.fxe3 with compensation for the sacrificed material (analysis Zaichik).

7. 9.Re1,exd4!? 10.Nxd4,Nc5 remains unclear.

8. 11.Bxd4!,Nc5 12.Ng3 is good for White.

9. 4.Be2,Bg7 5.g4,Na6 6.g5,Nd7 7.h4,c5 8.d5,c4 is unclear; 4.Nf3,Bg7 5.h3,0-0 6.Be3,c6 7.a4,a5 with equality.

10. 5...,c6 6.Bb3,0-0 7.Nf3,a5 8.a4,Na6 9.h3 with a small advantage for White.

11. 6...,Nxd4 7.exf6,Nxe2 8.fxg6,Rg8 9.Ngxe2,Rxg7 10.Bh6,Rg8 11.0-0-0,Be6 is unclear.

Other choices for White at move 4 mainly center around 4.Nf3 and 4.f4. These will be used in the next two cross-tables.

1.e4,d6 2.d4,Nf6 3.Nc3,g6 4.Nf3,Bg7 5.Be2,0-0 6.0-0

6	7	8	9	10	11	12
...	d5	h3	a4	Re1	Bf1	Nd2 ±
Nc6[1]	Nb8	c6[2]	a5	Na6	Qb6	
...	h3[3]	Be3[4]	a4	Qd2	dxe5	Rfd1 ±
c6	Nbd7	Qc7	a5	e5	dxe5	
...	h3[5]	Bxf3	Ne2	c3	b3!?	d5[8] ±/±
Bg4	Bxf3	Nc6	e5	Nd7[6]	Nb6?![7]	
...	Be3	Qd2	d5[9]	Rad1	Ne1	Nd3! ±
...	Nc6	e5	Ne7	Bd7[10]	b5[11]	

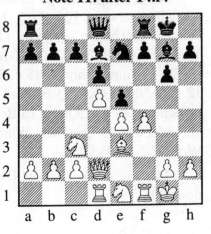

Diagram 69
Third line: after 7.h3

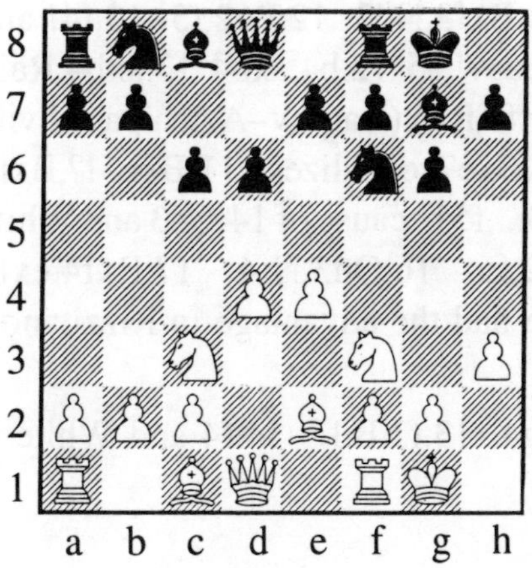

Diagram 70
Note 11: after 14.f4

229

1. 6...,c5 7.d5,Na6 8.Bf4,Nc7 9.a4,b6 10.Re1 and White is just a bit better.

2. 8...,e5 9.dxe6 e.p.,Bxe6 10.Re1,Nc6 11.Bf4,h6 12.Qd2 and White has a small advantage.

3. <u>7.a4</u>,a5 8.h3,Na6 9.Be3,Nb4 is unclear; <u>7.Re1!?</u>,Qc7 8.Bf4,Nbd7 9.e5,Nh5 10.exd6,exd6 11.Be3 and White has the edge.

4. <u>8.Bg5</u>,Nc6 9.Be3,e5 equalizes; <u>8.Bf4</u>,Nh5 9.Be3,e5 with an even game; <u>8.a4!?</u>,e5 9.dxe5,dxe5 10.Be3 which is OK for White.

5. <u>7.Bg5</u>,Nc6 8.Qd2,Nd7 9.Nd5!? is unclear; <u>7.Be3</u>,Nc6 8.Qd3?! (Better is 8.Nd2!?,Bxe2 9.Qxe2,e5 10.d5,Ne7 and White is a bit better.) 8...,e5 9.d5,Ne7 (Or 9...,Nb4 10.Qd2,a5 11.h3,Bd7 12.Bg5 and White has an edge.) 10.h3,Bc8 11.Nd2,Nd7 12.Nc4,f5! 13.f4,exf4 14.Rxf4,g5 with an unclear position in Gligoric - Nunn, Vienna 1980.

6. 10...,Re8 11.d5! and White has a slight advantage.

7. 11...,Qe7!? with the idea of playing Rae8 is quite OK for White (Ivanchuk).

8. 12.d5,Ne7 13.c4,f5 14.Nc3,Nd7 15.Rb1,a5 16.a3,Nf6 17.b4,axb4 18.axb4,fxe4 19.Nxe4,Nxe4 20.Bxe4,Nf5 21.g3! and White was better in Ivanchuk - Timman, Linares 1989.

9. 9.dxe5,dxe5 10.Rad1,Qc8 (If 10...,Qxd2 11.Rxd2 White has an edge.) 11.Qc1,Rd8 12.Rxd8+,Qxd8 13.Rd1 and White is doing OK.

10. <u>10...,Nd7</u> 11.Ng5!,Bxe2 12.Nxe2,h6 13.Nh3 and White has a small advantage; <u>10...,Bxf3</u> 11.Bxf3,Nd7 12.Be2,f5 13.f4! and White is a bit better; <u>10...,b5!?</u> 11.a3?!,a5 12.b4,axb4 13.axb4,Ra3! 14.Bg5!,Rxc3 15.Bxf6,Bxf3 16.Bxf3,Ra3 (Karpov - Azmaiparashvili, USSR Championship 1983.) 17.Bxe7 equalizes; 11.Bxb5!?,Bxf3 12.gxf3,Nh5 13.Kh1,Qc8 (Not 13...,f5 because of 14.Qd3 and White is better.) 14.Rg1,Qh3 15.Be2,f5 16.Qd3,Nf4 17.Bxf4,exf4 18.Nb5,fxe4 19.Qxe4 and White had the advantage in Rizzitano - Wolff, USA 1983.

11. 11...,Ng4 12.Bxg4,Bxg4 13.f3,Bd7 14.f4 and White is doing OK.

			1.e4,d6 2.d4,Nf6 3.Nc3,g6 4.f4,Bg7 5.Nf3[1]				

5	6	7	8	9	10	11	12
...	dxc5	Bd3	Qe2	Be3	0-0[4]	h3	Qxf3
c5	Qa5	Qxc5	0-0[2]	Qa5[3]	Bg4	Bxf3	Nc6 =
...	Bb5+	e5[5]	e6[6]	exf7+	Nxb5	Nc3	Nxd4
...	Bd7	Ng4	Bxb5	Kd7	Qa5+	cxd4	h5!?[7] ∞/±
...	e5[8]	dxe5	Kxd1	Bc4	Be3	Rf1	Be2
0-0	dxe5[9]	Qxd1+	Nh5	Nc6	Bg4	Na5	f6[10] =
...	Bd3	e5[12]	dxe5[13]	Bd2	Qe2	Be4	
...	Nc6[11]	dxe5	Nd5	Nb6	Nb4	f5!? ∞	

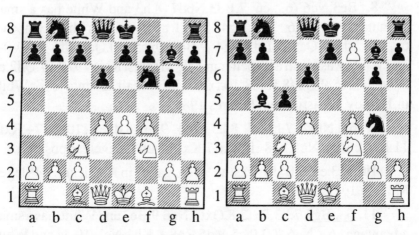

Diagram 71	**Diagram 72**
Main line: after 5.Nf3	**Second line: after 9.exf7+**

1. 5.e5,Nfd7 6.Nf3,c5 7.exd6,0-0 8.dxc5,Qa5 9.Be2,Bxc3+ 10.bxc3,Qxc3+ 11.Bd2,Qc5 12.dxe7,Re8 with an unclear position in Ivanovic - M. Gurevic, Lucerne, Team World Championship 1989.

2. 8...,Bg4 9.Be3,Qa5 10.0-0,0-0 11.h3,Bxf3 12.Qxf3,Nc6 13.a3,Nd7 14.Bd2,Qb6+ 15.Kh1,Nc5 16.Rab1,Nxd3 17.cxd3,f5 sharp, unclear and probably even position in Sax - Seirawan, Skellefteå World Cup 1989; 17...,e6 18.f5,exf5 19.exf5,Nd4 20.Qg3,Nxf5 21.Rxf5,gxf5 22.Nd5,f4 was unclear in Tolnai - M. Gurevic, Lucerne, Team World Championship 1989.

3. 9...,Qc7 10.0-0,Nbd7 (If 10...,Bg4 then 11.Qe1!? gives a slight edge to White.) 11.Kh1 and White is a bit better.

4. 10.h3!?,e5 11.0-0-0!?,Nbd7 12.g4,d5 13.exd5,e4 14.Ne4,Qa2 15.Nc3,Qa1+ 16.Kd2,Qxb2 17.Bd4,Qb4 18.Rb1,Qa5 19.Ra1,Qc7 20.Ne5 and White is better and has compensation for the sacrificed material in Judit Polgar - Azmaiparashvili, Amsterdam 1989.

5. 7.Bxd7+,Nfxd7 8.d5 and White has a small advantage.

6. 8.h3,cxd4 9.Qxd4 is unclear.

7. 13.h3,Nc6 14.Ne2,Nh6 15.Be3,Raf8 (15...,h4 16.0-0,Qf5 17.Qd2,Nxf7 18.Nd5,e6 19.Ndc3,Rac8 10.a4,Ke7 21.Rf2! and White had the advantage in Dolmatov - Lein, New York 1989.) 16.Qd3,Nf5 17.Bf2,Rxf7 18.0-0-0,h4 19.Kb1,Rc8 20.Qe4!,b6 21.a3,Nd8 22.Rhe1 and White had a slight edge in Belyavsky - Tal, Brussels World Cup 1988.

8. Be3,Nc6 (6...,c6 7.Bd3,Nbd7 8.h3 and White has a small advantage; 6...,Na6 7.e5,Ng4 8.Bg1 and White is slightly ahead; 6...,c5 7.dxc5,Qa5 8.Bd3,Ng4 9.Bd2,Qxc5 10.Qe2,Nf6 11.0-0-0 and White was again a bit better in Tal - Mednis, Riga 1979.) 7.Qd2,e5 8.dxe5,dxe5 9.Qxd8,Rxd8 10.fxe5 with a small advantage for White in Karpov - Kristiansen, Linares 1981.

9. 6...,Nfd7 7.h4,c5 8.h5,cxd4 9.hxg6,dxc3 10.gxf7+,Rxf7 11.Bc4,e6 12.Ng5,Nf8 13.Nxf7,Kxf7 with an unclear position.

10. 13.exf6,Bxf6 was an even game in Unzicker - Pfleger, Munich 1979.

11. 6...,Bg4 7.h3,Bxf3 8.Qxf3,Nc6 9.Be3 and White has a small advantage; 6...,Na6 7.0-0,c5 8.d5,Rb8 9.Kh1,Nc7 10.a4 and White has a small edge.

12. 7.0-0,Bg4 (7...,e5 8.dxe5,dxe5 9.f5 and White is a bit better.) 8.e5,dxe5 9.dxe5,Nd5 10.h3 with a slight advantage for White.

13. 8.fxe5!?,Nd5 (8...,Nh5!? 9.Be3,Bg4 10.Be2,f6 is an even game.) 9.Nxd5,Qxd5 10.c3,Be6 11.0-0,Rad8 12.Bf4!,Qd7 13.Qe1 and White had a slightly better game in Ehlvest - Anand, Reggio Emilia 1988/89.

We come now to two of the main systems at the disposal of respectively White and Black in the Closed Openings: the **Queen's Gambit** which occurs after **1.d4,d5 2.c4**, and the **Slav Defense** which is a division or logical outflow of this set-up: **1.d4,d5 2.c4,c6**. It is impossible to understand the Closed Openings adequately if not some time is spent in understanding the ramifications. Basically Black tries to equalise, i.e. to offset the tempo advantage that White gets in the opening by closely matching the moves and countering the implied threats of White's moves. This classic opening is the oldest of all the closed openings. Although it seems that most of the systems of the Queen's Gambit theoretically have been resolved, tournament practice shows that continually new problems crop up. We shall cover in this book the main lines of the Queen's Gambit and the Queen's Gambit Accepted. Black traditionally played (after 2...,e6 3.Nc3) first **3...,Nf6** but nowadays most GMs accept that **3...,Be7** leaves White less choice, e.g. the immediate **4.Bg5** pinning the Knight is temporarily impossible.

QUEEN'S GAMBIT DECLINED

1.d4,d5 2.c4,e6 3.Nc3								

3	**4**	**5**	**6**	**7**	**8**	**9**	**10**	**11**
...	cxd5[1]	Bg5	e3	Bd3	Qc2[3]	Nf3	0-0[5]	Rab1
Nf6	exd5	Be7	0-0[2]	Nbd7	Re8	Nf8[4]	c6	Bd6[6] ∞
...	...	...	...	...	...	Nge2	0-0-0!?[7]	Kb1 ±
						Nf8	Be6	
...	cxd5	Bf4	e3	g4	h4!?	h5	Rb1	f3
Be7	exd5	c6	Bf5	Be6	Nd7	Qb6	Ngf6	h6 ±
...	...	...	Qc2	e3	Qd2	f3	Bh6!	exd4 ±/±
			g6	Bf5	Nf6	c5	cxd4	

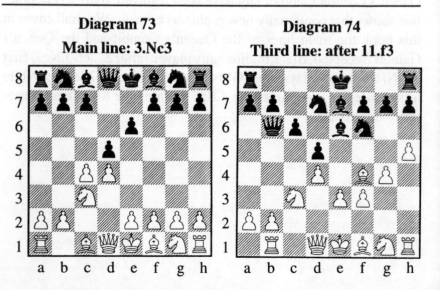

Diagram 73
Main line: 3.Nc3

Diagram 74
Third line: after 11.f3

1. 4.Nf3,c6 5.cxd5,exd5 6.Bg5,Be7 7.Qc2,g6 8.e4,dxe4
9.Bxf6,Bxf6 10.Qxe4+,Kf8! 11.Bc4,Kg7 12.0-0,Re8 13.Qf4,Be6
14.Bxe6,Rxe6 15.Rad1,Qd6 and a draw was agreed in Georgadze-
Oll, Odessa USSR Championship 1989; 7...,Na6 8.e3 (8.a3,g6
9.e4!?,Nxe4?! 10.Nxe4,Bf5 11.Bxa6,Bxe4 12.Qc3! and White was
better in Lautier-Geller, Sochi 1989; 9...,Nc7!? would be an improve-
ment for Black, though White still keeps a small edge.) 8..,Nb4
9.Qd1,Bf5 10.Rc1,a5 11.Be2,0-0 12.0-0,Nd7 13.Bxe7,Qxe7
14.Qb3,Rfb8 15.Na4,Na6 16.Bxa6,Rxa6 17.Nc5 and White had a
small edge in Karpov-Yusupov, Rotterdam World Cup 1989.

2. 6...,c6 7.Bd3,Nbd7 8.Nf3,0-0 9.Qc2,Re8 10.0-0 (Here
10.h3,Nf8 11.Bf4,Ng6 12.Bh2,Bd6 13.Bxd6,Qxd6 14.0-0,Qe7
15.Rab1,Ne4 16.Rfe1,Qf6 was unclear but White had a small
advantage in the rest of the game Gavrikov-Inkev, Palma de Mallorca
1989.) 10...,Nf8 11.h3,g6 12.Bh6,Nh5 13.Rab1,Ng7 14.b4,a6
15.Bxg7,Kxg7 16.Na4,Bd6 17.Nc5,Qf6 18.Rfc1,Ne6 19.Qd1,h6
20.a4,Re7 with an unclear position but a slight edge for Black in
Karpov-Short, Lucerne Team World Championship 1989.

3. 8.Nge2,Re8 9.0-0,c6 10.a3,a5!? 11.Rb1,Nf8 12.b4,axb4
13.axb4,b5!? 14.Qc2,Be6!? 15.Nf4,N6d7 16.Nxe6,fxe6
17.Bxe7,Qxe7 18.e4,Nb6 19.Rfe1 (Belyavsky recommends:
19.f4!?,Nc4 20.Bxc4,dxc4! 21.d5,Rad8 which is unclear.) 19...,Qf6
20.e5,Qh4 (Speelman - Belyavsky, Barcelona World Cup 1989.)
21.Ne2,Nc4 22.Ra1,Qe7 23.Qc3 with the idea Reb1 and then the
manoeuvre Nc1-b3-c5 (analysis of Belyavsky.)

4. 9...,c5?! 10.dxc5,Nxc5 11.Bb5,Bd7 12.Bxd7,Qxd7
13.Rd1,Nce4 14.Nxe4,Nxe4 15.Qxe4,Bxg5 16.Qxd5,Qxd5
17.Rxd5,Bf6 18.Ke2 and White was better in Gruenberg - Lputian,
Moscow World Cup 1989.

5. 10.h3,c6 11.0-0-0,a5 12.g4,a4! 13.Nxa4,Qa5 14.Bxf6,Bxf6
15.b3,b5 with an even game in Georgadze - Spassky, USSR 1981.

6. 11...,a5 12.a3,Bg4 13.Nd2,Bh5 14.b4 and White is slightly
ahead; 11...,Ng6 12.Bxf6!,Bxf6 13.b4,Be7 14.b5 with a slight edge
for White; 11...,Bd6!? 12.Rfe1 (If here 12.b4,Bg4! 13.Nd2,Bd7 is
unclear.) 12...,Bg4 13.Nd2,Ng6 14.e4,Bf4! was unclear in Sveshnikov
- Yusupov, USSR Championship 1982.

7. 10.h3,c6 11.g4,Bd7 (In the game Hulak - Spassky, Toluca 1982 was played: 11...,a5 12.0-0-0,b5 13.Kb1,a4 14.Ng3,a3 which was unclear.) 12,0-0-0,Rc8 13.Kb1,b5 14.Nf4,a5 15.Bf5,a4 in Kristiansen - Spassky which was also an unclear position; 10.0-0,c6 11.f3 (Alternative is 11.Rab1,a5 12.a3,Ng6 13.Ng3,Ng4!? 14.Bxe7,Qxe7 with a sharp position in which White has slightly better chances as played in Vaganian - Kharitonov, USSR 1982.) 11...,Be6 12.Rae1,Rc8 13.Kh1,N6d7 14.Bxe7,Rxe7 15.Nf4 (Kasparov - Andersson, World Cup Belfort 1988.) 15...,Nf6!? 16.Qd2,Rd7 17.b4 and White has a small advantage (analysis of Kasparov.)

QUEEN'S GAMBIT ACCEPTED

1.d4,d5 2.c4,dxc4 3.Nf3,Nf6 4.e3,e6 5.Bxc4,c5 6.0-0

6	7	8	9	10	11	12	13
...	a4[2]	Qe2	Rd1	exd4	Nc3	Ne5	Bf4 ±
a6[1]	Nc6	cxd4[3]	Be7	0-0[4]	Nb4[5]	Bd7	
...	Qe2	Bb3[7]	Nc3	dxc5	e4	e5	exf6[8] ±
...	b5[6]	Nc6	Be7	Bxc5	b4	bxc3	
...	...	...	Rd1[9]	Nc3	e4	Rxd4	Rd3 ±
...	...	Bb7	Nbd7	Bd6	cxd4	Bc5	
...	...	...	...	...	Ne5[10]	Nxd7	d5[11] ±
...	...	...	...	Qb6	Bd6	Nxd7	

<table>
<tr><td align="center">**Diagram 75**
Main line: 6.0-0</td><td align="center">**Diagram 76**
Note 8: after 17.Rad1</td></tr>
</table>

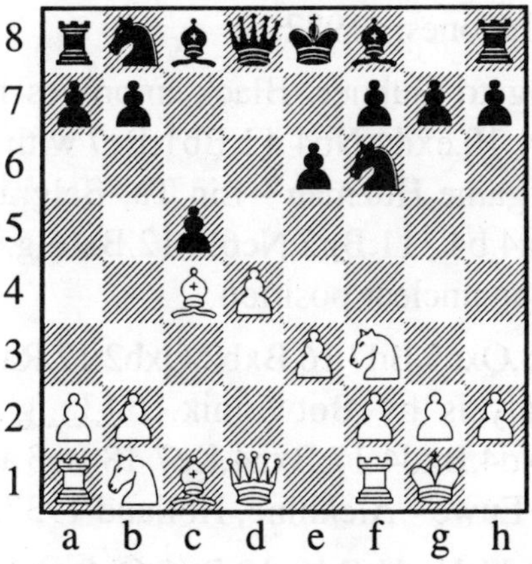

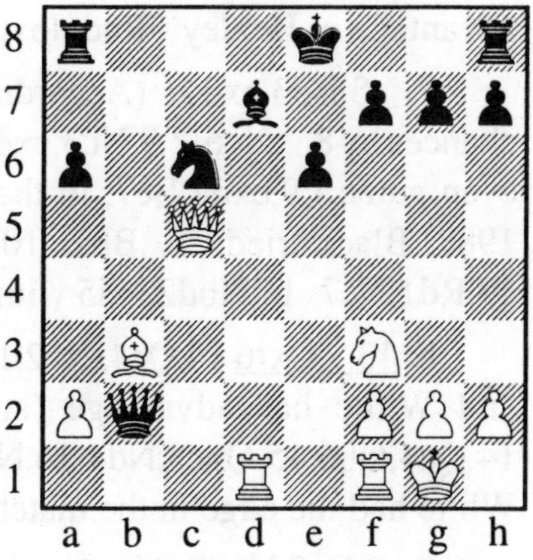

1. 6...Nc6 7.Qe2,cxd4 8.Rd1,Be7 9.exd4,0-0 10.Nc3 and White has the edge; 6...,cxd4 7.exd4,Be7 8.Qe2,0-0 9.Nc3,Nbd7 10.Rd1 and White is doing OK.

2. 7.Nc3,b5 8.Be2,Bb7 9.dxc5,Qxd1 10.Rxd1,Bc5 equalizes; 7.e4,Nxe4 (Also possible is 7...,b5 8.Bd3,Bb7 9.e5,Nfd7 10.Bg5,Qb6 equalizes.) 8.d5,Be7 9.dxe6,Bxe6 10.Qxd8,Bxd8 11.Bxe6,fxe6 12.Re1,Nf6 13.Ng5,0-0 gives an even game; 7.dxc5,Qxd1 8.Rxd1,Bxc5 9.b3,b5 10.Be2,Bb7 11.Bb2,Nbd7 12.a4,bxa4 13.Rxa4,0-0 was an even game in Spassky - Nikolic, Barcelona World Cup 1989.

3. 8...,Qc7 9.Nc3,Bd6 10.Rd1 (10.Bd3,0-0 11.dxc5,Bxc5 12.Ne4,Be7 13.b3!?,Nd5 14.Bb2,Bd7 15.Rfc1,Qb6 16.Nd4 was unclear in Lin Weigus - Lin Ta, Chinese Championship 1989.) 10...,0-0 11.h3,Re8 12.dxc5,Bxc5 13.e4,Nd7 14.Ba2 and White had a small edge (Lputian - Hübner, Rotterdam 1988).

4. 10...,Nb4 11.Ne5,0-0 12.Ra3!?,Nfd5 13.Qh5,f6 14.Rh3,fxe5 15.Qxh7+,Kf7 16.Bh6 and White had the advantage with compensation for the sacrificed material in Haba - Pekarek, Czechoslovakia Championship 1988.

5. 11...,Nd5 12.Bd3,Ncb4 13.Be4,Nf6 14.Ne5!,Nxe4 15.Qxe4,Nd5 16.Qf3! with a small advantage for White in Hjartarson - Marjanovic, Belgrade 1987.

6. <u>7....cxd4</u> 8.exd4,Nc6 9.Rd1,Be7 10.Nc3,Na5 11.Bd3,b5 12.Bg5 and White was OK in Raikovic - Marjanovic, Yugoslavia 1982; <u>7...,Nc6</u> 8.dxc5,Bxc5 9.a3,b5 10.Bd3 and White had a slight advantage in Henley - Radulov, Indonesia 1982.

7. 8.Bd3,cxd4 (According to Hübner, Black improves his chances by 8...,Nc6!? 9.Nc3,cxd4 10.exd4,Nb4 11.Bb1,Be7 with an even game.) 9.exd4,Be7; in the game Huzman - Lin Ta, Belgrade 1988, Black tried: 9...,Bb7 10.a4,b4 11.Bg5,Nc6! 12.Bxf6,gxf6 13.Rd1,Ne7 14.Nbd2,Nd5 with an unclear position.

8. <u>13....Qxf6</u> 14.Qc4,cxb2 15.Qxc5,Bd7 16.Bxb2,Qxb2 17.Rad1 and White has advantage (analysis by Botwinnik.); <u>13...,gxf6</u> 14.Qc4,Qb6 15.Qxc3,Nd4 16.Nxd4,Bxd4 17.Bxa4,Ke7 18.Be3 and White had the edge in the match Euwe - Alekhine, Holland 1937.

9. <u>9.Nc3</u>,Nbd7 10.e4,cxd4 11.Nxd4,Bd6 12.Rd1,Qb8 and an even game according to Polugaevsky; <u>9.a4</u>,Nbd7 10.axb5,axb5 11.Rxa8,Qxa8 12.Nc3,b4 13.Nb5,Qa5 is unclear.

10. 11.d5!?,exd5 (11...,c4 12.dxe6,fxe6 13.Bc2,Bc5 with a sharp position.) 12.Nxd5,Nxd5 13.Bxd5,Bxd5 14.Rxd5,Rd8 15.e4,Be7 16.Be3,0-0 17.b4! and White holds a small advantage as in Portisch - Ribli, Skellefteå World Cup 1989.

11. 13...,e5 14.a4 and White has an edge.

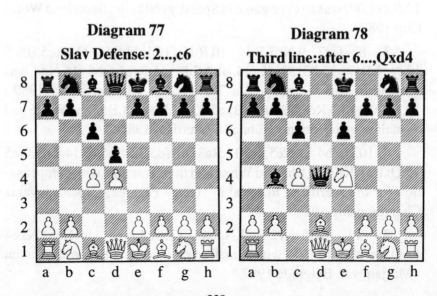

Diagram 77

Slav Defense: 2...,c6

Diagram 78

Third line:after 6...,Qxd4

SLAV DEFENSE

1.d4,d5 2.c4,c6							

3	4	5	6	7	8	9	10
cxd5	Nf3	Nc3	Bf4	e3	Bb5[1]	Qa4	0-0[3] ±/=
cxd5	Nf6	Nc6	Bf5	e6	Nd7[2]	Rc8	
...	...	...		e3	Bd3	0-0	Be5
...	...	...	e6	Be7	0-0[4]	Nh5	f5[5] ±/=
Nc3	e4	Nxe4	Bd2[6]	Bxb4	Be2	Bc3	Qd2
e6	dxe4	Bb4+	Qxd4[7]	Qxe4+	Na6[8]	Ne7	0-0[9] ∞
...	e3	cxd5	Bc4	Nge2	e4	Nxc3	
Nf6[10]	Bf5	Nxd5[11]	e6	Nd7	Nxc3	Bg6	=

1. 8.Qb3,Bb4! equalizes; 8.Ne5,Nxe5 9.Bxe5,a6 equalizes.

2. 8....,Bb4 9.Ne5,Qa5 10.Bxc6+,bxc6 11.0-0!,Bxc3 12.bxc3,Qxc3 13.Qc1!,Qxc1 14.Rfxc1,0-0 15.f3,h6 16.Nxc6,Rfe8 17.a4,Nd7 18.Bd6 and White had advantage in Botwinnik-Tal, Moscow title match 1961.

3. 10.Bc6?!,Rxc6 11.Qxa7,Qc8! 12.Qa5,Ra6 13.Qc7 (The alternative is: 13.Qb5,Rb6 14.Qe2,Ba3!) 13...,Qa8 and Black had advantage in Tomaszewski-Borkovsky, Poland 1979; 10.0-0,a6 11.Bxc6,Rxc6 12.Rfc1!,Be7 13.Ne2!,Qb6! 14.Rxc6,bxc6 15.Rc1,Bd3! 16.Qd1,Bxe2 17.Qxe2,0-0 18.Ne5,Nxe5 19.Bxe5,Rc8 with equality in Hausner-Dolmatov, Hradec Kralove 1981.

4. 8...,Nh5 9.Be5,0-0 10.g4,Nf6 11.h4,Qb6 12.Bxf6,Qxb2 13.Bxe7,Qxc3+ 14.Kf1,Nxe7 15.Rc1,Qa3 16.Rc7,Qd6 17.Qc2 with compensation for the sacrificed material in Safin - Dreev, Kramatorsk 1989.

5. 11.Rc1,Nf6 12.Bxf6,gxf6! with an even game in which White may have some chances.

6. 6.Nc3,c5 equalizes.

7. 6...,Bxd2+ 7.Qxd2,Nf6 8.Nxf6+,Qxf6 9.Nf3 and White has a small advantage.

8. 8...,Qxg2?! 9.Bf3 (9.Qd4!? is also an interesting alternative.) 9...,Qg6 10.Ne2,Na6 11.Ba3,Ne7 12.Rg1,Qf6 13.Nc3,Nf5 14.Ne4 and White had the advantage in Wood - Alexander, England 1948.

9. 11.Nf3,Ng6 12.0-0-0,Qf4 13.Qxf4 (Nice move is also 13.h4!?) 13...,Nxf4 14.Bf1,b6 15.g3,Ng6 16.Bg2,Bb7 17.h4 with compensation for the sacrificed material in Pfleger - Cherniak, Bucharest 1967.

10. 3...,dxc4 4.e4,e5!? 5.Nf3,exd4 6.Qxd4,Qxd4 7.Nxd4 with an even game in which White has some chances; 3...,e5 4.cxd5,cxd5 5.Nf3,e4 6.Ne5 and White has an edge.

11. 5...,cxd5 6.Qb3,Bc8 (Not 6...,Qb6? 7.Nxd5! and White is ahead.) 7.Nf3,e6 8.Ne5,Be7 9.Bd3 with a slightly better game for White.

What remains to be discussed are the two main openings in the Open and Half-Open Systems: the **Sicilian Defense** and the **Ruy Lopez** or **Spanish Opening**. Both have featured in the first two parts of this book, but they need closer scrutiny. Both of them have become so extensive in theory that monographs today are not capable of dealing with them separately but are split up. The monstrosity of 'over-information' is thus obvious. Our main concern is thus to guide the beginning chess player in what to do if confronted with each of them.

For the Ruy Lopez we have decided to give the main lines only of the **Exchange Variation** which occurs after **1.e4,e5 2.Nf3,Nc6 3.Bb5,a6 4.Bxc6** (reasonably uncomplicated and thus instructive), the **Open Variation** where White continues **4.Ba4** with the logical moves **4...,Nf6 5.0-0,Nxe4**, the **Closed Ruy Lopez** (as above but with) **5...,Be7 6.Re1,b5 7.Bb3**; and finally the **Marshall Attack** that was discussed in Part One, a logical outcome of the Closed Variation after **7...,0-0 8.c3,d5**. These four choices will be more than sufficient to at least reach equality and playable positions in the middle game against experienced opponents and assure survival beyond the many traps and pitfalls inherent in this opening. Although it belongs to the Open Games, strategy and positional insight are of vital interest. If you can play the Ruy Lopez, you can play just about any opening, provided you do it cautiously!

RUY LOPEZ (SPANISH OPENING) - EXCHANGE VARIATION

1.e4,e5 2.Nf3,Nc6 3.Bb5,a6 4.Bxc6,dxc6 [1] 5.0-0 [2]

5	6	7	8	9	10	11	12	
...	d4	dxe5	Rxd1	Rd3	Nbd2	Nc4	Nfxe5	
f6	Bg4 [3]	Qxd1	fxe5	Bd6	Nf6	0-0	Be2	=
...	...	c3	Be3	Nbd2	Re1	h3	Qb3	
...	...	Bd6	Nh6	Nf7	Qe7	Bh5	Nd8 [4]	±
...	h3	d3 [5]	Nbd2	Re1	d4	hxg4	Nh2	
Bg4	h5	Qf6	Ne7	Ng6	Bd6	hxg4	Rxh2 [6]	±
...	d3 [8]	Be3	Nbd2	Qe2	Rfb1!?	b4	a4	
Qd6 [7]	f6	Be6 [9]	0-0-0	g5	Ne7	Ng6	g4 [10]	±

Diagram 79

Exchange Variation: 5.0-0

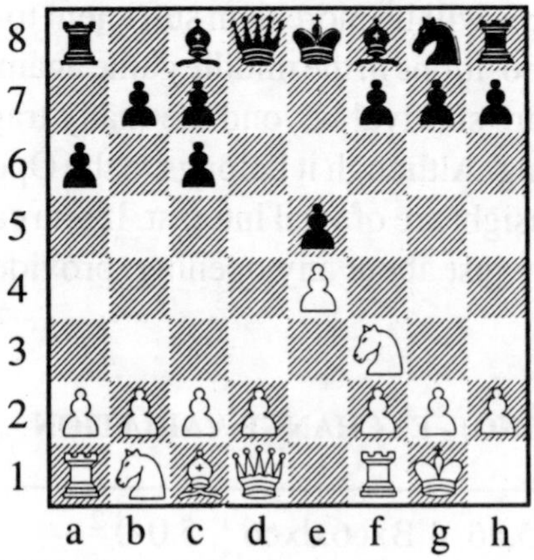

Diagram 80

Third line: after 7...,Qf6

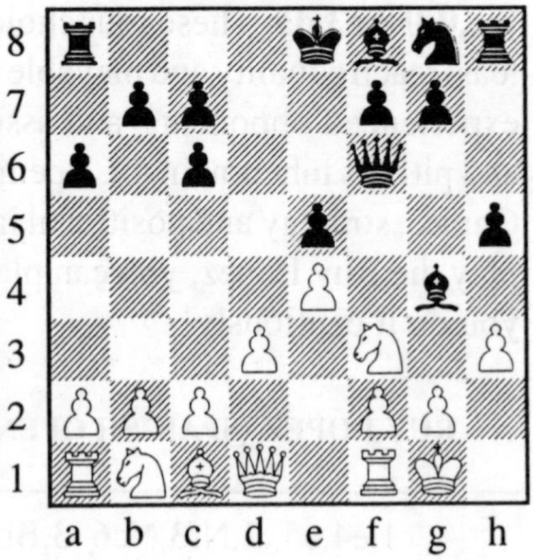

1. 4...,bxc6?! 5.d4,exd4 6.Qxd4 and White has the edge.

2. 5.d4,exd4 6.Qxd4,Qxd4 7.Nxd4,Bd6 8.Nc3,Ne7 9.Be3,f6 10.0-0,Bd7 with an even game; 6...,Bg4 7.Qc3!?,Qf6 8.Ne5!?,Be6 9.Nd2,Ne7!? 10.Ndf3,h6 11.Be3,0-0-0 12.0-0 with a sharp unclear position in Kiril Georgiev - Ivanchuk, Thessaliniki Olympiad 1988.

3. 6...,exd4 7.Nxd4,c5 8.Nb3,Qxd1 9.Rxd1,Bg4!? 10.f3,Be6 (In the game Ljuboevic - Karpov, Seara 1980, White got a very slight edge after 10...,Bd7 11.Nc3,0-0-0.) 11.Nc3 (Other move is 11.Be3,b6 12.a4,Ne7! 13.Bf4,c4 14.Nd4,0-0-0 15.Nc3,Rxd4 16.Rxd4,Ng6 17.Be3,Bc5 as played in Chandler - Ivanchuk, Thessaloniki Olympiad 1988.) 11...,Bd6 12.a4,0-0-0 13.Be3,c4 14.Na5?! (Better is 14.Nd4!?) 14...,Ne7 15.Nd5,Bxd5 16.exd5,c3! and Black had the advantage in Malyutin - Ivanchuk, Kramatorsk 1989.

4. 13.dxe5,fxe5 14.Bg5,Qe6 15.Bxd8,Qxb3 16.Nxb3,Rxd8 17.Na5 with a good game for White.

5. 7.c3!?,Qd3 8.Re1,Bxf3 9.Qxf3,Qxf3 10.gxf3,0-0-0 11.Kf1! followed by Ke2, d3 and Rd1 after which White is doing fine; 7...,Qf6 8.d4!?,Bxf3 9.Qxf3,exd4 10.cxd4,Qxd4 11.Nc3,Bd6 12.Bf4! and White has a small advantage.

6. 13.Qxg4!,Qh4 14.Qxh4,Rxh4 15.Nf3 and White is slightly better.

7. <u>5...,Qe7</u> 6.d4,exd4 7.Qxd4,Bg4 8.Bf4,Bxf3 9.gxf3,Rd8 10.Qe3 with a small advantage for White; <u>5...,Bd6</u> 6.d4,exd4 7.Qxd4,f6 8.e5 and White is a bit better (Alternative is 8.b3! with the idea 9.Ba3); <u>5...,Ne7</u> 6.d4,exd4 7.Nxd4,g6?! (Probably better is 7...,Ng6!?) 8.Nb3! and White is doing OK.

8. 6.d4,exd4 7.Nxd4,Bd7 8.Be3,0-0-0 9.Nd2,Nh6 with an unclear position.

9. 7...,Bg4 8.Nbd2,0-0-0 9.Rb1,Ne7 10.b4,g5 11.a4,Ng6 12.b5! and White has a small edge.

10. 13.Ne1 intending c4!? and White is just a bit better.

RUY LOPEZ - OPEN VARIATION (SOME OF THE MAIN LINES)

1.e4,e5 2.Nf3,Nc6 3.Bb5,a6 4.Ba4,Nf6 5.0-0,Nxe4 6.d4

6	7	8	9	10	11	12	13	14
...	Bb3	dxe5[2]	Qe2	Rd1	c4[5]	cxb5	Qf1	axb3
b5	d5[1]	Be6	Be7![3]	Nc5[4]	d4	d3	Nxb3	Nb4[6] ±
...	...	...	...	...	c4	Bxc4	Nc3	bxc3
...	...	...	...	0-0	bxc4	Qd7[7]	Nxc3	f6[8] ∞
...	...	...	Nbd2[9]	c3	Bxe6[11]	cxd4	Ne4[12]	Be3
...	...	...	Nc5	d4[10]	Nxe6	Ncxd4	Be7	Nf5[13] ±
...	Re1	dxe5	Bb3+	Nc3!?	bxc3	a4		
Be7[14]	f5	0-0	Kh8	Nxc3	h6	b6[15] ±		

Diagram 81
Main line:5...,Nxe4

Diagram 82
Second line: after 12.Bxc4

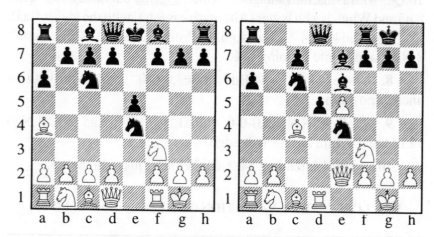

1. 7...,exd4 8.Re1,d5 9.Nc3,Be6 10.Nxe4,dxe4 11.Rxe4,Be7 12.Bxe6,fxe6 13.Nxd4!,0-0 14.Qg4 and White was clearly better in Fischer - Trifunovic, Bled 1961; 7...,Be7 8.Nxe5!,Nxe5 9.dxe5,Bb7 10.Qg4,0-0 11.f3,Ng5 in Tal - Smyslov, USSR Championship 1997; after 12.Nc3!?,Kh8 13.f4 White appears to have a slight edge.

2. 8.Nxe5,Nxe5 9.dxe5,c6! 10.c3,Be7 11.Be3,0-0 12.Nd2,Nxd2 13.Qxd2,Bf5 is an even game.

3. 9...,Na5 10.Nd4,c5 11.Nxe6,fxe6 12.c3,Nxb3 13.axb3,c4 14.b4,a5 15.f3 and White is better (Euwe); 9...,Bc5 10.Be3,Qe7 11.Rd1,Rd8 12.a4! and White has an edge; 9...,Nc5 10.Rd1,Nxb3 11.axb3,Qc8 12.c4! with a better game for White.

4. 10...,Na5?! 11.Nd4,c5 12.Nf5!,Bxf5 13.Bxd5,Ng5 14.Bxg5,Bxg5 15.Qf3 with a winning advantage for White.

5. 11.Bxd5!?,Bxd5 12.Nc3,Bc4! (12...,Nb4?! 13.Ne1!,c6 14.a3,Nxc2 15.Nxc2,Nb3 16.Rb1,0-0 17.Ne3,Rc8 18.Ncxd5,cxd5 19.Nxd5,Nxc1 20.Nxe7+,Qxe7 21.Rbxc1 with a better game for White in Kotkov - Kortchnoi, Poltava 1956.) 13.Rxd8+,Rxd8 14.Qe3,b4 15.b3,Be6 16.Ne4,Rd1+ 17.Ne1,Nd4 18.Bb2,Nxc2 19.Qe2,Rxa1 20.Bxa1,Nxa1 with a sharp, unclear position in Suetin - Geller, Riga 1958.

6. 15.Bd2,Nc2 16.Rxa6,Rxa6 17.bxa6,Bxb3 18.Bg5!,Bc4!

19.Bxe7,Qxe7 20.a7 and White had a small advantage in A. Greenfeld - Pernik (1983).

7. 12....,dxc4?! 13.Rxd8,Rfxd8 14.h3!? and White is OK (Boleslavsky); 12....,Bc5 13.Be3,Bxe3 14.Qxe3,Qb8 15.Bb3,Na5 16.Nbd2,Qa7! 17.Nd4,Nxd2 18.Qxd2,Qb6! as played in Kavalek - Karpov, Montreal 1979.

8. 15.exf6,Bxf6 16.Ng5 (Good is also 16.Bg5,Kh8! 17.Bxf6,Rxf6 18.Ng5,Na5 19.Qd3,Bg8 equalizes.) 16...,Bxg5 17.Bxg5,h6! 18.Be3,Qd6 19.Bb3,Ne5 20.Rd4,c5 21.Rf4,Nd7 22.Rd1,Qc6 23.Qd2,Nf6 24.Rh4,Ra7 with an unclear position.

9. 9.Be3,Be7 10.c3,Qd7 11.Nbd2,Rd8 12.h3,Nxd2 13.Qxd2,Na5 14.Bg5,c5 15.Rfe1,Nc6 16.Rad1,h6 17.Bxe7,Qxe7 18.Bc2 with a sharp position where White has slightly better chances as played in Short - Ljuboevic, Linares 1989.

10. 10....,Be7 11.Bc2,Bg4 12.Re1,Bh5 13.Nf1,0-0 14.Ng3,Bg6 15.Be3,Qd7 16.h4 with an unclear position in Anand - Torre, Thessaloniki Olympiad 1988; 10....,Bg4 11.Bc2,Be7 12.Re1,Qd7 13.Nf1 (A bit better for White proved here: 13.Nb3,Ne6 14.h3,Bh5 15.Bf5,Ncd8 16.Be3,a5 17.Nc5,Qc6 18.Nd3 in Ehlvest - Hjartarson, Belfort World Cup 1988.) 13...,Rd8 14.Ne3,Bh5 15.Nf5,0-0 16.Nxe7,Nxe7 17.Be3 with a sharp, unclear position in van der Wiel - Hjartarson, Rotterdam World Cup 1989.

11. 11.Ng5!? (Novelty by Zaitsev.) 11...,Qxg5 (If 11...,dxc3 12.Nxe6,fxe6 13.bxc3,Qd3! 14.Nf3,Qxd1 15.Bxd1 is good for White.) 12.Qf3,0-0-0 13.Bxe6+,fxe6 14.Qxc6,Qxe5!? 15.b4,Qd5! 16.Qxd5,exd5 17.bxc5,dxc3 with a sharp position that later favoured Black in Timman - Smyslov, Germany 1979.

12. 13.a4,Be7 14.Nxd4,Nxd4 15.Ne4,0-0 16.axb5,Nxb5 17.Be3,Qc8 18.Qc2,Qe6 19.f4,f6 20.exf6,Bxf6 21.f5,Qe5 22.Bc5 and White was OK in Ivanchuk - Yusupov, Linares 1989.

13. 15.Qc2,0-0 16.Rad1,Nxe3 17.fxe3,Qc8 18.Rd3!,c5 19.Nd6 with a slight advantage for White in Short - Belyavsky, Barcelona World Cup 1989.

14. 6...,exd4 17.Re1,d5 18.Nxd4,Bd6 9.Nxc6,Bxh2+ 10.Kh1!,Qh4 11.Rxe4+,dxe4 12.Qd8+,Qxd8 13.Nxd8+,Kxd8

14.Kxh2 and White was just a bit ahead in position and on material in Capablanca - Eduard Lasker, New York 1915.

15. 12...,a5?! 13.Rb1,b6 14.Bd5 and White was better in Geller - Kurajica, Yugoslavia 1977; the move 12...,b6!? is a novelty by Geller.

RUY LOPEZ - CLOSED VARIATION (SOME OF THE MAIN LINES)

(as above) 4.Ba4,Nf6 5.0-0,Be7 6.Re1,b5 7.Bb3,0-0

8	9	10	11	12	13	14
c3	d4	Be3	cxd4	Bc2	Bc1	b3
d6	Bg4	exd4[1]	Na5[2]	Nc4[3]	c5	Nb6[4] ∞
...	...	d5	Bc2	h3	Qxf3	exd5
...	...	Na5	c6[5]	Bxf3[6]	cxd5	Nc4[7] $\infty/\pm$
...	d3[8]	Bc2	Nbd2	Nf1	Ne3	a4
...	Na5!	c5	Nc6	Re8	Bf8	Bb7 =
a4	d3[10]	Bd2!?	c3	Nxc3	d4	Qxb3
Bb7[9]	d6[11]	b4	bxc3	Na5	Nxb3	Rb8 =

1. 10...,d5!? 11.exd5,exd4! 12.Bxd4!? (If 12.Bg5,Nxd5 with an unclear position.) 12...,Nxd4 13.cxd4,Bb4 14.Nc3,a5 15.a3,Bxc3 16.bxc3,a4 17.Ba2,Qd6 18.h3 as in Gulko - Geller, Lvov 1978; after 18...,Bh5!? it remains an unclear position says Ravinsky; 10...,Bh5!? 11.Nbd2 (Also OK is 11.h3.) 11...,d5!? 12.exd5,Nxd5 13.dxe5,Nxe5 14.Bg5,Nd3 15.Bxd5,Bxg5 16.Bxa8,Nxe1 17.Qxe1,Bd2 with an

Diagram 83
Main line: after 9.d4

Diagram 84
Alternative: 8.a4

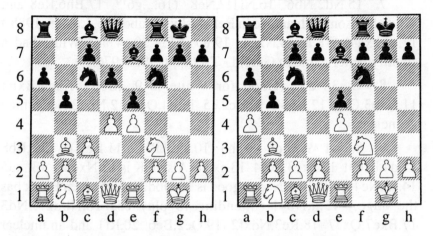

even game in Chandler - Romanishin, Leningrad 1987.

2. 11...,d5 12.e5,Ne4 13.h3,Bh5 14.Nc3,Nxc3 15.bxc3,Bg6 16.Qd2,h6 17.e6!,fxe6 18.Bxh6 with a sharp position that gives White better chances in Haba - Tolnai, Debrecen 1988.

3. 12...,c5 13.dxc5,dxc5 14.Nbd2,Nc6 15.Rc1,c4 16.h3,Bh5 17.g4,Bg6 18.Nh2,Nb4 19.f4,Nxc2 20.Qxc2,Nd5! 21.f5,Nxe3 22.Rxe3,Bc5 23.Rce1,Bxf5 24.exf5,Bxe3+ 25.Rxe3,Qb6 with compensation for the sacrificed material in M. Fernandez - Spassky, Vina del Mar 1989.

4. 14...,Na5 15.d5!,Nd7 16.Nbd2,Bf6 17.Rb1,Bc3 18.Re3 and White had the edge in Marjanovic - Ivkov, Yugoslavia 1988; 14...,Nb6!? 15.Nbd2,Nfd7 16.h3,Bh5 17.g4!?,Bg6 18.Nf1 was unclear in Tal - Portisch, Biel 1976.

5. 11...,Qc8!? 12.h3,Bd7 13.Nbd2,c6 14.b4!,Nb7 (Even better for White is 14...,Nc4?! 15.Nxc4,bxc4 16.Bg5.) 15.dxc6,Bxc6 (Also OK is 15...,Qxc6.) 16.Nf1,Re8 (16...,Nd8 17.Ng3,Ne6 18.Bb3,Rd8 with a sharp position tending to favour White as in Khalifman - Belyavsky, Moscow USSR Championship 1988.) 17.Ng3,h6!? (Maybe better is 17...,g6 18.Bg5 which is still OK for White.) 18.Nh4!,Nxe4 19.Rxe4,Bxe4 20.Bxe4,Bxh4 21.Nf5 after which White had the advantage in van der Wiel - Ivan Sokolov, Haninge 1989.

6. 12...,Bc8 (Not 12...,Bd7?! 13.Ne5!) 13.dxc6,Qc7 14.a4,b4!? 15.cxb4,Nxc6 16.b5 when White has a small edge.

7. 15.Nd2,Nb6 16.Nf1!?,Ne8 (16...,g6!? 17.Bh6,Re8 and White had some advantage in Belyavsky - Ljuboevic, Linares 1988.) 17.a4,bxa4! 18.Bxa4,Nxa4 19.Rxa4,f5 20.c4 and White had a slightly better game in Gufeld - Tsetlin, USSR 1976.

8. 9.a3,Na5 (Good for White is 9...,Be6 10.d4,Bxb3 11.Qxb3,Qb8 12.Bg5.) 10.Bc2,c5 11.d4,Qc7 12.Nbd2,Nc6 which is unclear.

9. 8...,b4 9.c3,d6 10.h3 (10.a5!?,Rb8 11.Bc4.) 10...,Rb8 11.d4,bxc3! 12.bxc3,exd4 13.cxd4 (Also OK is 13.Nxd4.) 13...,d5 14.e5,Ne4 15.Ba3!? (Not so good is 15.Nbd2?! Na5 when Black has the edge.) 15...,Nb4! (intending to play c5) 16.Nbd2!?,Nd3 17.Bxe7,Qxe7 18.Re3,Ndxf2 19.Qe2,Be6 20.Rf1 and an unclear position as occurred in Zapata - I. Zaitsev, Moscow World Cup 1989.

10. 9.c3,d5! is unclear; 9.Nc3,Nd4! equalizes.

11. 9...,Re8!? 10.c3,d6 11.Nbd2,Na5 12.Ba2,c5 13.Nf1!,c4!? was unclear Klinger - Nunn, Biel 1986.

MARSHALL GAMBIT (ALL INITIAL MOVES AS ABOVE PLUS:)

8.c3,d5!? 9.exd5,Nxd5[1] 10.Nxe5,Nxe5 11.Rxe5

11	12	13	14	15	16	17	18	
...	d4	Re1	g3	Be3	Qd3	Nd2	Qf1	
c6	Bd6	Qh4	Qh3	Bg4	Rae8[2]	f5[3]	Qh5[4]	±
...	...	...	...	Re4	Qf1[5]	f3	Re1	
...	...	...	...	g5!?	Qh5[6]	Bf5	Rae8	∞
...	Bxd5[7]	d4	Re3	h3	Qf3	Nd2	Nf1[9]	
...	cxd5	Bd6	Qh4[8]	f5	Bb7	g5	Rf6	⩱
...	d4	Re1![10]	h3	Qf3	Be3	Rxe3	Qxf4	
Nf6	Bd6	Ng4	Qh4	h5[11]	Nxe3	Qf4	Bxf4[12]	±

Diagram 85
Key position: 11.Rxe5

Diagram 86
Fourth line: 13.Re1!

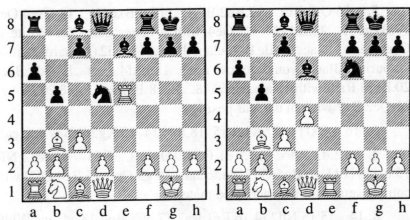

1. 9...,e4 10.dxc6,exf3 11.d4!,fxg2 12.Bg5 (12.Qf3 is best says Mikhail Tal.) 12...,Bg4 13.Qd3,Re8 14.Nd2,Nh5 15.Nf3 and White is better; in the game Vasyukov - Karaklaic, Belgrade 1961, Black tried: 13...,Bh5 14.Qh3!,Bg6 15.Nd2,Re8 16.Nf3,Ne4? 17.Rxe4,Bxe4 18.Bxf7+! with a winning advantage for White.

2. <u>16....Nxe3</u> 17.Rxe3,c5 18.Qf1!,Qh6 19.Nd2,Rad8 20.Nf3,Bxf3 21.Rxf3,cxd4 22.cxd4,Qd2 23.Rd3 and White was better in Fischer - Donner, Santa Monica 1966; <u>16....f5</u> 17.f4!,Kh8 18.Bxd5,cxd5 19.Nd2,g5 20.Qf1,Qh5 21.a4!,bxa4 22.fxg5,f4 23.Bxf4,Rxf4 24.gxf4,Rf8 25.Re5!,Bxe5 26.dxe5,h6 27.Qxa6,hxg5 28.Qd6,Rxf4 29.Rf1,Bf5 30.Qxd5 and White had a decisive advantage in Sax - Ehlvest, Skellefteå World Cup 1989.

3. 17...,Re6 18.a4,bxa4 19.Rxa4,f5 20.Qf1,Qh5 21.f4,Rb8 22.Bxd5,cxd5 23.Rxa6,Rbe8 24.Qb5!,Qf7 25.h3! (with the idea of 25...,Bxh3 26.Nf3,h6 27.Ne5,Bxe5 28.Rxe6,Rxe6 29.dxe5 and White would be better) as in Short - Pinter, Rotterdam 1988; 18.Bd1,Bxd1 19.Raxd1,f5! 20.Nf3!,Rg6 21.Qf1,Qh5 22.Ne5,Bxe5 23.dxe5,f4 with an unclear position in Ljuboevic - Nunn, Amsterdam 1988.

4. 19.f4,Kh8 20.Bxd5,cxd5 21.a4 (21.Qg2!?,g5 22.Qxd5,Rd8 23.Qc6,gxf4 24.Bxf4,Bxf4 25.gxf4,Be2 26.Kh1,Rde8 27.Rg1 and White was better in A. Sokolov - Nunn, Rotterdam World Cup 1989.)

21...,g5 22.axb5,axb5 23.fxg5,Rxe3! 24.Rxe3,f4 25.gxf4,Bxf4
26.Rg3,Qxg5 27.Kh1,Bd6 28.Qg2 and Timman had the edge as
White in his game against Nunn, Brussels World Cup 1988.

5. 16.Qf3,Bf5 17.Bc2,Bf4! (17...,Bxe4?! 18.Bxe4,Qe6
19.Bxg5,f5 20.Bd3,f4 21.Qe4 with a better game for White in
Georgiev - Lukacs, Baile Herculane 1982.) 18.Nd2 (A sharp position
favouring Black would follow after: 18.Bxf4,gxf4 19.Nd2,Bxe4
20.Bxe4,Rad8 with the idea Rd6.) 18...,Rae8 19.Rxe8,Rxe8 20.Ne4,g4
21.Qe2,Bc7 with an unclear position.

6. 16...,Qxf1+ 17.Kxf1,f5 18.Re1,f4 19.Kg2,Bf5 is unclear.

7. 12.d3,Bd6 13.Re1,Qh4 (Or 13...,Bf5 14.Nd2,Nf4
15.Ne4,Nxd3 16.Bg5,Qd7 is unclear.) 14.g3,Qh3 15.Re4,Qf5! with
compensation for the sacrificed material.

8. 14...,f5 15.Nd2,f4 16.Re1,Ra7 17.Nf3,Bg4 18.a4! and White
is just a shade better.

9. 18.Qe2!?,f4 19.Nf3,Qh5 20.Nxg5!,Qg6 21.Re6,Qxg5
22.Rxd6,Rae8 23.Re6,Kf7 24.Rxe5,Rxe5 25.dxe5 with a winning
advantage in Hübner - Nunn, Skellefteå World Cup 1989.

10. 13.Re2,Nh5! 14.Be3 (14.Qd3,Bg4! equalizes.) 14...,Bb7
15.Nd2,Kh8 16.d5,Nf6 17.c4,bxc4 18.Nxc4,Bd5 equalizes.

11. 15...,Nf2 16.Bd2!,Bb7 (Not 16...,Ng4? which wins for
White after 17.Re8.) 17.Qb7,Nd3 18.Re2,Qg3 (Not 18...,Rae8
19.Qf3 with a decisive advantage for White.) 19.Kf1,Nf4 20.Rf2,Qd3
21.Kg1,Ne2+ 22.Rxe2,Qxe2 23.Qf3,Qxf3 24.gxf3 and White is
better (analysis by the Swedish GM Wedberg).

12. 19.Re1,Bf5 20.Na3 and White is just a bit better says
Mikhail Tal.

What we said about the Ruy Lopez applies even more to the Sicilian Defense often called the Defense of the 20th century. Often 50% of the 1.e4 games in GM tournament are answered by 1...,c5. White thus must study some of the more important lines, be conversant with the most basic position in many variations, but most of all be able to decide at the outset whether he wants to become involved, and to what extent. To allow the beginning player this choice we have decided to include the following variations: the **Closed Sicilian** in which White (for the moment) declines to play d4 and thus does not allow opening of the c-line for Black by trading c5 for his center pawn d4. White plays **2.Nc3!** The Scheveningen which Kasparov himself calls the "classic" line is not discussed, because your Saitek/Kasparov/Radioshack computer has been programmed with the most important data. This variation is Kasparov's favorite, where as Black you are "subjected to persistence pressure on the K-side in return for counterplay on the Q-side and the c-line. The **Alapin-Sveshnikov** (see below) where White plays **2.c3** is one of the most potent weapons to get away from Black's opening preparations. The **Richter-Rauzer** is one of the main lines of the Open Sicilians and allows White to decide continuously how much struggle he wants. It occurs after **1.e4,c5 2.Nf3,Nc6 3.d4,cxd4 4.Nxd4,Nc6 5.Nc3,d6** (Black's moves second and fifth moves are often interchanged.) **6.Bg5.** The **Sveshnikov** is one of Black's most interesting attempts to completely change the emphasis in this defense, and occurs after the above first four moves followed by **5.Nc3,e5!?** It had long a dubious reputation, but the aging Russian GM after whom it was named earned it the hard way by proving in over 40 years of theory and tournament practice that Black always can at least equal White's improvements. A dangerous weapon if Black is patient. These four variations will introduce the reader to sufficient material to weather most storms and allow a choice. The games that will result can then be a stepping stone to improved understanding and growing playing strength.

1.e4,c5 2.Nc3

2	3	4	5	6	7	8	9
...	g3	exd5[1]	Bg2	d3[2]	Nge2	Ne4	Bxe4
e6	d5	exd5	Nf6	Be7	d4	Nxe4	0-0 =
...	f4[4]	Nf3	Bc4[5]	f5!?	fxe6	d3	0-0
Nc6[3]	g6	Bg7	e6	Nge7!?	dxe6[6]	0-0	Nd4[7] =
...	g3	Bg2	d3	Be3	Qd2	Nge2	0-0
...	g6[8]	Bg7	d6[9]	e6	Nge7	Nd4	0-0 =
...	...	...	...	f4[11]	Nf3	0-0	Be3
...	...	...	...	e6[12]	Nge7	0-0	Nd4[13] =

Diagram 87	Diagram 88
Key move: 2.Nc3	**Second line: after 6.f5!?**

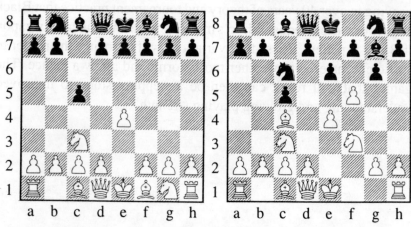

1. 4.Bg2,Nf6 5.d3,Be7 6.Nge2,dxe4!? 7.Nxe4,Nxe4 8.Bxe4,0-0 equalizes; 4.d3,d4 5.Nce2,f5!? is unclear in Kovacevic - Djuric, Yugoslavia 1989.

2. 6.Nge2,d4 7.Ne4,Nxe4 8.Bxe4,Nd7! 9.d3,Nf6 10.Bg2,Bd6 equalized in Spassky - Korchnoi, USSR 1968.

3. 2...,d6 3.f4,g6 (3...,Nc6 4.Nf3,g6 5.Bc4,Bg7 6.0-0,Nf6 7.d3,0-0 f5!? is OK for White.) 4.d4,cxd4 5.Qxd4,Nf6 6.e5,Nc6 7.Bb5,dxe5 with an even game.

4. 3.Nge2,e5!? 4.g3,d6 5.Bg2,g6 6.d3,Bg7 7.0-0,Nge7 8.f4,0-0 9.Be3,Nd4 10.Qd2,Be6 11.Rae1,Qd7 12.Nc1,Rae8 13.Nd1,b6 14.fxe5,dxe5 15.c3,Ndc6 was unclear in Korchnoi - Hübner, Barcelona World Cup 1989.

5. 5.Bb5,Nd4 6.0-0 (6.Nxd4,cxd4 7.Ne2,Qb6 8.Bd3,d6 would give an even game.) 6...,Nxb5 7.Nxb5,a6 8.Nc3,d6 9.d3,b5 10.Qe1,Bb7 11.Bd2,Qd7 with an unclear position as played in M. Pavlovic - Knaak, Erevan 1988.

6. 7...,fxe6 8.d3,d5 9.Bb3 is a bit better for White.

7. 10.Be3,Nec6 with an even game.

8. 3...,e6 4.Bg2,g6 5.d3,Bg7 6.f4,Nge7 7.Nf3,0-0 8.0-0,d6 9.Bd2 (Also possible is 9.Be3,Nd4 10.Bf2,b6!?) 9...,b5 10.a3,Rb8 11.Rb1,c4!? with a sharp position that tends to favour Black in Marjanovic - Lputian, Erevan 1989.

9. 5...,Rb8!? 6.f4,b5 7.Nf3 (Interesting is also 7.Nh3.) 7...,b4 8.Ne2,e6 9.a3,a5 10.axb4,axb4 11.0-0,Nge7 12.Be3,d6 13.d4,cxd4 14.Nfxd4,0-0 with an even game in Abramovic - Taimanov, Paris 1989.

10. 8.Bh6!?,Bxh6 (8...,0-0 9.Bxg7,Kxg7 10.h4 and White is OK.) 9.Qxh6,Nd4 10.Qd2 (Or 10.0-0-0!?) 10...,0-0 11.Nh3,f6 12.0-0,e5 13.f4,Qb6 14.Rab1,c4 15.Kh1,cxd3 16.cxd3,Be6 was unclear in Balashov - Timman, Rio de Janeiro 1979.

11. 6.Nf3,Nf6 7.0-0,0-0 8.h3,Rb8 9.a4,a6 10.Be3,b5 equalizes; 6.Nge2,e5 7.0-0,Nge7 8.Be3,0-0 9.Qd2,Be6 10.f4,Nd4 is an even game.

12. 6...,Nf6 7.Nf3,0-0 8.0-0,Rb8 9.h3,b5 is an even game;

<u>6....e5</u> 7.Nf3 (7.Nh3!?) 7...,Nge7 8.0-0,0-0 9.Be3,Nd4 equalizes.

13. <u>10.Rb1</u>,Nec6 11.Ne2,Nxf3+ 12.Bxf3,b6 equalizes; <u>10.Bf2</u>,Nxf3+ (Or 10...,b6!?) 11.Bxf3,Nc6 12.Bg2,Nd4 (12...,b6!? 13.e5,Bb7 would give Black an even game.) 13.e5!?,dxe5 14.fxe5,Bxe5 15.Ne4,f5 16.Nxc5 and White was just a bit better in Spassky - Gufeld, Wellington 1988.

The second way to avoid Black's opening preparation in the Sicilian is by answering 1...,c5 with 2.c3.

1.e4,c5 2.c3							
2	**3**	**4**	**5**	**6**	**7**	**8**	**9**
...	exd5	d4	Nf3	Bd3	0-0	cxd4	Nc3
d5	Qxd5	e6	Nf6	Be7	cxd4	Nc6	Qd6 =
...	e5	d4	cxd4[5]	Nf3[6]	Bc4[7]	Bb5	Nxe5
Nf6	Nd5	cxd4	d6	Nc6	Nb6	dxe5[8]	Bd7[9] ∞/=
...	...	...	...	...	a3!	Bd3	0-0
...	...	...	...	e6	Be7[10]	Nc6[11]	b6!?[12] ±
...	...	...	Qxd4	Nf3	Qe4	Nbd2	Nxe5
...	...	...	e6[13]	Nc6	d6[14]	dxe5	Nxe5! =[15]

1. <u>2....e6</u> 3.d4,d5 4.exd5 (If 4.e5 we transpose into the French Defense!) 4...,exd5 5.Be3,c4!? 6.Nf3,Nc6 7.b3! and White is slightly better; <u>2....e5</u> 3.Nf3,Nc6 4.Bc4,Qc7!? 5.d3 (Or 5.Ng5,Nd8.) 5...,Nf6 6.a3!?,Be7 7.b4,0-0 8.0-0,b6 9.Re1,Bb7 10.Nbd2,Rad8 with a sharp, unclear position that tends to favour White as in Sheshnikov - R. Sherbakov, Budapest 1989.

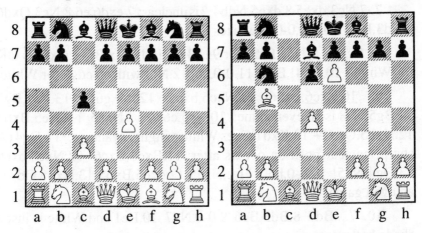

Diagram 89

Alapin key move: 2.c3

Diagram 90

Note 6: after 8.e6!

2. 4...,Nc6 5.Nf3,Bg4 (5...,cxd4 6.cxd4,e5 7.Nc3,Bb4 8.Bd2 is slightly better for White.) 6.Be2,cxd4 7.cxd4,e6 8.0-0,Nf6 9.Nc3,Qa5 and White has the edge; 4...,Nf6 5.Nf3,Bg4 6.Qa4!?+,Nc6 7.Bc4,Qd7 8.dxc5,Bxf3 9.gxf3,e6 10.Be3,Nd5 11.Bxd5,Qxd5 12.Qe4,Qh5 13.b4,Be7 14.Nd2 and White had a small advantage in Sveshnikov - Neverov, Moscow 1989.

3. 6.Be2!?,Nc6 7.0-0,Be7 8.c4 (8.Be3,Ng4!? is unclear.) 8...,Qf5 9.Nc3,cxd4 10.Nxd4,Nxd4 11.Qxd4,e5 12.Qd3,0-0 13.Qxf5,Bxf5 14.Be3,Rfc8 15.Rfd1 and White was doing fine in Sveshnikov - Sunie, Moscow World Cup 1989.

4. 7...,0-0 8.c4 (Unclear is 8.dxc5,Rd8.) 8...,Qd8 9.dxc5,Bxc5 10.Qe2 and White has a small edge; 7...,Nc6 8.dxc5!?,Qxc5 9.Be3 with a small advantage for White.

5. 5.Bc4,Nb6 6.Bb3,d6!? (6...,dxc3 7.Nxc3 with sufficient compensation.) 7.cxd4,dxe5 8.Qh5,e6 9.dxe5,Nc6 10.Nf3,Qd3 and Black has a small positional advantage; 5.Nf3,Nc6 6.Bc4,Nb6 7.Bb3,d5 8.exd6 e.p.,Qxd6 9.0-0,Be6 (Interesting is also 9...,Bf5.) 10.Bxe6,Qxe6 11.a4 and White was just a bit better in Sveshnikov - Levchenkov, USSR 1988.

6. 6.Bc4!?,Nb6 7.Bb5+,Bd7 8.e6!,Bxb5 9.Qh5,Qc8 10.Qxb5+,Kd8 11.Be3,Qxe6 12.d5,Qd7 13.Bxb6+,axb6

14.Qxb6+,Qc7 15.Qe3 and a small advantage for White in Rozentalis - Aseev, Klaipeda 1988.

7. 7.Nc3,dxe5 8.dxe5,Ndb4!? is unclear; 7.exd6,e6 8.Nc3,Qxd6 9.Bd3,Be7 10.0-0,0-0 equalizes.

8. 8...,d5 9.Nc3,Bf5 (Or 9...,Bg4 10.h3,Bxf3 11.Qxf3 is OK for White.) 10.Nh4!,Bd7 11.0-0,e6 12.Nf3 with an edge for White.

9. 10.Bxc6,Bxc6 11.Nxc6,bxc6 12.0-0,g6!? 13.Re1,Bg7 14.Bg5,Nc8 is an even game; 10.Nc3,e6 (10...,Nxe5 11.dxe5,Bxb5 12.Nxb5,Qxd1+ 13.Kxd1 gives White a slight advantage.) 11.Qg4 (A sharp, unclear position occurs after: 11.Bxc6,Bxc6 12.Nxc6,bxc6 13.Qg4,Nd5! 14.0-0,h5.) 11...,Nxe5 12.dxe5,Bxb5 13.Nxb5,Qd7 is an even game.

10. 7...,Bd7 8.Bd3,Bc6 9.0-0,Nd7 10.Re1 and White is just a shade better.

11. 8...,0-0 9.0-0,dxe5 10.dxe5,Nd7 11.Re1 and White is just ahead in position.

12. 10.Qc2,Bb7 11.Nc3 with a small edge for White.

13. 5...,Nc7 6.Nf3,Nc6 7.Qe4,g6 8.Bc4,Bg7 9.0-0 and White is doing fine.

14. 7...,f5 8.fxe6 e.p. (An even game develops after 8.Qe2,Qc7 9.g3,d6! 10.exd6,Bxd6 11.Bg2,0-0.) 8...,Nxf6 9.Qh4,Qc7 10.Bg5!?,Be7 11.Nbd2,Ne5 12.Nxe5,Qxe5+ 13.Be2 with a slight advantage for White in Kurajica - Popovic, Vrsac 1980.

15. 10.Qxe5,Nf6 11.Bb5!,Bd7 12.a4,a6! and it was an even game in Sveshnikov - Geller, USSR Championship 1979.

The following table/analysis/variation is nowadays mostly referred to as the Kalashnikov Variation. However, there is no doubt that the Russian GM Sveshnikov has contributed the most to all variations in the Sicilian Defense in which ...e5 is played by Black. This move was first ridiculed as being anti-positional; then its critics consistently proved that it had weaknesses, but invariably Black found improvements. It has now finally won universal acceptance and is regularly chosen by outstanding tournament players on the GM circuit.

	1.e4,c5 2.Nf3,Nc6 3.d4,cxd4 4.Nxd4,Nf6 5.Nc3,e5 6.Ndb5[1],d6					
7	**8**	**9**	**10**	**11**	**12**	**13**
Nd5	exd5	c4	Nc3	Be2	0-0	f4[2] ∞/±
Nxd5	Nb8	a6	Be7	0-0	f5	
...	...	c4[3]	Qa4	Qb4	Be3	h4 ∞/±
...	Ne7	Ng6[4]	Bd7	Qb8	b6	
a4	Na3	Bc4	0-0	Nxc4	Qd3[5]	Nxd6+[6] =
a6	Be6	Rc8!	Bxc4	Nd4	Nxc2	
Bg5[7]	Na3	Nc4	Nd5[8]	Bxf6!?	Qxd5	Qd2[9] ∞
a6	Be6	Rc8	Bxd5	gxf6	Nb4	

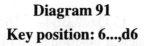

Diagram 91
Key position: 6...,d6

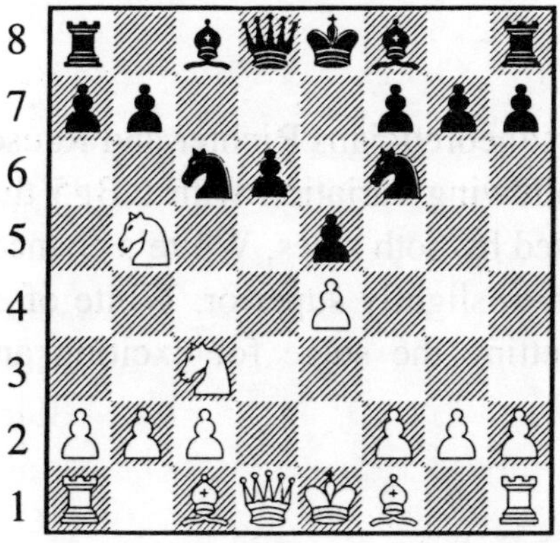

Diagram 92
Note 9: after 18..., Qb6

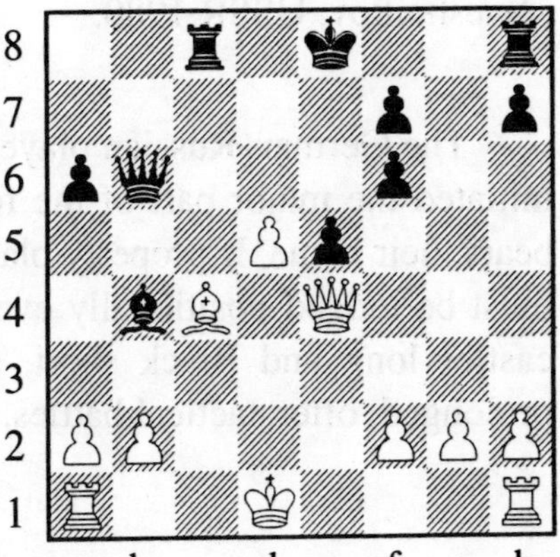

1. 6.Nb3,Bb4 7.Bd3,d6 8.0-0,Bxc3 9.bxc3,Bg4 was unclear in Vitolinsh - Dolmatov, Frunze 1979; 6.Nf5,d5!? 7.exd5,Bxf5 8.dxc6,bxc6 is unclear; 6.Nde2,Bc5 7.Ng3,d6 8.Be2,Be6 with an even game; 6.Nf3,Bb4 7.Bc4,Nxe4!? 8.0-0,Nxc3 (8...,Bxc3? 9.bxc3,Nxc3 10.Qe1,d5 11.Nxe5 and White is better.) 9.bxc3,Be7! with an even game.

2. 13...,Bf6 14.Qc2,Nd7 15.Kh1 with a small advantage for White in Tal - Tseshkovsky, Riga 1979.

3. 9.c3!?,Nf5 (Quite good for White proved: 9...,f5?! 10.Qa4,Kf7 11.Qb4!,Ng6 12.h4!,a6 13.Bg5,Qd7 14.h5 in Veselovsky - Zlotnik, Moscow 1978.) 10.a4,Be7 11.Bd3,Nh4 12.0-0,Ng6 13.f4! with a slight edge for White in Gulko - Gurgenidze, USSR 1979.

4. 9...,Nf5 10.Bd3,Be7 11.0-0,a6 12.Nc3,0-0 13.a4 and White had a slight advantage in Westerinen - Kirpichnikov, Jurmala 1978.

5. 12.Ne3,Be7 with the plan ...,0-0, ...Qd7 and ...Rfd8.

6. 13...,Bxd6 14.Qxc2,Bb4 15.Bg5 with equal chances.

7. 7.Be3,a6 8.Na3,Rb8!? 9.Nd5,Nxd5 10.exd5,Ne7 11.c4,Nf5 12.Bd2,Be7 13.Bd3,0-0 14.0-0,Bg5! 15.Nc2,Re8 16.Re1 and an even game.

8. 10.Bxf6!?,gxf6 (Also good for White is 10...,Qxf6 11.Nb6,Rb8 12.Bc4,Qd8 13.Ncd5.) 11.Ne3,Ne7 12.Bd3!? and White is slightly ahead.

9. 13...,d5!? 14.exd5,Nxc2+ 15.Qxc2,Bb4+ 16.Kd1,b5 17.Qe4,bxc4 18.Bxc4,Qb6 with an unclear position as in Filipenko - Sveshnikov, USSR 1980.

The German-Russian players/theoreticians Richter and Rauser initiated the major part of the following variation with 6.Bg5 that bears their name. If properly played by both sides, White's chances must be judged positionally ever so slightly superior. White often castles long and Black short, setting the stage for exciting and prolonged, often tactical battles.

1.e4,c5 2.Nf3,Nc6 3.d4,cxd4 4.Nxd4,Nf6 5.Nc3,d6 6.Bg5

6	7	8	9	10	11	12	13	14
...	Qd2	0-0-0	Qxd4	f4[2]	Bh4	e5!	Bf2!	Qxa7[5] ±
Bd7	Rc8[1]	Nxd4	Qa5	h6[3]	g5	Bg7[4]	Ng4	
...	Qd2	0-0-0	f4	Nf5	exf5	Kb1	Bxf6	Nd5 ±
e6[6]	Be7[7]	0-0	e5	Bxf5	Qa5[8]	Rad8	Bxf6	
...	...	...	...	Qxd4	Bc4	e5	fxe5	Bd2[10] ±
...	...	...	Nxd4	Qa5	Bd7	dxe5	Bc6	
...	...	...	...	Bh4	Nf5	exf5	Kb1	Bxf6[12] ±
...	...	...	h6	e5[11]	Bxf5	Qa5	Rad8	

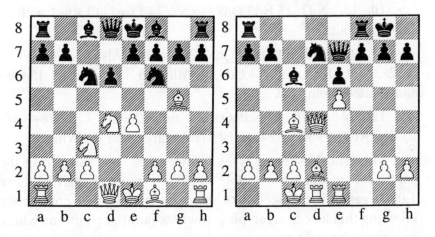

Diagram 93

Richter-Rauzer: 6.Bg5

Diagram 94

Note 10: after 17.Rhe1

1. 7...,Nxd4 8.Qxd4,Qa5 9.Bd2! (Unclear is 9.f4,Rc8 10.e5,Rxc3!?) 9...,e5 10.Qd3 and White has an edge.

2. 10.Bd2,e5 11.Qd3,a6 12.f3,Be6 13.a3,Qc7 14.Bg5,Nd7 15.Kb1,Be7 16.h4!,h6 17.Be3,b5 18.g3!,Nb6 19.Bh3 and White had a small advantage in Gipslis - Zaichik, USSR 1981.

3. 10...,Rxc3 11.bxc3,e5 12.Qb4,Qxb4 13.cxb4,Nxe4 14.Bh4,g5! 15.fxg5,Be7 16.Re1,d5 17.Bd3! with a good game for White; 10...,e6 11.e5,dxe5 12.fxe5,Rxc3 13.Bd2,Qxa2 14.Bc3,g6 14.b4! and White was better in Belyavsky - Ubilava, USSR 1978.

4. 12...,gxh4 13.exf6,e6 14.Be2 and White is doing OK.

5. 14...,Qxa7 15.Bxa7 with a small advantage for White in Timoshenko - G. Kuzmin, Krasnoyarsk 1980.

6. 6...,Qb6 7.Nb3,e6 8.Bd3,Be7 9.0-0,0-0 10.Kh1,h6 11.Be3,Qc7 12.f4,a6 13.Qf3,b5 14.Rae1 with a good game for White; 6...,g6 7.Bxf6,exf6 8.Bc4,Bg7 9.Ndb5 and White has the edge.

7. 7...,h6 8.Bxf6,gxf6 9.0-0-0,a6 10.f4,Bd7 11.Be2,h5 12.Kb1,Qb6 13.Nb3 and White is doing fine.

8. 11...,Rc8 12.Kb1,Nd4 13.Bd3,Qa5 14.g4,exf4 15.Bxf4,d5 16.g5 with a better game for White.

9. 11...,Rd8 12.Rhf1!,Bd7 13.f5,Rac8 (Not 13...,exf5 14.exf5,Bxf5 15.Nd5 and White has the advantage.) 14.Bb3,Qc5 15.Qd3 and White is slightly better.

10. 14...,Nd7 15.Nd5,Qd8 16.Nxe7+,Qxe7 17.Rhe1 with an edge for White.

11. 10...,Nxd4 11.Qxd4,Qa5 12.Bc4,Rd8 (Also good for White is 12...,e5 13.fxe5,dxe5 14.Qd3.) 13.Rhf1,e5 14.fxe5,dxe5 15.Qe3 and White is doing OK.

12. 14...,Bxf6 15.Nd5,Qxd2 16.Rxd2,exf4 17.Nxf6+,gxf6 18.Be2,Rfe8 19.Rf1,Re4 20.Bf3 is slightly better for White.

This finishes our survey of openings and will permit the persistent reader who is able to absorb a major part of these 1,000+ games in this section to enter any opening with confidence knowing that he can steer play towards familiar positions where he knows the right answers.

* * * *